India China Relations

Future Perspectives

India China Relations

Future Perspectives

Edited by

D. P. Tripathi

B. R. Deepak

Vij Books India Pvt Ltd

New Delhi, India

Published by

Vij Books India Pvt Ltd
(Publishers, Distributors & Importers)
2/19, Ansari Road, Darya Ganj
New Delhi - 110002
Phones: 91-11-43596460, 91-11-47340674
Fax: 91-11-47340674
e-mail : vijbooks@rediffmail.com
web: www.vijbooks.com

ISBN: 978-93-81411-15-5

Price in India: ₹ 995/-
Price outside India: US $ 55

Printed in India
at Narula Printers

CONTENTS

Acknowledgements *ix*

Introduction *xi*

India's Relationship with China 1
MANI SHANKAR AIYAR

Strengthening China-India Relations in an All-Round Manner 7
ZHANG YAN

Ji Xianlin: India-China Civilizational Dialogue and Intercultural Studies 11
B R DEEPAK

History of Sino-Indian Friendship and the Ideal of World Peace 30
WANG BANGWEI

Wen Jiabao: An impressive statesman in a Changing China 35
SUDHEENDRA KULKARNI

Experiences and Enlightenments: The Sixty Years of Diplomatic Relations between China and India 45
CHENG RUISHENG

Sino-Indian Border Mismanagement: An outcome of China's 'victim's psychology' and India's tough posture'? 58
B R DEEPAK

China through Indian Eyes 77
DP TRIPATHI

The Development and Issues in Sino-India Security Relations 86
MA JIALI

Imagining China 92
AMITABH MATTOO

Development of Education in China and India-A View from China 105
AN SHUANGHONG

India-China Relations 110
P. STOBDAN

India's Land System, A Revelation to China's Land System Reform 124
SHENG RONG

China's Strategic Forces' Modernisation 135
RAJIV NAYAN

Indian and Chinese Diaspora 153
RN DAS

The Road to Global Zero: China's and India's Perspectives 174
YANG XIAOPING & ZHANG GUIHONG

Power and Paradox: The Future of Sino-Indian Relations 184
C. RAJA MOHAN

India-China Relations: Could trade and Economics pave way for the Strategic Cooperation? 189
BINOD SINGH

The Sixty Years of India-China Relationship 207

1. Chronology of India-China Relations (1950-2010) 208
2. Economic Complimentarities between India and China 215
3. Panchsheel Agreement 219
4. Rajiv Gandhi's Goodwill Visit to China 223
5. Agreement between India & China on the Maintenance of Peace and Tranquility along the Line of Actual Control. 225
6. Agreement between India & China on Confidence Building Measures along the Line of Actual Control. 228

5. Documents signed between India and China during Prime Minister Vajpayee's visit to China 236

6. Political Parameters and Guiding Principles for the Settlement of the India-China Boundary Question 239

7. Highlights of the Joint Declaration issued after the talks between Prime Minister Manmohan Singh and Chinese President Hu Jintao 242

8. A Shared Vision for the 21st Century of the People's Republic of China and the Republic of India 244

9. 60th Anniversary of the Establishment of Diplomatic Relations between India and China 250

Appendix 252

Contributors 275

ACKNOWLEDGEMENTS

On the occasion of the 60th anniversary of establishment of diplomatic ties between India and China in 2010, the editorial committee of *Think India* brought out a special issue on India and China. This volume is the product of this special issue, albeit a few more chapters have been included. We would like to express our sincere thanks to *Think India* team for their continuous support and cooperation.

It would not have been possible without the help, support and patience of our contributors to have this volume. Many of whom irrespective of their preoccupation and other commitments agreed to contribute. The opening article by eminent parliamentarian Sh. Mani Shankar Aiyar is a reconstruct of his illuminating speech on India-China Relations in the JNU campus on 15th April 2010 organized by *Think India*, we record our sincere thanks to him for letting the speech to be reproduced here. We also thank Ambassador Zhang Yan, for being supportive and having contributed to this volume. We would like to thank Prof. Wang Bangwei, eminent columnist and media advisor to former Prime Minister A B Vajpayee, Sh. Sudheendra Kulkarni, Ambassador Cheng Ruisheng, Prof. Ma Jiali, Prof. Amitabh Matoo, Prof. C. Raja Mohan, Prof. An Shuanghong, Prof. P. Stobdan, Prof. Sheng Rong, Dr. Yang Xiaoping, Prof. Zhang Guihong, Dr. Rajiv Nayan, Dr. R. N. Das, and Binod Singh for their timely contributions and thoughtful insights. I would also like to thank Madurendera Kumar Jha, who translated Sheng Rong's article from Chinese to English. The good advice of our friends who have contributed to this volume has been invaluable on both an academic and a personal level, for which we are extremely grateful.

Last, but by no means least, we thank Vij Books, the publisher for their support and cooperation throughout the evolution of this book. Finally, for any errors or inadequacies that may remain in this work, of course, the responsibility is entirely the editors.

INTRODUCTION

India and China, the two giants of Asia are two of the oldest, living civilizations of the world. While Sindhu and Ganges gave birth to the Indian civilization and influenced South and Southeast Asia; Yellow River and Yangtze gave birth to the Chinese civilization and influenced Northeast and Southeast Asia. Being neighbours, India and China had established trade and cultural relations, since times immemorial.

It has been established by the historical records that Sino-Indian interaction was a two-way traffic and the two elements of this exchange were material and spiritual or cultural exchanges, which were facilitated by the four routes of communications, namely, the Central Asian Route or the so-called Silk Route, Assam-Burma and Yunnan Route or the famous Southern Silk Route, Tibet Nepal Route and the Sea Route or the so-called Maritime Silk Route.

The first credible information about the India-China interactions is provided by Si Maqian (BC 145 - BC 90), the great Chinese historian, in his masterpiece '*Records of a Historian*: *Foreigners in the Southwest*.' The record narrates that when Zhang Qian, a Han envoy in the western regions returned to the court in 122 BC, he reported to Han Emperor Wu Di (BC 140 - BC 87), that while in Bactria, he saw Sichuan silk and bamboo walking sticks. He also gathered that these were purchased by the local merchants from Indian markets, that lay several thousand kilometers in the Southeast. It could be established, from this fact, that India and China were already having trade relations in the second century BC. Ban Gu (32 AD - 92 AD), another Chinese historian writes in his book '*Early Han Annals*' about the state of affairs in Kashmir and its products like pearls, corals, lapis lazuli etc. The same book mentions about sea routes, connecting Southern India and China.

As regards the material exchanges, India supplied trade items such as corals, pearls, glass and fragrances. On the other hand, silk appears to be the major item transported from China to India. Trade relations further developed during Tang (618-907) Song (960-1279) and Yuan (1279-1368) dynasties. By this time, maritime activities were intense and it is reported in various sources that in Guangzhou (Canton) there were ships of Indians, Persians and Sri Lankan merchants. Meanwhile, Indian astronomy, calendars, medicine, music and dance, sugar manufacturing technology etc. made their way to China. Chinese silk products remained popular among the trade items. Silk was also transported to the Roman Empire through India where Indian merchants acted as intermediaries. During Ming Dynasty (1368-1644), Calicut and Cochin in India rose to prominence as new ports. References to other sea ports such as Mahabalipuram, Goa, Nagapattam, Quilon, Nicobar, Mumbai, Malabar, Calcutta and many more, could be found in various Chinese literary sources.

Beside material exchanges, it was perhaps the spiritual linkage i.e. Buddhism that altogether transformed and took the relationship to a new high. Though it is debatable when exactly Buddhism disseminated into China, the most prevalent version is the famous dream of "golden Buddha" by Han Emperor Ming Di (58AD-75AD). It was an outcome of this dream that the Chinese emperor dispatched a search team to India, whereby two highly proficient Buddhist scholar monks Kashyapa Matanga and Dharmaraksha were taken to China. The monastery, White Horse Monastery, which was built to accommodate them in Luoyang, attracts thousands of devotees and tourists even today. Initially, only the imperial house, aristocracy and other high-ranking officials practiced Buddhism, but gradually, especially from 3rd to 9th century, the influence of Buddhism in China broadened, and scholar monks from China to India and from India to China, visited both countries, by the thousands.

Though it is difficult to list all of them here, mention must be made of Kumarajiva (343AD-413AD) who established a great feat in the history of Sino-Indian cultural exchange. Kumarajiva, a Kashmiri by origin, reached China in 382 AD at a mature age of 40, attained high proficiency in Chinese language and translated many Sanskrit scriptures into Chinese. He was the first Indian scholar to head the Bureau for Sutra Translation. Another Indian who was high on popularity in China was

Bodhidharma,who went to China in 6th century AD and is believed to be the founder of Shaolin martial arts in China. Shaolin monastery in Luoyang still reminds us of this great Indian cultural ambassador to China.

On the other hand, Faxian (342AD-424AD), Xuanzang (600AD-664AD) and Yijing (635AD-713AD) shine bright among the Chinese cultural ambassadors to India. Faxian was the first Chinese to travel to India in search of Buddhist sutras with reliable literary sources. Faxian left Chang'an for India in 399 AD. He took the central Asian route, visited northern, central, western, eastern and southern India and returned to China by the sea route in 412 AD. In 414 AD, he completed his monumental work '*Accounts of a Buddhist Country.*' Xuanzang and Yijing had certain advantages over Faxian, as Tang Emperor Taizong (626AD-649AD) and Empress Wu Zetian (690AD-704AD) patronized them respectively. Xuanzang started to travel in western regions in 628 AD at a young age of 29. He crossed many cities along Xinjiang, former Soviet Union, Afghanistan, and Pakistan and finally reached Kashmir. He studied in Nalanda for a few years from 632AD-636AD and became proficient in Sanskrit. It is indeed heartening that the university where Xuanzang once studied is being rebuilt jointly by India, China, Japan and Singapore, and plans to offer courses in Buddhist studies. Xuanzang narrated the state of affairs of China to the Indian King Harshavardhana. Harsha was so impressed that he sent an embassy to the Chinese capital Chang'an that reached Tang court in 641 AD. The Chinese emperor Taizong responded positively and sent his envoy Wang Xuance to India. Xuanzang reached back in Chang'an in 645 at the age of 46 and engaged himself in the work of translating sutras. Xuanzang has narrated his Indian journey in the "Great Tang Records" later forming the classic '*Journey to the West.*' Had the works of Faxian and Xuanzang not been there, it would have been difficult to construct a major part of our ancient history. Yijing, a contemporary of Xuanzang, reached Tamerlipti of India via sea route in 673 AD, at the age of 39. The next year he reached Nalanda and studied Buddhist scriptures. He returned to China after 18 years and compiled biographies of the monks going to the western regions, in search of scriptures during Tang Dynasty, four year later.

Along with Buddhist linkage, Hinduism also made inroads into China.

This could be established from the discoveries of Hindu cultural relics from the sites such as Lopnor in Xinjiang, Kizil and Dunhuang grottoes in Gansu, Dali in Yunnan and Quanzhou in Guangdong provinces of China. Frescoes of Kizil and Dunhuang houses, the portraits of many Hindu deities such as Hanuman, Ganesha, Vinayaka, Laxmi and Shakti as also statues of Lord Krishna and Shiva have been unearthed from Quanzhou and Dali, in China.

Because of material and spiritual-cultural exchanges, both India and China benefited immensely in the field of literature as well as science and technology. Indian stories, fables, art, drama and medicine reached China. During Tang Dynasty, Chinese literary forms like *Chuanqiwen* and *Bianwen* were greatly influenced by the Indian literary style manifested in Panchatantra and Buddhist stories. Meanwhile, paper manufacturing techniques, silk, compass and gunpowder found their way from China to India. Above all, the cultural ambassadors from India to China and from China to India enhanced and strengthened mutual understanding, which acted as a catalyst in modern history of India and China, for rendering mutual support and sympathy to each other, during their respective national liberation struggles.

From Yuan (1271-1368) and Ming dynasties (1368-1644) onward until India and China launched their freedom struggles, the cross cultural currents between them were interrupted by the drastic domestic changes and more importantly by the gradual eastward expansion of western colonialism. Following this India was completely colonised by the British and China gradually transformed into a semi-feudal and semi-colonial society. Though colonisation did not result in severing of the centuries old ties between India and China, it did make its pace slow and sluggish. However, because of their long association and having suffered the same fate they extended moral support and sympathy to each other in their respective anti-imperialist struggle.

The anti-imperialist efflorescence of the Indian and Chinese people manifested, in a major way, as a challenge to the colonial order, for the first time, during the First War of Indian Independence (1857-59) in India and the Taiping Uprising (1850-1864) in China, as for the first time Indian soldiers stationed in China switched over to the Taipings and fought shoulder to shoulder against the imperialists and the Qing government. The reports of Indian soldiers joining the Taiping could be found in the memorials of the Qing army generals or other officials of the throne and with the foreigners who were directly involved in this peasant uprising.

The Indian soldiers were forced to fight a dirty war- The Opium War - much against their wishes. They joined the Taiping ranks out of sympathy as they found their sufferings similar to those of their own, but they failed to recognize the similarity between their objectives and establish links at organisational levels. However, on objective conditions, both the uprisings played an important role and inflicted heavy economic losses on the British. The involvement of Indian troops in the Taiping Uprising was the true beginning of rendering mutual support and sympathy, in their common struggle, among the Indian and Chinese people. This rapprochement continued when the more organised struggle for national independence was launched by the Indian and Chinese people.

It was due to the synergy between the cultures and the plight of the people of India and China that the nationalists and revolutionaries of both the countries developed deep mutual contacts and friendship amidst their anti-imperialist struggle. They became natural allies and devised various ways to dislodgc thc imperialists out of their countries. The supporters of Tilak, the leader of militant nationalists, carried out activities like Shivaji's commemorative meetings in places as far as Tokyo, in order to make the Indian voice of anti-imperialism reach outside India. These activities had active support of the Chinese nationalists such as Zhang Taiyan and Sun Yat-Sen. Sun Yat-Sen developed deep links with various Indian nationalists and revolutionaries and by using his good office, introduced them to the leading Japanese personages, thus enabling them to carry out their anti-British activities, unhindered. Nationalists like Surendermohan Bose, Rash Behari Bose, M.N. Roy, Barakatullah, Lala Lajpat Rai and many other outstanding pioneers of Indian freedom movement, maintained good contacts and friendship with Sun Yat-Sen, who, whole-heartedly supported the Indian cause and rendered all possible support.

Apart from operating from Japan, the Indian revolutionaries also made China one of their centres to carry out anti-British activities. Barring a few, most of them were members of the Ghadar Party. Much of the activities centred around Hankou, the centre of Kuomintang (KMT) government, and Shanghai and Hong Kong where Indian settlers, including policemen and troops, numbered maximum. The Ghadar activities during Siam-Burma Plan were directed from the United States, without any active outside help. The activities in the second phase found a link with the KMT and the Communist Party of China (CPC). The Ghadar support to the Chinese nationalist government and in turn, enlisting the latter's support, was the direct outcome of the formation of First United Front in China, between the KMT and CPC. Their activities came to an abrupt end with the collapse of the United Front in 1927, though some individuals continued to be active upto 1931-32.

With the rise of Gandhi in Indian politics, the entire Indian freedom movement turned into a mass movement. He stood for a spiritual world order and struggled to bring in this order, by civilized means, such as *satyagraha* and *ahimsa*. He wanted everybody to follow the path of truth and non-violence. For this, he even wrote to Hitler and to the Japanese militarists. He made non-violence his principal creed and never compromised with it. He was upheld by the Chinese people as a symbol of 'eastern civilization'. The Chinese media paid utmost attention and widely covered the Indian freedom struggle in various newspapers and journals. *Eastern Miscellany* took the lead and introduced Gandhi and the Gandhian movement to the Chinese people. It covered extensively the Non-Cooperation Movement of 1920-22 and Civil Disobedience Movement of 1931-34. Roughly from 1905-1948, it carried close to 65 articles covering different aspects of the Indian National Movement. The Chinese people showered both encomiums and criticism on Gandhi when he led the Non-Cooperation and Civil Disobedience Movements. Sun Yat-Sen, however, never approved of non-violence, for he was of the view that an armed struggle was indispensable for national liberation. He, nevertheless, approved of Gandhi's pacifist techniques such as non-cooperation and civil disobedience. Gandhi even suggested the techniques and principle of non-violence to the people of China, but came round to the Chinese viewpoint that it cannot be applied to China's national situation, especially when it was engaged in an armed struggle with the Japanese.

A new chapter was written in the history of Sino-Indian relations during the War of Resistance (1937-45) and the Second World War. So long as China suffered at the hands of the Japanese militarists, the reverberations were felt in India too. India dispatched a medical mission to China, in 1938, to help them in their War of Resistance. Dr. Kotnis, a doctor of this mission became a martyr when he died a hero's death while serving the wounded soldiers of Eighth Route Army and other Chinese people. Nehru made the bonds of friendship even stronger when he visited China in 1939. The Chinese people at first supported the Indian viewpoint that it should not join the War unless it was declared free. Later, they asked for support from India for the war effort of allied powers, as the whole situation had changed with the formation of India-China-Burma War theatre. President Chiang Kai-Shek visited India in 1940 specially to break the ongoing deadlock between the British and the Congress and met Gandhi.

The period from 1905-1947 was the duration when both the people of India and China extended support and sympathy towards each other, in their common struggle. It was Nehru's vision that the tremendous potential of economic cooperation would necessarily bring India and China closer to each other in a new world order, after the war and that politically too, the two would unite against any outside aggression and play an important role in the world affairs. Soon after the end of the War, China plunged into civil war. In this period of crisis, India wished for the unity of China and hoped that it would resolve its problems peacefully. It appears that the ground realities in China during and before the civil war were not clear to the Congress. Its leaders underestimated the hold of the Communist Party, over the masses. This could possibly be due to the relationship that Nehru and other Congress leaders had established with the leaders of the ruling Kuomintang (KMT), that never controlled more than 27% of the total area of China. Another factor could be the uniformity of interests and goals that the Indian National Congress and KMT had established during Nehru's visit of China in 1939. Actually, non-resistance to Japan and the extermination campaigns by KMT against the communists, had made it very unpopular amongst the masses. Also, corruption within the KMT ranks was said to have reached extraordinary proportions. Despite American assistance, the well-equipped army of KMT was routed and forced to flee to Taiwan.

India kept its faith with China despite the defeat of the nationalists in the civil war. Nehru also accepted the failure of Chiang Kai-Shek and his corrupt army. He was convinced that public opinion in India was against KMT and lending support to a bankrupt government in China, would be condemned in India. Thus, respecting the victory of Communist Party of China over KMT, India recognized the People's Republic of China as the legitimate government of China on April 1, 1950. India was the first country in the non-communist block to recognize China and establish diplomatic relations.

The post-independence history of Sino-Indian relations has been that of friendship hype (1947-1958), animosities (1959-1969), normalization (1970-1998), setbacks (1998-2000) and cooperative partnership (2001-date).

After establishing diplomatic ties, both India and China expressed common concern and understanding on major international issues, and cooperated with each other on various diplomatic fronts. China respected the Indian stand of not siding with any block and for expounding its own policy of peace, neutrality and non-alignment, even though Mao was averse to the idea of remaining neutral. Some of the Chinese suspicions towards India, were done away with, when on 29 April 1954, India and China signed an Agreement on Trade and Intercourse between the Tibet Region of China and India. India accepted Tibet as a part of China. In other words, India relinquished the British responsibilities and obligations in Tibet. The preamble of the Agreement advocated the so-called Five Principles of Peaceful Coexistence or Panchsheel. From 1954 to 1957, Chinese Premier Chou En-lai visited India thrice and Nehru visited China once. India advocated for the restoration of China's permanent seat in the United Nations Security Council. From 1950 to 1958, the Indian delegation to the United Nations (UN) General Assembly appealed to the UN at least 30 times, sponsored resolutions year after year advocating that the Peoples Republic of China should represent China, at the UN. During the Korean War (1950-1953), India voted against the UN draft resolution which vilified China as an aggressor and abstained from voting for the draft resolution for putting an embargo on China. On its part, China named India as the chairman of the repatriation committee for Prisoners of War (POW) after the Korean War.

However, due to the unsettled border and other problems left over by the history, Sino-Indian relations took a nosedive. It could be argued that the Indian stand on the boundary question was a reflection of its stand on the issue of Tibet, which itself had many lacunae and was unsustainable given the strength of India. The British could sustain Tibet as a buffer, for it was the most powerful nation at that time. The conclusion of Sino-Indian agreement on Tibet, in 1954, was wrongly perceived in India, as acquiescence of India's position in the Eastern Sector. The subsequent cartographic changes by both the countries, further complicated the issue. In 1958, when Chou En-lai formally laid China's claim to Arunachal in Eastern Sector and Aksai Chin in the Western Sector, Nehru was greatly surprised. The 1959 Tibetan revolt, Indian sympathy towards Tibet and the political asylum to the Dalai Lama made China furious - they started taking anti-India posture at regional as well as international levels. The official talks on the border issue in 1960-61, ended in a failure. The Sino-Soviet split and increasing bonhomie between India and Russia was perceived by China, as essentially a military alliance, directed towards her. The growing mistrust and animosities resulted in a limited border conflict in 1962. The ensuing diplomatic freeze also jeopardised the boundary issue and heightened the tensions along border areas.

Between 1962 and 1969, Sino-Indian relations remained in a deep freeze. Emboldened by its easy victory over India, China initiated a vitriolic and vituperative campaign against India, which deepened India's suspicion about the intentions of China even further. India's mistrust in China was further confirmed when China befriended Pakistan and began to extend military and political support to it. China also used the opportunity to aggravate internal insurgency in India - incited and encouraged the Naxal violence, trained the Nagas and Mizos in China and sent them back to foment trouble in India. China justified its actions as she accused India of supporting Tibet and Taiwan independence. The relations between the two countries touched its lowest ebb when China supported Pakistan during the latter's military adventure against India, in 1965 and 1971 and threatened India of similar actions. During the so-called Cultural Revolution, thousands of red guards demonstrated outside the Indian embassy in Beijing and shouted anti-India slogans. Some of the slogans included, "Down with the Indian reactionaries!", "Resolutely eliminate all spies of imperialism, revisionism and reaction!" There are some Chinese scholars who believe that the anti-India propaganda germinated from the "ultra leftist policies" of China, during the cold war.

After the border war, the mutual trust and sympathy was completely lost. The Indo-Pak conflict of 1965 and 1971 further added fuel to the fire, as China now sided with Pakistan on various issues, including Kashmir. However, there were attempts to restore the bilateral relations, from both the sides. The then Indian Prime Minister, Indira Gandhi expressed India's desire to improve relations with China. On May 1, 1970 while receiving diplomats from various countries at Tian-an-men, Mao Zedong (1893-1976) warmly shook hands with the Indian envoy Brijesh Mishra.

Relations improved gradually from mid-1970s onwards when diplomatic relations were restored at ambassadorial level. Since then, the cultural exchanges between the two countries have been on the rise. In 1978, Wang Binnan headed a delegation of Chinese People's Association on a Goodwill visit to India. Following this, the first batch of Indian students were sent to China on an exchange programme. In 1979, the then Foreign Minister Atal Behari Vajpayee visited China. The visit happened to be a short one as China invaded Vietnam while Vajpayee was still in China. Once again the officials of both the countries began to put in their efforts to resolve the unsettled boundary issue. However, despite the nine rounds of talks from1981 to 1988, they could not reach any conclusion, for the issue is too intricate and sensitive. However, both the countries felt that the border question should not be a hindrance in the development of relations in other domains.

Sino-Indian relations took a major stride after Rajiv Gandhi visited China in December 1988. It was the first by an Indian Prime Minister, in three decades. In the meeting with Rajiv Gandhi on December 21, 1988, the then Chairman of China's Central Military Commission, Deng Xiaoping remarked, "Let us forget the unpleasant phase in our past relations and do everything with an eye on the future." Both sides expressed their hope to join hands to cooperate for mutual development. Agreements for scientific and technological cooperation, civil aviation, and the plans for executing cultural exchange and cooperation for the year 1988, 1989 and 1990 were signed, and a Joint Working Group (JWG as set up to resolve the boundary issue.

Following Rajiv Gandhi's visit, Chinese Premier Li Peng paid a return visit to India in 1991; it was the first visit by a Chinese Premier after Chou En-lai's 1960 visit. During his visit, Li signed five agreements with his Indian counterpart Narasimha Rao - these being: Consul treaty between India and China, Agreement on Restoration of Consulate General in Bombay and Shanghai, Memorandum on the Restoration of Border Trade, Sino-Indian Trade Protocol for the year 1992 and Scientific and Technological Cooperation in Outer Space for the peaceful use by the aviation ministries of India and China. Beside, both sides opined that the border issue should not become an obstacle in the improvement of bilateral relations. Bilateral relations were further strengthened by the visits of the then President of India, R. Venkataraman and Minister of Human Resource and Development Mr. Arjun Singh, to China in May 1992 and February 1993 respectively.

Prime Minister Narasimha Rao's September 6, 1993 China visit is hailed as another landmark in the bilateral relations. If Rajiv Gandhi was successful in cutting the ice, then Narasimha Rao's visit brought about a thaw in India-China relations, by signing India-China accord on the Line of Actual Control (LAC). The Agreement on Maintenance of Peace and Tranquility along the LAC, in the Sino-Indian Border Areas stipulated that the border issue should be resolved through peaceful and friendly negotiations; neither side should use force or threaten to use force against the other; the two sides should strictly respect and observe the LAC before the border issue is settled and each side should keep its military forces in the areas along the LAC, to a minimum level. Narasimha Rao made it clear in his speech at Beijing University that both the countries had been through a long period of misunderstanding and misapprehension, but once again they were entering into an era of mutual understanding and cooperation.

Chinese President Jiang Zemin's 1996 India visit further strengthened the bilateral relations between the two countries. Jiang was the first *de facto* and *de jure* head of the Chinese government to visit India. During his visit, India and China signed four important agreements: 1) The Agreement on Confidence Building Measures (CBMs) in the field of military deployment along the LAC in the India-China border areas; 2) The Agreement concerning the maintenance of the Consulate General of India in Hong Kong Special Administrative Region of the People's Republic of China; 3) The Agreement on cooperation for combating illicit trafficking in narcotic drugs and psychotropic substance and other crimes; and 4) the Agreement on maritime transport. Among all these, the agreement on CBMs was of foremost importance. The agreement pronounced that the suggested measures aim at "a fair, reasonable and mutually acceptable settlement" of the boundary question. The very first article of the agreement is very significant, which says, "neither side shall use its military capability against the other side". Some of the national newspapers at that time reported these pronouncements as "a virtual no-war pact". However, the agreement cannot be considered a no-war pact, for the same things were reiterated, though faintly, during Narasimha Rao's 1993 China visit.

Normalisation of relations appeared to be going in the right direction for India and China, until India did its nuclear test on May 11th and 13th, 1998. China raised its concern, saying that the explosions ran against the international trend and was "detrimental to the peace and stability of the South Asian region". China's initial reaction to the Indian tests was mild; however, it grew strong and harsh when Prime Minister Vajpayee 's letter to the US President Bill Clinton appeared in the media, citing "China threat" in defence of its nuclear tests of May 11 and 13. In fact, "China threat" perception was spelled out by the Indian Defence Minister George Fernandes, before the May 11 tests. At that time China had targeted Fernandes alone and had rebuffed his views and accusation as irresponsible. Many leading political parties also had termed Fernandes' remarks as 'irresponsible and baseless.'

Partly bitten by Fernandes' China bashing and more so by Vajpayee's letter to the US President Bill Clinton, China's reaction to the second series of nuclear explosions of May 13th was harsh. It accused that India's nuclear tests reflected "an outrageous contempt for the common will of the international community" and accused India of seeking "hegemony" in South Asia. In India, people felt that citing of 'China threat' was unnecessary and that the controversy created by Fernandes's remarks was entirely avoidable; however, India at once refuted the Chinese charges that it sought hegemony in South Asia or that its action would entail serious consequences to the peace and security in the region and the world at large. Ridiculing China's objection to India's tests, a statement by the government spokesman drew attention to the fact that "India has legitimate security concerns" and that it could not but take into account the offensive nuclear weapon and missile capability in the region nor "the well documented history of proliferation through clandestine acquisition taking place in our neighbourhood." These remarks obviously referred to China and its help to Pakistan. The spokesman further added that China had conducted 45 tests till date, since it exploded its first nuclear device, while India, after a restraint of 24 years, just exploded five devices.

The bickering over the nuclear issue continued for some time, which put the Sino-Indian relations in jeopardy. However, as the post nuclear negotiations with major world powers paid dividends, China also understood the futility of remaining aloof or alienating India. The two sides officially resumed talks in February 1999, after a gap of 9 months. Both sides agreed to resume the 11th JWG meeting, that was slated to be held in the second half of 1998 but had to be postponed due to the setbacks. The June 1999 China visit of Indian Foreign Minister, Jaswant Singh, further brought about a thaw in the frosty relations. China on its part expressed its willingness and readiness to discuss any matter arising out of India's security concerns. Jaswant Sigh during his China visit, clarified it to the Chinese authorities that India does not consider China as a threat to it.

India initiated a more pragmatic approach as regards its China policy since Rajiv Gandhi's 1988 China visit. India embarked on the road of reforms in the 1990s that also demanded an overhauling of its foreign policy. The most striking change is its abandonment of Nehru's approach to the boundary question. India is willing to engage China and negotiate with it the knotty boundary question. The eight rounds prior to 1988 and 15 rounds of JWG talks since then, is an example of this. It has deemed it sensible to develop trade and economic relationship with China, and not let the boundary issue become an obstacle in the development of relations, an obvious departure from its pre-1980s China policy. The visits of Narasimha Rao and Atal Behari Vajpayee to China, in 1993 and 2003 respectively, reflect this new approach of the Indian government. Opening more of the border regions for trade, including the Nathu La in Sikkim, exemplify the greater maturity in the relationship between the two countries, in the backdrop of China recognizing Sikkim as a part of India.

Another high level visit that gave boost to the momentum of earlier visits at the highest levels was the visit of Chinese Premier Wen Jiabao to India between April 9 and 12, 2005. Premier Wen was visiting India at a time when both India and China were being swept by tremendous economic changes, in their respective countries. Owing to the drastic economic and political changes in the domestic and international arenas, the negotiation on various issues of common concern were held in a constructive atmosphere, and a new level for comprehensive development of economic and political relations, was created. Building on the Declaration on Principles for Relations and Comprehensive Cooperation between the Indian and Chinese Prime Ministers on 23 June 2003, the two sides reiterated that India-China relations have now acquired a global and strategic character, and that there was a need to resolve the outstanding issues in a proactive manner, without letting them come in the way of the continued development of bilateral relations. A total of twelve agreements were signed to pave the way for a future course of sound and fruitful relations between the two countries. These are: 1) Agreement on Political Parameters and Guiding Principles for the Settlement of the India-China Boundary Question; 2) Report of India-China Joint Study Group on Comprehensive Trade and Economic Cooperation; 3) Protocol on Modalities for the Implementation of CBMs in the Military Field along the Line of Actual Control in the India-China Border Areas; 4) Agreement on Mutual Administrative Assistance and Cooperation in Customs Matters; 5) MOU on the Launch of the India-China Financial Dialogue; 6) MOU on Civil Aviation; 7) Protocol of Phytosanitary Requirement for Exporting Grapes from India to

China; 8) Protocol of Phytosanitary Requirement for Exporting Bitter Gourds from India to China; 9) MOU on Provision of Hydrological Information of the Sutlej/Langqen Zangbo River in Flood Season by China to India; 10) Protocol on India-China Film Cooperation Commission; 11) MOU on Cooperation between the Indian Council of World Affairs and the Chinese People's Institute of Foreign Affairs; and 12) Memorandum on the Construction of an Indian-style Buddhist Temple on the Western side of the White Horse Temple in Luoyang, China.

Keeping in view, the amazing growth rate of the bilateral trade, the two sides recognized the importance of strengthening mutual connectivity and agreed to jointly work towards further enhancement of direct air and shipping links, tourism and people-to-people contacts. A MOU on major liberalisation of civil aviation links between India and China, was also concluded during the visit. The outcome of this was that direct flights operated by Air China, China Eastern and Air India flew from Beijing to New Delhi and from Shanghai to Mumbai and New Delhi.

After Wen's visit, though the trade relations improved substantially, as the bilateral trade crossed 60 billion US dollars in 2010; however, the political thrust seems to have been marred by the jittery border issue, and more so by the Chinese insistence on handing over ofTawang in Arunachal, to China, for a final settlement of the border issue. Hu Jintao's India visit in 2006, Prime Minister Manmohan Singh's China visit in 2009 and Wen Jiabao's India visit in 2010, could not break much ice, owing to the deepening mistrust and India's resolve to strengthen its border infrastructure, of late. Though the JSG has recommended an India-China Regional Trading Arrangement, but the political trust deficit has played a spoiler. Now the matter has been referred to a Joint Task Force (JTF) that will study in detail, the feasibility and the benefits of such an agreement. Other issues such as China's intention to divert Brahmaputra water, border incursions, malpractices of the Chinese telecom companies in India, China-Pak nexus, opening of dozens of China Study Centres in Nepal and its tacit support to the Maoists, China's building of naval infrastructures and ports in Bangladesh and Sri Lanka, etc have once again eclipsed the good neighbourly relations between the two countries.

It is not possible not to have problems between the neighbours. The need of the hour is to build mutual trust, and to build this trust, we must explore possibilities. India has supported China in the UN, over 30 times even after the 1962 war, so China's support to India's bid for a permanent membership of the UN Security Council will win enormous goodwill for China in India and would take the bilateral relations to a new high. China's guarded and cautious approach on this issue has not gone down well with India. Other possibilities could be more and more people-to-people contacts and a relaxed visa regime. The media-to- media relations need to be strengthened and direct access to news channels in either country is another possibility. In this regard, India needs to increase its reporter strength in China, so that the Indian public get more and objective news stories about the different aspects of China. The initiation of conducting Cultural Festivals on either side of the Himalaya is another activity that will enhance mutual understanding. Last but not the least, it is time for India and China to resurrect their centuries old sentiments with a new zeal and exploit their potential and usher in a New World of economic cooperation. This seems quite realistic as both India and China have initiated economic liberalisation and have given priority to economic development. The icon of China's reforms and 'sinicized socialism', Deng Xiaoping remarked, "If China and India are developed, we can say that we have made our contribution to mankind." It is this vision which India and China should emulate, to bring out the millions of people from the morass of poverty and hunger. Moreover, in order to reduce their technological dependence on western countries, both India and China need to cooperate in the fields like space, application of nuclear energy for constructive purposes, computer software, genetic engineering, agriculture, hydroelectricity generation etc. Today when we talk of this cooperation and future of India China relations, the same must be viewed in the larger perspective of India China historical bonds vis-à-vis their interests and future outlook. There is hope that these two Asian giants would forge closer ties as they did, during their struggle for freedom and embark on the road of development, peace and good neighbourly relations.

-D.P. Tripathi
-B.R. Deepak

Mani Shankar Aiyar

India's Relationship with China*

The most essential element in building our relationship with China is that we must be clear in our mind as to what is the bottom line. Is the McMahon line the bottom line? Is there scope of any kind of adjustment on that? What we want from the Chinese becomes more meaningful only when we know exactly what we want from ourselves. From the days of Mahatma Gandhi, if not earlier, it has been clear to us that like we cannot ask for the moon and get it, similarly violence and destruction lead nowhere. If we do not engage with the Chinese then perhaps it betrays more, a moral act of self-confidence in our own country than it does any recalcitrance on the part of our neighbour. The fact of the matter is that a self-confident country that knows its own bottom line, should have no difficulty in engaging with any country in the world, especially with a neighbour and specially with such a large, populous, powerful and growing neighbour as the People's Republic of China. Happily, in the India-China relationship, unlike the India-Pakistan relationship, there is no historical competition. While there were cultural and civilizational contacts in the past, there were very few political contacts. Indeed if there was any strong contact in economic terms between India and China, it was much more in Southern India on the coast of Kerala and Tamil Nadu, with the seaports of China, than there was across the land.

China really came looming onto our horizon with the revolution of 1911 that Sun Yat-sen led against the Chinese emperor, which inaugurated the Republican period of China's life and Chiang Kai-shek was certainly, until about 1947, a very significant Chinese leader, regarded as the Chinese patriot who stood up firmly against the Japanese invasion of China. He was regarded as the comrade-in-arms, by Jawaharlal Nehru on the grounds

---

*This article is based on Shri Aiyar's talk on 'India-China Relations' organised by *Think India* in the JNU campus on 15 April, 2010.

that if we have such relationships with China, Asia will be able to re-establish itself. And that it was not a purely political or sectarian relationship was revealed when the Maoist revolution succeeded and India wished to be the very first country to recognise the new People's Republic of China. But we had a request from Myanmar (Burma) that we should give them the courtesy of being the first to recognise the Maoist Republic and Jawaharlal Nehru with his usual gentleness, conceded that demand and that is why India became the second country in the world to recognise People's Republic of China. And the hopes were so very strong, of a relationship being built between India and China, that when in 1950, (as we now know, due to a revelation made by K.R. Narayanan, when he was the President of India) the Americans offered us the Chinese permanent seat in the UN Security Council. Jawaharlal Nehru rejected the idea and argued that it was China and not India that had the legitimate claim on the seat. There were those in India who feared that the relationship between India and China was bound to deteriorate as China consolidated itself and started making disturbing claims.

Given the fact that independent India perceived at least in some quarters its security interests, as being influenced by the same factors that had driven the great game between Russia and India when Czars were in power in Russia and the British were in power here in India, there were warnings sounded, the most renowned of them being that made by Sardar Patel, who was then, at the end of his life. I think it was only few days before he died, Sardar Vallabhbhai Patel's letter to Jawaharlal Nehru on 7 November 1950 not only deplored Indian Ambassador KM Panikkar's action but also warning about dangers from China, when he wrote to Jawaharlal Nehru, warning him that misplaced expectations of the Chinese could be dangerous to our security and ever since then, a lot of Indian elements, hostile to China had picked upon that letter and shown it as an example of Jawaharlal Nehru's naivety[1]. However he was aware of the complication posed by the Tibet question as it were between us and them. Therefore, in 1954, a formal agreement was entered into, between India and China, with respect to Tibet, in which while the suzerainty of China

---

[1] See Appendix 1

over Tibet was accepted, it was hoped that the cultural and spiritual identity of Tibet would be maintained and in some sense, in terms of contemporary 20th Century understanding of international politics, Tibet would continue to function as the buffer between India and China. And it was in the context of that agreement signed in April 1954, that the five principles of peaceful co-existence - The Panchsheel - was agreed upon. So the choice before India today, in my opinion, is either to restore our relationship with China on the basis of 'Panchsheel'[2], or to abandon the principles of 'Panchsheel', to accept I do not know what. I think it is necessary to ask those who point accusatory fingers at China, as to what it is that should constitute the principles of the India - China relationship if 'Panchsheel' is not going to serve the purpose. As far as I am personally concerned, as something of a Nehruvian, I think the five principles of peaceful co-existence essentially say that two sovereign countries will not interfere in each other's internal affairs, and they will have mutual respect for each other and try to promote their relationship on the basis of mutual cooperation and evolution of the mutual interest. For all the years of the Nehru era and the Indira Gandhi era, we had no hesitation whatsoever in affirming or continuing the commitment to the principles of 'Panchsheel'.

Except for a brief border conflict in 1962, India and China have had a long history of peaceful coexistence and therefore the relation between them has the potential to blossom into a major relationship. And here I must halt and go back to Nehru's vision of Asia. Nehru in his capacity as the External Affairs Member of the Viceroy's Council, had convened in the March 1947 Asian Relations Conference[3], in a continent which had virtually

---

[2] From 31 December 1953 to 3 April 1954, India and China conducted negotiations on Tibet and concluded the "Agreement between the Republic of India and the People's Republic of China on Trade and Intercourse between Tibet Region of China and India" on 29 April 1954. The preamble of the Agreement advocated the so-called Five Principles of Peaceful Coexistence or *Panchsheel*, these are: 1. Mutual respect for each other's territorial integrity and sovereignty, 2. Mutual non-aggression, 3. Mutual non-interference in each other's internal affairs, 4. Equality and mutual benefits, and 5. Peaceful coexistence.

[3] In early 1947, the Indian Council of World Affairs convened an Asiatic Conference in Delhi and extended invitation to over 30 countries including Tibet. During the conference Tibet like other nations had Tibetan flag on its table. Chinese envoy launched a protest when they pointed to the map in the conference hall that showed Tibet outside China. Matter was addressed when brought to Nehru's notice.

no independent country. So it was the leaders of freedom movements taking place all around Asia, that were summoned together because Nehru had the vision to see that these were going to be imminently the leaders of Asia and the era of colonialism with which we lived for 250 years, was about to draw to an end. And it was Chiang Kai-shek's China that became the key party to the representatives' meet.

Here I must mention the influence of Viswa-Bharati, Rabindra Nath Tagore's university at Shantiniketan, where for the first time, scholars from Korea, Japan, China, Persia and from the Arab world were brought together, along with the Indian scholars, in one single place to try to rediscover the self-respect which, in many ways, had gone out of Asian hearts, particularly in the 19th century. Take for example the case of Mahatma Gandhi going to London, as a 17-18 year old boy and asking himself why it was that a few thousand English men were able to rule over 200-300 million Indians and coming to the conclusion that it was because they ate meat. There was a complete collapse of the Indian belief in India and it was much worse for the Chinese, because as a result of exported opium from India to China, the Chinese manhood had been leached. A typical image of a Chinese was that of one who was reclining upon his sofa with an opium pipe stuck to his mouth and drugged for life. And this was true not of hundreds of Chinese but true of a huge proportion of their population, not only male but also female. All over Asia, starting from Eastern Mediterranean and extending right up to Japan, (where the memory of Commodore Perry entering the Tokyo Bay and opening up that country to western influence was very strong) there was a complete loss of self-confidence in Asia in the fact that they were a worthy people. There was a tendency to look west to discover the sources of intellectual and emotional vigour, the ability to run military campaigns and the ability to conduct the affairs of the state. Now, how much of a contrast this was, with only a 150 years earlier, is illustrated by a letter I came across, the other day. Written by Aurangzeb to his Prime Minister the letter read, 'you had told me that the Firangi king was a small landlord but I now understand that he is as great an emperor as myself.' There was an India of the 17th century which believed itself to be at the top of the world. Indeed the India of the 11th century, as Al Beruni testifies, was also one that believed itself to be at the top of the world and this was perhaps true for most of the countries of Asia, since it was they who had been in the vanguard of the advancement of the human civilization.

So it is not surprising that there had been this loss of self-respect, this loss of self-confidence. Even reformers life Raja Ram Mohan Roy (1772-1833) were tending to look towards the European examples rather than take inspiration from within, to see how our society could be reformed in the direction of restoring ourselves to past glory. And this is also reflected in the Muslim thought where a lot of very reactionary Muslim theologians who had been virtually ignored through the 18th century, suddenly became figures of immense importance in Muslim thinking, during the 19th century, because they too were wondering what had become of us. Iqbal's Shikwa and Jawab-e-Shikwa is a reflection of that.

So, in this period of a lack of self-confidence, along came Rabindranath Tagore, established Viswa-Bharati and said 'I don't need European scholars except those who wish of their own accord to come and join us'. He brought together, thinkers from all over Asia and started what in effect was an Asian Renaissance. So what Nehru was attempting to do was to convert this Asian renaissance into an Asian resurgence. I think this larger vision is often missed by those who are hostile to our relationship with China. They don't realise that Asia is not going to restore itself until and unless the two major Asian countries come together along with Iran and the Arab world.

Therefore, India-China relationship has to be worked upon. For it is not enough only to have a vision. One has to face the ground realities and the ground realities include the fact that China is a huge nuclear weapons' power. We have to face the fact that they are insisting every now and then that McMahon line is not acceptable to them and all of NEFA, now called Arunachal Pradesh, belongs to them. We have the problem of Tsangpo, which rises in Tibet and flows into Arunachal Pradesh as Dihang and becomes Brahmaputra when it enters Assam - it is a river which could be diverted into the direction of mainland China, leaving the whole of North-East, which has highest forest cover in India, to turn into desert. We have the problem in Ladakh, where a third of our territory, Aksai-Chin is occupied by China and claimed by them as the legitimate part of their country. So there are problems, but when you put them on the scale beside what is the vision of what you wish to achieve, then there is no comparison between the weight of the problems and the weight of what will be achieved. The point is, we either resolve the problems or at least learn to live with them. And if we learn to live with them, and India and China come together, I have no doubt, that in the rest of South-East Asia, much of East Asia and progressively through Iran into West Asia, we can build ourselves and then restore this continent to the position that it has always held through history, of being the vanguard not just of economic prosperity, but of the advancement of human civilization.

So are you confident that you will protect the sovereignty of your country? Are you confident of your own bottom line? Are you confident of your capacity to hold that bottom line? If your answer is 'yes', then you must negotiate with the Chinese with patience and imagination, rooted in ground realities, with an eye on the future, to restore Asia to its glorious past.

Zhang Yan

Strengthening China-India Relations in an All-Round Manner

This year marks the 60th anniversary of the establishment of diplomatic relations between China and India. On this auspicious occasion, it is indeed a great pleasure for me, through the journal *Think India Quarterly*, to express my sincere gratitude to Indian friends from all walks of life, who have worked tirelessly for the development of China-India relations. In the more than 2000 years of history, good-neighbourliness and friendly interactions have been the main features of China-India relations. The liberation and independence of China and India in the middle of the last century not only changed the destinies of the two countries, but also the political landscape of the world. The establishment of diplomatic ties between China and India on April 1, 1950 ushered in a new era for the development of the bilateral relations. Since then, China and India have enjoyed mutual understanding and support in their respective endeavour of safeguarding independence and sovereignty, as well as in nation building. The catch phrase of "Hindi-Chini Bhai-Bhai" has been deeply rooted in the hearts of the peoples of the two countries. The famous 'Panchsheel', the Five Principles of Peaceful Coexistence, initiated by China and India during 1950s, continues to be one of the guiding principles of international relations. In spite of the temporary ups and downs, China-India relations on the whole, have been progressing positively, thanks to the leadership of the succeeding generations of the two countries. Today, China and India have emerged as the two rapidly growing economies and their relationship has gone beyond the bilateral dimension and assumed global and strategic significance.

Looking into the future, despite all kinds of positive and negative hypotheses, I am optimistic about China-India relations for the following reasons:

First, the leaders of both the countries have taken long-term strategic perspective about mutual relationship which provides a clear guidance and solid political basis for the sustained development of relations.

Second, China-India relations have acquired new dimensions. The two countries established the Strategic and Cooperative Partnership for Peace and Prosperity in 2005, formulated the Ten-Pronged Strategy in 2006, and signed A Shared Vision for 21st Century in 2008. All these have provided guidelines and roadmaps for the development of strategic partnership.

Third, China-India relations are expanding and deepening in an all round manner, and have extended into almost all human endeavours which have yielded tangible benefits to the people of both the countries.

Fourth, China and India enjoy growing shared interests. As two emerging economic powers, China and India have become important trade partners. They also share similar views on many important global and regional issues and closely coordinate and cooperate with each other within the framework of BRICS, BASIC, G20 and other fora and on issues like the financial crisis, climate change and international trade negotiations. Both are committed to the idea of promoting and building a harmonious world order for common prosperity.

Fifth, China-India relations have matured over the years. While striving to seek mutually acceptable solutions to the boundary issue and other differences, both sides agree not to let these differences stand in the way of cooperation. Furthermore, the two countries have set up relevant mechanisms, such as Special Representative Talks on border issue, strategic dialogues and so on. All these platforms have played very useful roles in addressing relevant issues and maintaining stable relations between the two countries.

The past 60 years have clearly proved that when China and India live in amity and understand and support each other, the two countries grow faster and people benefit. When China and India join hands, they make positive impact on the world peace and prosperity. It has also proved that cooperation, communication, consultation and dialogue are the best means to handle relations. There are no fundamental differences and conflicts between China and India. We have more common interests than differences. Chinese President Hu Jintao has emphasised that 'the good-neighbourly friendship and cooperation between China and India and their common development, not only benefit our two peoples but also serve the peace and development of Asia and the entire world.' Indian Prime Minister Dr. Manmohan Singh has time and again said that 'there is enough room in the world for India and China to prosper together.'

In order to take the China-India relations forward, I am of the view that efforts should be made in the following areas:

First, further enhance mutual trust. I share the view that China and India need to enhance their mutual trust which is vital to a sound and stable relationship. Without trust there can be no genuine relations. Without trust, there can be no sustained and meaningful cooperation. The two countries should maintain the momentum of high-level interaction; expand exchanges and cooperation at all levels and in all fields. The very recent visit by the Indian President to China, will surely enhance mutual trust and cooperation between the two countries.

Second, upgrade the level of economic cooperation. As two fast growing economies, China and India hold great potentials for cooperation in trade and investment. The two sides should expand the scope of trade, improve trade configuration, and strive to reduce the trade imbalance. At the same time, the two countries should endeavor to reach a regional trade arrangement and take effective measures to remove trade and investment barriers, in order to foster an environment conducive to sustainable development of bilateral economic cooperation and achieve a win-win outcome.

Third, expand people-to-people exchanges to cement public support for our relations. The two countries should enhance exchanges and cooperation in the fields of education, tourism, religion, science and technology, and increase interactions between the academic communities and media sectors of the two countries. Exchanges between youths of both sides should be further expanded. The China Festival in India and Indian Festival in China which have recently opened, will surely serve as an invaluable platform for promoting mutual understanding and friendship.

Fourth, further strengthen cooperation at multilateral fora. China and India must remain important partners in regional and global affairs, strengthen coordination and cooperation, and continue to play an active role in promoting multi-polarisation and democratisation of international relations and safeguard the common interests of developing countries.

Fifth, properly address each other's concerns. The two countries should respect and accommodate each other's interests and concerns and appropriately manage the outstanding issues through consultations on equal footing and in a spirit of mutual understanding. The two sides must follow the political parameters and principles that both have agreed upon, including the Five Principles of Peaceful Co-existence, and strive to seek a fair and reasonable solution acceptable to both the sides.

Sixth, properly handle public opinion. Public opinion is vitally important to the development of our relations. We must provide correct guidance to the public opinions and avoid war of words. Efforts should be made on both sides to create an objective, friendly and mutually trusting environment. A good and conducive public environment will not only provide the necessary condition for stable development of our relations, but also create conditions conducive to the settlement of historical issues and other differences.

The populations of China and India account for 40 per cent of the world's total population. A meaningful cooperation between China and India will not only benefit the two countries and its people, but also the peace and prosperity of Asia and the world at large. At the beginning of a new cycle of 60 years, China-India relations is poised for a major breakthrough, with new and rare opportunities. The two countries must join their efforts to take our relations to greater heights.

BR Deepak

Ji Xianlin: India-China Civilizational Dialogue and Intercultural Studies

This chapter systematically expounds Ji Xianlin's contribution to Indian studies in China. It discusses that being a pioneer of Indian studies in China, Ji Xianlin promoted civilizational dialogue between India and China. The very authorship, translation, annotation and compilation of a large number of literary works, including Buddhist literature by him is a testimony to his extraordinary feat in this area. His advocacy of the two-way traffic between India and China is vividly reflected in this chapter when the author discusses Ji Xianlin's studies in various facets of cultural and material linkages between India and China. Besides discussing Ji Xianlin's destiny with India, his contribution to Indian studies and his approaches towards research, the chapter concludes that he is a true ambassador of India-China cultural exchange and friendship.

Baidu, China's largest search engine, introduces Ji Xianlin as a well-known scholar of classical Chinese, paleographer, historian, Orientalist, thinker, translator, Buddhist scholar, proficient in 12 languages, so on and so forth. In China, some people have crowned him with the titles such as the 'maestro of Chinese culture', 'academic leader', and 'national treasure'. However, he has refused to be crowned with such titles, and has requested such people "to take these crowns off his head and return his freedom (*Wenhui Bao*, June 13, 2007)." This author, perhaps others in India also, has come to know Professor Ji Xianlin as a well-known professor of Peking University, a prolific translator, having great expertise in Sanskrit, Pali and the history of Sino-Indian cultural exchanges. Ji Xianlin is not only respected in mainland China, but equally revered and adored by people of other countries and regions, especially the Indian people. This is amply demonstrated by the fact that in 2008, the Government of India conferred on him, India's third highest civilian honour, the Padma Bhushan. Reacting to this news, Wang Bangwei, Professor at the Institute of Oriental Studies of Beijing University said (Shi Jianfeng 2008), "This is a matter of great significance. The conferment of this award will have a very positive impact on how the ordinary Chinese people perceive India." While interacting with the Indian media, Professor Jiang Jingkui, Deputy Director of India Research Centre at Beijing University also expressed that "the important decision [of conferring Padma Bhushan] is one of the important aspects in the development of Sino-Indian friendship. This is bound to change the perception of many Chinese people towards India." Professor Jiang Jingkui believes that "from a certain point of view, the contribution of Ji Xianlin to the Sino-Indian relationship parallels that of Xuan Zang." No wonder, China Confucius Foundation established Ji Xianlin Research Institute under the auspices of Shandong University to pursue research on "The Studies of Ji Xianlin" five years back, when the gentle academic giant of China turned 94 years old.

Ji Xianlin's Destiny with India

In India, many people are of the view that Ji Xianlin's tryst with oriental research happened either in China or India. However, to everyone's surprise, his destiny with India started in Germany. Ji Xianlin joined the Department of Western Literature of Tsinghua [Qinghua] University in 1930. In 1935, he was successful in securing an exchange programme scholarship between the Tsinghua University and University of Gottingen, Germany, and left for Germany. In Goettingen, the first problem he encountered was the selection of courses. Recollecting his arrival in Goettingen, Ji Xianlin (1986:440-41) records, "I was a bewildered man. However, one day when I saw an announcement before the dean's office, I was excited. I noticed that Professor Waldschmidt was offering a course in Sanskrit. This aroused my old passion for Sanskrit and Pali. From then on, I devoted ten years to the studying of Sanskrit and Pali, in this small town of just 100,000 people." Ji Xianlin believed that since Chinese culture was deeply influenced by the Indian culture, it was impossible to understand that culture without understanding Sanskrit. He undertook studies in Sanskrit and Pali at the Institute of Sanskrit Studies, at the University of Goettingen. The teachers he owed most were Prof. Emil Sieg and Prof. Waldschmidt. The latter asked him to study the *Mahabhashya* of Patanjali, the *Rigveda* and Dandin's *Dasakumaracharita* etc. There were more than 40 lessons every week. In the 5th semester, he read *Fragments of Buddhist Texts* in Sanskrit, found in Turpan, Xinjiang. In the 6th semester, he proposed a synopsis for his doctoral thesis entitled *The Finite Verb Change in Mahavastu* and subsequently got his doctoral degree in philosophy in 1941.

Due to the outbreak of the World War II, he could not return to China at once and decided to stay on in Goettingen. In October 1945, he got a teaching assignment at the Institute of Sinology, University of Goettingen, which he pursued alongside his study of Buddhist Sanskrit. Recalling his student days at Goettingen, Ji Xianlin says, "This was the golden age of my life-long academic life, I never had the same time again." Soon after the close of the War, Ji Xianlin returned to China in October 1945. His studentship in Germany was the turning point of his academic career. It was here that Ji Xianlin decided to tread the road of Oriental Studies. Upon reaching China, at the recommendation of Professor Chen Yinge (1890-1969), Ji Xianlin was appointed as a professor at Peking [Beijing] University, and was assigned the task to set up the Department of Oriental Languages.

Ji Xianlin and the Civilizational Dialogue

My university days' teacher, Prof. Tan Chung (2005:8) once lamented that the "contribution made by Ji Xianlin to further civilizational dialogue between India and China has been underestimated by the people." I think he is right in his assertion; this is particularly true of Indian scholars, many of whom are not even familiar with his name. Forget about the scholarship engaged in the geopolitical studies, people in the field of literature have hardly referred to his works. In order to get a feel of his contribution, it is desired that we take a look at his works and the circumstances under which he promoted such a dialogue. After returning from Germany, he focussed on the history of Buddhism and the history of Sino-Indian cultural relations, published a series of academic papers full of innovation. The following are some of his representative works, in the field of translation and Sino-Indian cultural studies.

Translations

- *Kalidasa's Shakuntala (1956)*
- *Panchatantra (1959)*
- *Kalidasa's Vikramorvasiyam (1962)*
- *Ramayana (1980-1984)*
- *Tagore at Home (1985)*
- *Maitreyasamiti (1991)*
- *Jataka Stories (1998)*

Academic works and edited books

- *Collected Essays on the History of Sino-Indian Cultural Exchange (1957)*
- *A Brief History of India (1957)*
- *Collected Papers on the History of Sino-Indian Cultural Relations (1982)*
- *Modern Buddhist Sects (1984)*
- *1857-1859 - National Uprising of India (1985)*
- *Annotated Journey to the West during Great Tang (1985)*
- *History of Sino-Indian Cultural Exchange (1991)*
- *Dunhuang-Turpan Tocharian Studies (1993)*
- *Studies in Oriental Culture (1994)*
- *Literary History of the Orient (1995)*
- *History of World Cultures (1996)*
- *Discussions on the Eastern and Western Cultures (Two Volumes 1997)*
- *The Road of Cultural Exchange: History of Chinese Sugar (1997)*
- *Dictionary of Dunhuang Studies (1998)*
- *Tocharian Text Maitreyasamiti-Nataka (1998)*
- *Zen and the Oriental Culture (2000)*

In addition to the above mentioned works, there are many works of prose and other writings. It could be discerned that Ji Xianlin made significant contribution to the resumption and promotion of the Sino-Indian cultural dialogue. As early as in 1956, he spent considerable time in writing a million characters strong, *History of Sino-Indian Relations.* Later, due to various political reasons, this project of the Chinese Academy of Social Sciences, was aborted.

However, the translation of *Ramayana* proved most time-consuming as the classic epic containing 20 thousand odes took 10 precious years of Ji Xianlin's life. This was an unprecedented event in the history of translation in China. The translation of *Ramayana* started in those turbulent years of the so called Cultural Revolution (1966-76) when such works were rated as "poisonous." Ji Xianlin also suffered the brutal persecution at the hands of the "Gang of Four" in Peking University. He was termed a "counter-revolutionary" and thrown into the "cow shed." He felt as if he was "ostracized" from the "nationality of a human being." When I met him in 1993, he narrated to me how he was paraded around with a huge drum slinging from his neck, and felt he was "neither a human being nor a ghost" and at the same time "a human being as well as a ghost." In the face of brutal criticism, inhuman treatment and humiliation, he thought about committing suicide. On one occasion when he was about to commit suicide by consuming sleeping pills, he was dragged out by the red guards for those struggle sessions. He was kicked and beaten up badly. This was the moment when he decided to live on by upholding his convictions. It was under such circumstances that he ventured forth, with the translation of *Ramayana*. In 1979, parts of this translation were published by the Foreign Languages Publishing House, Beijing. When Professor Yu Longyu (2004:3), a student of Professor Ji Xianlin asked Ji Xianlin about the motivational force behind the translation during Cultural Revolution, Ji Xianlin responded, "I would like to emphasise a point that while gauging the strength of a country, there is a parameter, and that is, its culture and academia. We have to see whether these are flourishing or not. Just gauging the richness of cultural treasure-house is not enough, we also have to see whether a country understands the cultural heritage of other countries or not ... The oriental studies in Europe are very strong and the level, very high. Europe has produced a huge number of Orientalists, who have delved into the studies of China, India, Egypt and Mesopotamia. However, at present, the kind of momentum they have had in the past, is being lost. Therefore, it is for us to take over from them and do a good job in taking the oriental studies to a new high."

In early 1958, Ji Xianlin wrote a comprehensive article entitled "Indian literature in China" and introduced in detail, the influence of Indian literature on Chinese literature, by going through the relevant records in the 24 histories of China. The pre-Qin era, asserts Ji Xianlin, especially the Spring and Autumn Period (5th Century BC to 6th Century BC) could be regarded as the golden period of fables in China. China produced literary works such as *Zhuangzi, Liezi, Han Feizi, Yanzi, Chunqiu, Lushi Chunqiu, Zhanguoce etc.* which are full of fables. On the Indian literary stage, works such as *Panchatantra, Puranas* etc. could be regarded as the Chinese counterparts. Ji Xianlin posits that many Indian fables have found their way into Chinese literature. A few examples could be found in Qu Yuan's *Tianwen* (Heaven Questioned). For example, the line *Tianshi zongheng, yangli yuansi ofTianwen* implies that God released his disc [*sudarshanchakra*], and decapitated head from the body. According to Su Xuelin (Yu 1987: 72), this expression has its origin in the *Sagara Manthan* story of *Mahabharata*, more precisely the execution of Rahu by Indra after the former drank the *amrita.* Another expression *Jueli wei he, er gutu zai fu*, according to Ji Xianlin (1987:116), has its origin in India. He posits that "gutu" since Han Dynasty (206 BC to 220 AD) has been regarded as a rabbit, and the "rabbit in the moon" in *Tianwen* is not a Chinese concept but an Indian, as the concept is found in the Rig Vedas, dating back to 15th century BC. Moreover, the same concept is found in the *Jataka* and other Buddhist literature, argues Prof. Ji. Eminent Buddhist scholar monk Xuan Zang, who came to India during the 7th century, also mentions about the "Rabbit in moon" story in his monumental work, *Datang Xiyuji* (Ji et. al. 1985:579)

During the northern and southern dynasties, the influence of Indian mythology and other literary forms had far reaching influence on the Chinese literature. The phenomenon of ghosts, gods and supernatural beings of this time has very rich Indian content. The most striking theme was that of '*yinsi diyu*' meaning '*naraka*' or hell and '*yinguo baoying*' meaning rewards based on '*Karma*'. In the words of Prof. Ji (1987:118), it is not to say that China did not have the concept of '*naraka*' before the arrival of Indian concept in China. It was there, but somewhat ambiguous and blurred. With the arrival of Indian people in China, the Chinese concept of '*naraka*' took a definite shape, so much so that '*yanwang*' meaning the '*Yamaraja*' is a term shipped from India. Various works of Six dynasties vintage, such as Shun Shi's *Linghun Zhi* (About Soul), Zu Taizhi's *Zhiguai* (Spirits) and *Shenguai Lu* (About Gods and Ghosts), *Liu Zhilin's Shenlu* (About Gods), Xie Shi's Guishen *Liezhuan* (Of gods and Spirits), Zhi Shi's *Zhiguai Ji* (Records of Spirits), Cao Pi's *Zhiguai* (Spirits) etc. are full of Indian influence. Most of the above-mentioned works revolve around the philosophy of '*naraka*' and '*Karma*' and '*Phala*'. The stories like "Parrot extinguishing a mountain fire", found in *Zabao Zangjing* has also found its place in Xuan Zang's *Datang Xiyuji* (Journey to the West during Tang Dynasty). However, the parrot has been replaced by a king called Zhu Wang (Ji 1985:442-3).

The literary genre '*Chuanqi*' of Tang period (short stories or poetic dramas) and '*Bianwen*' (narrative literature with alternate prose and rhymed parts for recitation and singing) have also very strong Indian content. The new Chinese style vividly depicted the Indian classics such as *Mahabharata*, *Ramayana*, and other works such as *Jataka* and *Panchatantra*. The same thing is true to '*Bianwen*', which has prose as well as rhyme in its narration. '*Chuanqi*' and '*Bianwen*' besides having a striking similarity with Indian literary style are also rich in Indian content. The '*karama*' and '*phala*' theme appears to dominate the content. Some of the famous '*Chuanqi*' works are *Zhenzhongji, Liaoyizhuan, Huoxiaoyuzhuan* and *Yingyingzhuan* etc. As regards the '*Bianwen*', some examples are *Taizi Chengdao Jing, Taizi Chengdao Bianwen, Baxiang Bianwen, Pomo Bianwen, Jiangmo Bianwen, Damugan Lianmingjian Jiumu Bianwen* etc. The same style has been found in Buddhist Sutra narration (Jiang Jingwen). A few examples are *Prajnaparamita Sutra and Sadharamapundarika Sutra* narration.

Some of the works of Yuan dynasty especially the Yuan Qu, was also influenced by the Indian themes, according to Ji Xianlin. The theme of Ma Zhiyuan's '*huangliang meng*' has been borrowed from '*Zhenzhongji*' of previous years that has very rich Indian content. Similarly, Zheng Dehui's '*Qiannu Lihun*' has borrowed its theme from '*Lihuiji*'; Shang Zhonxian's '*Liuyizhuan shi*' again has been written on the basis of '*Liuyizhuan*'. Quoting Xu Dishan (Ji 1987:34), Ji Xianlin says that the Indian drama had also left its influence on the Chinese drama. Even today, the puppet drama of Quan Zhou in Fujian province is very popular. One form of puppet drama is known as '*Butai*' in *Minnan* dialect, which is similar to '*Putali*' word of Sanskrit.

The novels written during Ming and Qing dynasties especially Wu Chengen's *Xiyouji (Journey to the West)*, asserts various Chinese scholars including Ji Xianlin, Chen Yinke (Ji 1987: 63-7), Wu Xiaoling etc. that the character '*Sun Wukong*' of the *Journey to West* is not entirely a Chinese product, but has been heavily influenced by the character of '*Hanuman*' in *Ramayana. Sun Wukong*'s enormous power, including his 10,800 li[1] leap in one somersault, 72 different magical appearances, and his style of fighting the evil, resembles that of '*Hanuman*' *of Ramayana.*

As regards the Sino-Indian cultural exchanges, Ji Xianlin accumulated a great deal of information and wrote prolifically on the subject matter. The *Collected Papers on the History of Sino-Indian Cultural Exchange*, published in 1982, is worth mentioning. There are path breaking articles such as the dissemination of paper, paper-making technique, and advent of silk into India. Concerning the questions of when and how the paper and paper making techniques disseminated to India, Ji Xianlin (1982:11-39; 1991:19-20) believes that the word 'paper' finds mention in Indian languages by the end of 7th century. As regards the question of silk, Ji Xianlin tries to prove its dissemination to India from linguistic as well as archaeological viewpoints. He substantiates his argument by citing *Arthashastra* and *Manusmriti, Mahabharata and Ramayana, Kumaar-sambhavam, and Ritusamhara* (Ji Xianlin 1982:76-96).

Another work which is worth mentioning is the annotation of *Journey to the West during Great Tang* written by Xuan Zang. Ji Xianlin wrote an extraordinary foreword for this book that ran into more than 100,000 words. The annotation is so detailed that it increased my personal knowledge about my hometown Kuluta (present Kullu) in the book. *The History of Sugar* was completed in 1996. The book gives a detailed account of the material as well as cultural exchanges between countries such as China, India, Persia, Arabia, Egypt, South-East Asia, Europe, and Africa. Ji Xianlin is the strongest upholder of the "two way traffic" theory between India and China, which has been beautifully expounded by him in his various works. In the process of compiling *The History of Sugar*, Ji Xianlin conducted the

[1] Li is a unit of measuring length; one li is half a km.

study of sugar manufacturing technology and its dissemination from India to China and vice versa. After going through piles of Chinese and foreign historical records, he concludes that the "technology of manufacturing white sugar" disseminated from China into India. "The technology reached India by sea route; even if we rely entirely on linguistic evidences, this can be proved (Ji Xianlin 1982:3; Ji Xianlin 2006:3-4). The evidences to this effect are also found in the *History of the Ming Dynasty* which reiterates that the technology travelled from China to India's Bengal, during the Ming dynasty. His article, which was translated by this author into English, appeared in the 1994 special issue of '*India Horizon*' published by the Indian Council of Cultural Relations (ICCR) under the editorship of Prof. Tan Chung (Ji Xianlin 1994:5-9). This is another major contribution of Ji Xianlin to the history of India-China cultural and material exchanges.

Since Buddhism is one of the most important linkages between India and China, Prof. Ji Xianlin's commitment to Buddhist studies has yielded excellent results. Ji Xianlin is one of the very few scholars in China and beyond, capable of using original Buddhist texts along with Sanskrit, Pali, Buddhist Sanskrit, ancient Chinese translations of Buddhist texts etc. classical resources to conduct studies in Buddhism. His representative works in this field are: *The Language Question of the Classical Buddhism, Classical Indian Languages, Buddhism* etc. He also fills the gap that exists in India and China by venturing in the studies of Tocharian language. The representative works in this area are *Studies in Tocharian Script; Fragments of the Tocharian A Maitreyasamiti-Nataka of the Xinjiang Museum.*

Ji Xianlin has combined the changes in India's medieval languages with his studies in Buddhist history, and has attempted to find out the origin of the Buddhist texts, their transformation and dissemination; by doing so, he has attempted to establish the origin of major Buddhist sects and their dissemination to other places. *Futu and Fo* published in 1947, reveals that the Sanskrit word Buddha (*Fotuo*) which appeared in the early Chinese translations of Buddhist texts as '*Futu*', was in fact borrowed from a Tocharian slang. In another article entitled '*Revisiting Futu and Fo*' written in 1989, he further expounded that the origin of '*Futu*' could be found in Bactarinanic languages.

It could be discerned that for several decades, Ji Xianlin immersed himself into the studies in Sino-Indian cultural exchanges. His feat in the Sino-Indian studies is extraordinary and admirable. There is a general belief in China that Ji Xianlin's academic achievements could be categorized in 10 major areas of research. Besides his studies in Sino-Indian cultural exchanges, he delved into the studies in Chinese culture, oriental and occidental cultural systems, oriental and occidental cultural exchanges, prose etc. Ever since the grand old man of 92 was admitted to Beijing 301 Hospital in 2002, he wrote scores of articles and essays. In the year 2007, New World Publishing House published his "*Memories from the Hospital Bed*". He renounced the titles such as 'master of Chinese culture', 'academic leader', and 'national treasure' in these notes (Wenhui Daily June 13, 2007). Ji Xianlin wrote: "I have never thought of becoming a Sinologist ... I am not even entitled to be 'small master of Sinology' let alone be the grand master. Please dethrone me of the titles such as the 'great man of Sinology', 'academic leader' and 'national treasure' and return my freedom." In 1998, Jiangxi Education Publishing House published 24 volumes of the *Selected Works of Ji Xianlin*, containing more than 8 million words. There are another 8 volumes under publication that would make it an impressive 12 million words collection. The following volumes have already been published:

Volume 1	*Prose (I)*
Volume 2	*Prose (II)*
Volume 3	*Ancient Indian Languages*
Volume 4	*Sino-Indian Cultural Relations*
Volume 5	*Indian History and Culture*
Volume 6	*Chinese Culture and Oriental Culture*
Volume 7	*Buddhism*
Volume 8	*Comparative Literature and Folklore*
Volume 9	*History of Sugar (I)*
Volume 10	*History of Sugar (II)*
Volume 11	*Tocharian Text Maitreyasamiti*
Volume 12	*Tocharian Language Studies*
Volume 13	*Prefaces, Postscripts and Others (I)*
Volume 14	*Prefaces, Postscripts and Others (II)*

Volume 15	*Translations of Sanskrit and other Language Tests (I)*
Volume 16	*Translations of Sanskrit and other Language Tests (II)*
Volume 17	*Ramayana (I)*
Volume 18	*Ramayana (II)*
Volume 19	*Ramayana (III)*
Volume 20	*Ramayana (IV)*
Volume 21	*Ramayana (V)*
Volume 22	*Ramayana (VI a)*
Volume 23	*Ramayana (VI b)*
Volume 24	*Ramayana (VII)*

Ji Xianlin on Research Methods

It could be discerned from his writings and translations that Ji Xianlin was a prolific language expert and translator who had never slackened his efforts in his 70-year-long academic career. The above mentioned collection is an outcome of his pre-1994 writing; however, his academic feat after 1995 is yet to be published. His academic achievements are brilliant, and abound in great spiritual wealth; his academic approach is equally of great spiritual wealth and worth emulating. According to Prof. Yu Longyu (2004:516), one of the students of Professor Ji Xianlin, Ji Xianlin's academic approach could be summarized in the following words: valuing time, trend setting, scanning piles of resources to extract an iota of truth, and academic morality. Valuing time has been the secret of Ji Xianlin's success; trend setting his immortal soul; scanning piles of resources to extract an iota of truth; and academic morality, the foundation of his uprightness. As regards academic approaches of Ji Xianlin, many books have attracted the attention of readers; some of these include *Ji Xianlin on Academic Research and Methodology; Ji Xianlin on Human Life; and Ji Xianlin on Composition.*

As regards valuing time, Prof. Yu (2004:516) says that it is not due to Ji Xianlin's wisdom that he became a world renowned academic, but more so due to his tenacity and perseverance. It is said that "genius is nothing but labour and diligence." Ji Xianlin agrees to this notion and says that "it is 70-80 percent diligence and 20-30 percent of genius." Ji Xianlin does not consider himself a genius. However, he underpins the diligence factor. According to him (Yu 2004:516), "It does not matter which profession you pursue, nothing succeeds without diligence." In 1993, when I visited Professor Ji Xianlin for the first time, I discovered that his entire drawing room was full of heaps of books; it took us a while in making some space to sit down. Later on I discovered that the situation was not better in other rooms as well. When I enquired about his routine, he said, "I just require a sleep of 5-6 hours. I get up at 4:30, have breakfast at 5:00, and then begin my work. I do not like to take a nap after lunch; I would rather devote it for my writings."

Ji Xianlin on Academic Research and Methodology is a book devoted to Ji Xianlin's personal experience towards research and learning. The book also introduces the experiences of his predecessors such as Chen Yinge and Hu Shi. In one section he writes: "Since I do not have enough time to engage in writing, I dig out those waste materials in the corner of my mind and utilise the time before, after and even during the middle of those customary speeches at the conferences, and write articles. There are useless speeches at various meetings and seminars, the dissemination of information is limited, I only lend an ear or a half at such meetings, the rest I would devote to writing articles. Of course, I also take every opportunity whether in a plane, train, car or bicycle, especially when I am on a stroll, to ponder and reflect on the resources I have gone through."

Secondly, blazing new trails in his profession is Ji Xianlin's passion. Ji Xianlin says that "If one cannot break ground, it is useless to write (Huang Yaming 2008)." In *Ji Xianlin on Academic Research and Methodology*, he writes about one of his experiences in Germany as to how he once completed a long article after lot of efforts. He was satisfied with his efforts. However, when his teacher went through the article, not only did he not receive the expected praise, the article was returned to him with complete rejection. The Professor said to him, "no doubt you have put lot of efforts and referred to many books, but where are your individual viewpoints? It is full of others' viewpoints. It looks exhaustive but has no real value." Ji Xianlin says that when he suffered such a severe blow, he reached a conclusion that "if you do not have ideas or if you lack creativity, you should not write." He supports the views of Chen Yinge on creativity. He says that (Yu 2004:518) 'if one lacks creativity, one lags behind and becomes rigid and stagnant. A person with creativity forges ahead, has the vigour and vitality to take flight'. Ji Xianlin's research in Sino-Indian Studies have been path breaking; his works such as *Rig Veda, Ramayana*; *Journey to the West during Great Tang*, and *The History of Sugar* is a testimony to this.

Thirdly, Ji Xianlin canonizes Hu Shi's philosophy of "having bold thoughts, but being meticulous about the findings." The key is being "bold and careful." Ji Xianlin maintains that things under heaven are very complex; therefore, one needs to be extremely careful and avoid jumping to conclusions, while viewing things from the surface. We must proceed from the surface to the inner core; get to the heart of the matter, by exploring authenticity of the issues from all possible dimensions. Bold assumptions and inferences are the same; however, bold assumption should be followed by careful scrutiny of the facts, and inference should be followed by mastering and applicability of the research material. As regards mastering the source material, Ji Xianlin advocated the concept of "fishing by draining the pond approach." According to Ji, if we really want to live up to the expectations reflected in these four characters, we must have the following conditions: One, we must have supra language ability; secondly, possess rich experience of life; three, to have the opportunity to make use of first hand authentic records and four, a variety of reference materials.

Above mentioned preconditions are not everyone's cup of tea; however, we can say that Ji Xianlin has them all. "Fishing by draining the pond" have been the first principle of Ji Xianlin's academic pursuit. However, this is only one side of the things; accessibility to the records does not necessarily mean that your perceptions and methods could be right. Therefore, one needs to have correct perception and methodology to reach irrefutable logic and conclusions. This is what Ji Xianlin calls "careful verifications of the facts." In the process, some assumptions require gradual amendments, not just once, may be ten, a hundred or even thousand times before reaching a conclusion (Yu 2004:520-21).

Finally, Ji Xianlin attaches great importance to academic ethics or moral conscience. In 1997 while writing on academic ethics, Ji Xianlin maintained (Ji Xianlin 1997), "Academics is all about honesty, which cannot be adulterated and faked. Honesty in scholarship, whether individual or collective, should be based on seeking truth from the facts. This is what I call academic moral conscience. To plagiarise others' achievements, or fishing for fame by creating new theories or a school of thought on the basis of tampering with the truth and forged research, is the deed of out-and-out academic thugs." Ji Xianlin maintains that these types of thugs exist not only in China but also in the world. However, this kind of fraud cannot be hidden for a long time, for one day the truth is revealed to the world. "Once the truth sees the light, these thugs would be despised by the intellectual milieu, and we have witnessed the cases of suicides by such frauds." Ji Xianlin believes that we have been living with such academic thugs since the ancient times, but this kind of blatant cheating should not be permitted by any means.

Ji Xianlin further says that in addition to some big thugs, there exists a variety of small time swindlers and frauds. Some of them write articles after listening to some lectures and academic papers; while others steal others' perceptions and approaches after reading books and journals, without acknowledging their names, as if they themselves are the innovators of these views and perceptions. There are many such people around us." These are the people who have no academic ethics or academic moral conscience. As for himself, he says that "I have never done any academic fraud, and neither will ever do it in the future." Ji Xianlin also quoted Liang Qichao who wrote in his book entitled *An Outline of Qing Academics,* "concealment or distortion of evidence is immoral". He says that these words are in conformity with the academic ethics discussed in the preceding sections. This also proves that the Qing academia attached importance to academic ethics.

An Ambassador of India-China Cultural Exchange

It is evident that the 24 volumes of *Collected Works of Ji Xianlin* come down to his research on India. It would not be wrong to assert that Ji Xianlin devoted his entire life to Indology. To this end, he visited India several times. No matter whenever and wherever he went, Ji Xianlin carried the feelings of the Chinese people towards their Indian brethren and was accorded a warm welcome by the Indian people. During his speeches in India, he told the Indian people about the Chinese culture. Upon returning to China, he wrote down his travelogues about India, published articles and thus made these available not only to the Chinese people, but to the people of the world as well. The *My Impressions of India* section of *Collected Essays* of *Ji Xianlin* is attributed to his impressions about India. In these memoirs, one can see the splendid culture of India; we can see the aggression suffered by the Indian people at the hands of the imperialists and the heroic spirit of the Indian people amidst their anti-imperialist struggle. More importantly, we can also take a glimpse at the Sino-Indian friendship running down from generation to generation, over centuries, in the historical records.

In the words of Ji Xianlin (1986:134-35), had he not written down his Indian experiences, it would have been tantamount to a criminal offence towards the Indian as well as Chinese people, at least a selfish act. Recollecting his impressions about India, he writes, "While in India, I always mentioned to Indian people that I have brought with me the fraternity of the Chinese people to the Indian people; I will also carry the friendship of the Indian people to the Chinese people. However, how should friendship be carried back to China? No doubt, friendship exists between our two people, but it is invisible, shapeless, colourless, odourless and carries no mass. There is no way we could carry it in packets. The only way to carry it is through our actions. For a person like me who loves inking down things, the best way is to write it down and let the people of China read it. Although not all of them can visit India, they can enjoy our feelings and happiness and the friendship of the Indian people towards the Chinese people." In 1951, when Ji Xianlin visited India for the first time, he penned down his impressions in the following words: (1986: 138): "There was an ocean of people at the airport supporting red banners. When we stretched our hands for hand shake, they were received by those pairs and pairs of warm hands; when we stretched our necks, these were laden with garlands of red, yellow, purple, green etc. fresh flowers. The scent and fragrance of these flowers left an indelible impression on me for the rest of my life."

Ji Xianlin's second and third visit to India took place in 1955 and 1974 respectively. He was invited to participate in international conferences on both the occasions. Since the duration of his stay was relatively short, and the places of visits fewer, Ji Xianlin's contacts with the Indian people were limited. In the words of Ji Xianlin, there were very few impressions.

The fourth time he visited India was in 1978. This time, owing to India-China border conflict, the entire scenario had changed. Recalling this visit, Ji Xianlin notes, (1986:139): "India had become a mystery to me. In the past, as regards India, I had gone through the process of - from strangeness to familiarity; however, during this visit, it was reversal of the process, I realised that I was going through the process of - from familiarity to unfamiliarity." It could be imagined that more than 30 years of severed diplomatic relations between the two countries had produced adverse effects for the promotion and mutual understanding between the people of China and India. Ji Xianlin has described the 1962 border conflict as an "unpleasant episode." According to him, this little unpleasant happening can only be regarded as a bubble in the long history of cultural exchanges between China and India (1986:137). He further recollects that during this visit when the Chinese delegation emerged from the New Delhi airport, the welcome they received from the Indian people matched the welcome they received during their first visit, and once again feeling of going from familiarity to unfamiliarity, vanished in no time.

Ji Xianlin not only penned down the factual account of fraternity between the Indian and the Chinese people, but also talked about the long history of cultural exchanges between the two people. In some of his articles, we get to know about Ji Xianlin's exchanges with his Indian friends. While visiting the University of Delhi and Jawaharlal Nehru University, he made very passionate speeches. He records (1986:144-47), "After concluding his welcome address, the Chairman announced my name. Though relaxed, I was not prepared, and did not know what to say. When the Chairman was delivering his address, I was listening attentively, however, was also thinking about what to speak on such forums. What could be the most appropriate things for such occasions? I thought since I have delved into the studies in Sino-Indian culture exchange, and have accumulated some source materials...why not talk about it. I decided to talk about cultural exchanges between China and India ... Such a simple speech of mine aroused the interest of the audience. I was a relaxed man, thought would visit a few places after the meeting was over. However, after the ceremony, I was surrounded by the enthusiastic teaching and student community, and was showered with questions pertaining to the cultural exchanges between China and India. Their questions were not limited to the cultural exchanges alone, but also came down to the four tones of the Chinese language; ancient China's foreign contacts; questions related to records of tributes from the Western Ocean. Some asked about the translations of the Sanskrit texts, and others about the Chinese version of Buddhist scriptures. Some even asked about the People's Communes education system in China and so on. It appeared as if my Indian friends have caught hold of an old dictionary, and wanted to search for anything they could find in it ... I wished I could perform the wonders of the 'Sun Wukong', the monkey king of the novel *Journey to the West*, who, in one stroke, could shed a cluster of hair, blow them up and create equal numbers of his own replicas instantly, and could satisfy the myriad requests of my Indian friends." I did not find an iota of criticism about India in his writing, irrespective of the fact that there were very bitter feelings between India and China, after the war. Prof. Tan Chung told me that when Ji Xianlin's car departed after a lecture at Delhi University, it was roughed up by the Tibetan and Indian protestors. Being the organisers of the event, Prof. Tan and others escorted the Chinese guests to safety. Ji Xianlin has never mentioned this episode in his writings and neither has he talked about it in my conversations with him.

In the same vein, Ji Xianlin has vividly described all historical sites which he visited, so that the Chinese people could know about India's splendid culture and its rich heritage. While in Nalanda, he wrote (1986:177-81), "For centuries, this place was not only a centre of Buddhism, but was also the centre of Indian academics. From the Jin Dynasty to the Tang Dynasty, many Chinese Buddhist monks such as Fa Xian, Xuan Zang and Yi Jing came here in the pursuit of knowledge". While mentioning Xuan Zang, Ji Xianlin wrote, "This Chinese scholar monk from Tang Dynasty took a long assiduous journey, defying death and reached India; he stayed in Nalanda for a long time, studied Buddhist and other classical texts. He received extremely favourable treatment from the Indian people and its king alike. Upon reaching China, he wrote his monumental work *Journey to the West during Great Tang* that gave an extremely detailed and accurate account of ancient India. This monumental work is still considered by the academia in India and the world at large, as a rare treasure. In China, Xuanzang's name is almost a household name; while in India we often heard people making mention of him."

Finally, Ji Xianlin tells us why we should pay attention to the cultural exchanges between China and India. He justifies it by citing the following arguments (Ji 1991:185-86): "First and foremost, the history of Sino-Indian cultural exchange tells us that our two countries have been engaged in cultural exchanges over the past two thousand years, have learnt from each other, and have developed and enriched each other's cultures. Even today we are reaping the benefits of this exchange. This sort of exchange is full of advantages rather than disadvantages. Secondly, the history of Sino-Indian cultural exchange tells us that the cultural history of mankind is the creation of all of us; it has never been created by a particular nation or country. Recognition of this fact will bring great benefits that can enhance friendship and understanding between the people. Finally, the history of Sino-Indian cultural exchange tells us that the cultures of China and India belong to the oriental culture." Ji Xianlin believes that the twenty-first century would be the century of Oriental culture. It would become world's leading culture and would take the human and cultural development to a higher level. Precisely because of these views, Ji Xianlin has furthered the cause of his predecessors by devoting his entire life to the civilizational dialogue and inter-cultural studies. While blazing new trails in the area, he has also opened up many new areas of research and enquiry.

To conclude, people like Ji Xianlin and my teacher Tan Chung have set examples for us in the area of India-China civilizational dialogue. They would continue to encourage and educate generations and generations of scholars on both sides of the Himalaya. There is no doubt that these are the ambassadors of friendship and cultural exchanges between China and India, and will inspire and educate people like us, forever.

References:

Yaming, Huang (2008), *Five Tastes of Ji Xianlin: Reading Ji Xianlin on Research Methods* http://blog.sina.com.cn/s blog_4a06f127 0100050k.html (August 14, 2008).

Xianlin, Ji (1982), *Collected Papers on the History of Sino-Indian Cultural Exchange*, Xinzhi Sanlian Publication, Beijing.

Xianlin, Ji (1985), Xuan Zang *The Journey to the West during Great Tang.*

Preface of the (Ji Xianlin et.al. 1985) annotated version of the Journey to the West during Great Tang, Zhonghua Shuju, Beijing.

Xianlin, Ji (1986), Collection of Ji Xianlin's Essays, Beijing University Press, Beijing.

Xianlin, Ji (1991), *The History of Sino-Indian Cultural Exchange*, Xinhua Press, Beijing.

Xianlin, Ji [Tr. Deepak, B. R] (1994), *Endless Flow of Cross-cultural Currents between India and China, India Horizon*, special issue of Indian Council for Cultural Relations, New Delhi.

Xianlin, Ji (1997), *Ji Xianlin on Academic Ethics* (excerpts) http://tieba.baidu.com/f?kz=107763550. (Accessed on January 18, 2010)

Xianlin, Ji (2006), *Ji Xianlin on Sino-Indian Cultural Exchange*, New World Press, Beijing.

Xianlin, Ji (2006), *Ji Xianlin on Research Methodology,* Dangdai Zhongguo Press, Beijing .

Jianfeng Shi, (2008), *Padma Bhushan, India's highest honour conferred on Ji Xianlin Dongfang Zaobao*, January 29, 2008 .

Zhong Tan , Yinzeng Geng (2005), *India and China: Interface and Surge of the Two Great Civilizations*, Shangwu Press, Beijing.

Shuying Wang, (1994), *Eminent Chinese Writers on Tagore*, Zhongguo Huaqiao Press, Beijing.

Shuying Wang, (2006), Ji Xianlin and Sino-Indian Cultural Exchange, china.com.cn, December 12, 2008.

Wenhuibao (June 13, 2007), *Ji Xianlin's Sickbed Diaries: Return My Freedom.*

Longyu Yu, (2004), *India and China: Indian Writers and Chinese Culture*, Ningxia Press, Ningxia.

Wang Bangwei

History of Sino-Indian Friendship and the Ideal of World Peace*

In world history, India and China are the only countries having such a close proximity or strikingly similar experiences. Both China and India are ancient civilizations with long history and uninterrupted cultural development. Both are Asian, as well as world giants with vast territory and large populations. The combined population of the two, accounts for one-fourth of the world population. We are neighbours, with the Himalayas as the natural boundary between us. There are many commonalities between us; we have had a history of friendly contacts for over 2000 years. In the history of 2000 years, it was only in the early 1960s that we had an unfortunate but very brief conflict. Looking at the world around us, can we find such an example in Asia, Europe or America whether in the remote past or present? Probably there is none. In the history of mankind, there have been many civilizations, but their traditions only live in the distant memories of the people, for they have long been discontinued. From ancient times to the present, there have been protracted conflicts, big and small wars between various countries or regions, and some of the conflicts even rage on till date. Looking at it, from this point, the history of contacts between China and India is indeed very different from other countries.

'Zhongguo' is translated as China in English. If one traces the origin of this word, then in fact, it originates form the Sanskrit word Cina [Cheena]. The name 'China' in Western languages mostly comes from here. What does it indicate? This, at least, explains one fact, that most of the people, across the globe, understood China through Cina; therefore, it would not be wrong to assert that in the process of the world knowing and understanding China, our neighbour India played an important role.

* Translated from Chinese by Avijit Banerjee, Reader, Visva Baharati, Santiniketan.

'Yindu' in English is translated as India. The origin of this name also lies in the Sanskrit word 'Sindhu', meaning 'River' or the 'Indus River.' Initially, the Persian people used this word for India. Later, it spread to Greece, and the distortion in pronunciation finally made it 'India'.

Till today, although the Chinese call China as 'Zhongguo', and the Indian people call their country 'Bharata', for most of the people or most of the countries in the world, our two countries are known as China and India. Today if we say the globe or the world is big, it is also small. Comparing ancient times, since the communication and exchanges between the people and countries are more frequent and intimate, hence, 'China' and 'India' came to be known as most commonly used nomenclatures for 'Zhongguo' and 'Yindu', by the world.

I admire Mr. Jairam Ramesh, his inspiration and his coinage of the term 'Chindia'. The coinage cannot be pronounced as purely fictitious but has its basis; not only has it the basis, but it is the example of "hearts beating in unison". This forced me to ponder over the fact that even though this coinage is new, however, the relationship of the Indian and Chinese culture imbuing one another, has long existed between India and China in the history of more than two thousand years of interactions. There may be many concrete examples to illustrate this point; however, I believe that Buddhism is a major and probably, the foremost one, followed by Language and Art. Obviously, there are still many more.

Buddhism originated in India, but spread to China and was accepted by the Chinese people around two thousand years back. According to this viewpoint, it can be said that India is the root of Buddhism. China's Buddhism is the trunk and leaves that sprouted from the Indian root. However, merely to say this will not illustrate the issue. A story in the history of Chinese Buddhism is just an example. During the mid-Tang Dynasty, a monk called Bu Kong (Amoghavajra) came to China from India. Amoghavajra propagated the Esoteric Buddhism in China and was highly revered by the Chinese people. Among the Buddhist monks who came to China from India during Tang Dynasty (618-907), there were three monks who were revered as the "First Three Great Buddhist Masters of Kai Yuan Era" and Bu Kong is one of them. Bu Kong had a Chinese disciple named Han Guang. After reaching China, Bu Kong returned to India with Han Guang. The 27th Juan of *Biographies of Eminent Monks of Song Dynasty*

(Song Gaoseng Zhuan) is attributed to the Biography of Han Guang. According to the biography, upon returning from India, Han Guang went to Wu Taishan during the period of Tang Tai Zong. At Wu Taishan, lived an eminent monk called Zhan Ran; Zhan Ran enquired from Han Guang about India and his experiences in India. Han Guang briefed him about a part of his experiences in India: "There was a monk of high order in India; he was well versed in Buddhism. When I asked him about the *shunyabad*, he replied 'it differentiates between good and evil, flat and round, and knows which one is suitable.' He repeatedly told me 'if destined to meet again, please translate Chinese Buddhist sutras into Sanskrit, so that I could study it.' He held my hand and repeatedly urged me for this."

This is to say, generally speaking, it was the Chinese people who always learnt Buddhism from India. However, by now, after understanding China's condition, the Indian monks showed their willingness to learn Buddhism from China. This is a very interesting fact. Although some people have doubted the credibility of this story, but the entire story is sensibly trustworthy. Zan Ning, the compiler of the *Biographies of Eminent Monks* in the Song Dynasty, after narrating the above story penned down the following paragraph:

> "After all how many people went from China to India to preach Buddhism? How many Chinese went over to western regions to preach Buddhism is not known. It is said that Tuyuhun King Kualu Khan dispatched an embassy to Liang and sought Sakyamuni Buddha Statue including 14 Buddhist Sutras that included Parinirvana Sutra, Prajna Sutra etc. His emissaries were well versed in Chinese, both oral and written. After obtaining the Sutras, they translated them to local languages and disseminated into various kingdoms north of western Qinghai. Following this, undoubtedly these were disseminated into India. Mao Poetic genre, Analects of Confucius, Filial Piety Sutra were translated into local languages and studied in Gucheshi in Xinjiang. Scholar monks who went to the western region during Tang translated Dao Dejing into Sanskrit. An intense debate started between the Buddhists and the Taoists over Bodhi as Dao but had to be abandoned due to various diverging viewpoints. Having translated the classic so beautifully is hard to imagine! The western region where Buddhism originated is the root and trunk of the Buddhism, it flourished with

> its branches and leaves during eastern Xia. Chinese people are agile and thrift, they talk less and do more, Indian people are simple and honest, but are good at reciting texts. The advantage of the Indian people lies at memorising, whereas the Chinese are apt at explanation."

Zan Ning used the root and branches of "Nigrodha" tree as a metaphor to illustrate the relationship between Buddhism and Culture of China and India, both discussing the common points and also the differences, what a witticism! The words of Zan Ning again made me recollect the experience of Xuan Zang in India. Xuan Zang went to India with an objective to study from the Great Masters of India, but at the same time he himself contributed to the development of religion and culture in India. Xuan Zang studied *Yogachara Sutra* from Silabhadra at Nalanda. Moreover, he travelled far and wide in India and acquired vast knowledge.

In Nalanda, Xuan Zang wrote *Huizong Lun* (Arthasasthra) and *Po EJian Lun* (Treatise on getting rid of evil) in Sanskrit. While the former reflects the fusion of the Madhyamika and Yogachara School of Mahayana Buddhism and expounded Xuan Zang's personal views on the subject, the latter argues in favour of the theory of Mahayana and received much appreciation from the Indian scholar monks. Siladitya (Harshavardhan), the contemporary Indian King had the highest esteem for Xuan Zang's moral character and knowledge, he held a mass assembly at his capital, Kanyakubja (present day Kannauj) and invited Xuan Zang as the key speaker. He also invited twenty Kings, and more than four thousand Buddhist Monks across India; more than two thousand disciples of other religions also participated in the assembly. Xuan Zang presented his paper at the assembly; it is said that for eighteen days no one could refute Xuan Zang's arguments in the assembly. Therefore, the monks of Mahayana Buddhism gave Xuan Zang the name of "Mahadeva"; the monks of Hinayana faith also gave Xuan Zang a name and called him "Mokadeva". A Chinese monk coming to India and being conferred the title of "Deva" owing to his scholarship, only Xuan Zang can be worthy of such an honour. We know that the people of India showered encomiums on Rabindranath Tagore, the great poet and writer of modern India, and called him 'Gurudeva'.

In the course of a two millennia history of interaction between China and India, there are many instances of "root" and "branches", "branches" changing into "roots", and vice versa. In Sanskrit, some words like Cini (sugar), Cinaja (steel), Cinaputra (pear), Cinani (peach) etc are all related to China. If this is the case, why can not 'China' and 'India' become 'Chindia'? Using Zan Ning's metaphor, the cultural interaction between India and China could be described as a big "Nigrodha' tree, the roots crisscrossing, with luxuriant foliage, and emitting that vitality even today. As a matter of fact, both the people of China and India are living under the same big tree.

In China, we had a great debate on the world peace and harmony just before the Warring States period. However, the world and its scope were rather limited in the hearts and minds of the Chinese people. Following this, China and India came into direct contact with each other. As far as the Chinese people are concerned, the scope of the world, including India, gradually widened. China and India coexisted peacefully all along till the modern times. For two thousand years, notwithstanding the unceasing conflicts between various countries, nationalities and social strata, peace and friendship have, all along, been the mainstream between the people of China and India. The pursuit of peace and harmony in the world has all along, been the ideal of the people of the two countries.

In today's world, peace and tranquility are not to be found everywhere. On the contrary, it is discordance and tension all around. Fortunately, in Asia, we have had common understanding in the past between Chinese and Indian people; this has been strengthened, of late. Peaceful coexistence, friendly contacts, mutual learning, common development these are the only and essential things necessary. In today's situation, if India and China can handle their affairs well, we can conclude that almost one-third of the world affairs will have been managed properly. So, what is preventing the people of India and China and the peace loving people of the world, from making joint efforts and setting up such an example?

In short, I believe that all friends in China and India hold unanimous views on this point. In this new century, let the 'nigrodha' tree of Sino-India friendship have deep roots and luxuriant leaves. Under the big tree, China and India can come together, and make a historic contribution to world peace.

Sudheendra Kulkarni

Wen Jiabao: An Impressive Statesman in a Changing China

It is often dismaying to see the Indian media's fixation with the West. More than six decades after gaining freedom from the British empire, our media continues to display influences of a colonised mindset. Aping the contents and trends of the western media, our newspapers, magazines and TV channels portray the world around in such a way as to make the reader or the viewer unconsciously believe that the centre of the universe lies in the West. Be it arts, culture, cinema, music, business, intellectual debates, social mores or politics, the domination of USA and Europe over our media's international coverage is nearly complete. Not just Barack Obama and George Bush II, but even second-rate politicians from Britain and France (and their wives) get so much coverage in the Indian media that one is forced to contrast it with the scant attention that is paid to leaders from and socio-political developments in countries such as China, Brazil, Russia, South Africa, Turkey or Iran.

In the past, this was perhaps attributable to the fact that certain countries in the West indeed dominated the world's economy, politics, diplomacy and strategic affairs. But, for God's sake - indeed for our own sake - let us realise that the world is changing. The West's power is rapidly declining. New countries - and their leaders - are emerging on the global scene and leaving their mark on the evolving new world order.

China is changing the World Order

No country is transforming the contemporary world order so radically as China has been doing in the past twenty years. Surging past several European economies in the last decade and most recently Japan, China has now become an economic colossus whose GDP ($ 5 trillion) is surpassed only by that of USA ($ 14 trillion). Within the next 10-15 years, it is poised to beat even the US to become the largest national economy in the world. It is already the world's largest exporting nation. A recent poll conducted by the Pew Research Centre in Washington DC shows that as many as 44% Americans now say that China is the world's leading economic power, while just 27% name the United States. Also, the number of Americans having a negative attitude towards China is declining. Indeed, the number of people with a positive view of China is steadily rising in Africa, Latin America and Asia. Already, people in most African countries think that China is more important for their future development than their erstwhile colonial masters such as France, Britain, Portugal or Italy. All this dramatic change could not have come about by chance. The people and the leadership of China at various levels have worked hard, and with single-minded determination, to achieve China's internal transformation and external influence.

And yet, how much of China do we see in Indian newspapers, journals and on TV channels? How much do even educated and politically aware Indians know about China's leadership ? Its President, Hu Jintao, who is also the general secretary of the Communist Party of China (CPC); its Prime Minister Wen Jiabao; and others? Or about their predecessors? Or about their likely successors? The reason cannot be that China's communist regime keeps a tight lid on information. True, the political debate and functioning of the media in China are not as free as in India or in the West. Nevertheless, it isn't true that nothing of significance can be known about the social and political happenings in China. With the emergence of the internet, a great deal of credible information, coming from both unofficial and official sources, is now available. I strongly believe that the Indian media and intellectual bodies have a duty to better inform the Indian public about the various aspects of China's remarkable rise.

In writing positively about the political developments in China, one observes a certain diffidence among Indian commentators. Many of those who belong to the communist left are quite befuddled by the social and economic developments in China and find themselves unable to explain or justify them from a Marxist perspective. Many non-left commentators, on the other hand, still carry a negative image of China, a sour hangover from the Chinese military aggression, and India's defeat, in 1962. The unresolved border dispute, and the uncertainty over how it might ultimately get resolved or get played out in the near or medium-term, makes many educated Indians unprepared to see, or acknowledge, the positive aspects of China. They view any laudatory information about China as an attempt to mislead Indians into trusting an "untrustworthy neighbour", who, according to them, has "evil designs on our country". This "trust deficit" must be overcome. I believe that our two great Asian nations are required by destiny itself, to build friendly and cooperative relations for the greater good of the world of tomorrow. Of course, we Indians should not forget lessons of the past. However, we shouldn't remain prisoners of the past bitterness and insecurities either. As a nation, we should engage China with self-confidence and on an equal footing, learning from its strengths and successes and also proudly communicating India's own strengths and successes to the fraternal people of China.

My eye-opening China visit in 2003

It is from this perspective that I am penning this essay about the one contemporary Chinese leader who has impressed me the most and because of whom my own perception of China underwent a major change, for the better, in recent years. It is Wen Jiabao. I had watched him closely when I had accompanied Prime Minister Atal Behari Vajpayee, as a member of his delegation on the latter's state visit to China in 2003. Wen Jiabao, who looked gentle, earnest and friendly, had succeeded Zhu Rongji as China's premier only a year earlier, just as Hu Jintao had succeeded Jiang Zemin as the party boss a year earlier, at the 16th congress of the CPC in 2002.

My first impressions of China were formed by three observations during the visit. The first, of course, was that China had progressed spectacularly, going by the urban landscape of Beijing and Shanghai. The second was on account of an edit-page article in China Daily, an English language newspaper, which contrasted the simple, non-showy working style of the Hu-Wen leadership with that of their immediate predecessors in the communist party (who, of course, remained unnamed). The article gave the example of how the new leaders had ordered an end to the grand ceremonial send-offs and receptions at the airport, accompanied by long cavalcades of cars carrying ministers and government officials, whenever the President or the Prime Minister went on, or returned from, a foreign tour. It also mentioned Premier Wen Jiabao's "pro-people" approach as evidenced by his frequent visits to farms, factories and project sites, to directly speak to workers and peasants.

My third notable observation, which left an indelible impression of a changing China, was when Vajpayee visited the White Horse Buddhist Temple in Luoyang in central China. It honours two Indian monks, Kashyapa Matanga and Dharma Raksha, who had travelled all the way from a monastery in Madhya Pradesh to China in the third century BC, carrying the message of Buddhism. Hundreds of Buddhist cave-temples dot the hills around Luoyang. According to legend, many Chinese emperors received the wisdom to rule from these sacred hills. As I and other members of the Prime Ministerial delegation climbed from one cave-temple to another, I was intrigued to find that a highly placed Chinese diplomat, obviously a communist party member, was engrossed in meditative prayers at each stop. I later asked him if he had religious beliefs. "In China, many people are religious," he replied. "My 90-year-old mother in Shanghai has built a Buddhist temple at home. Chinese people feel affinity towards India because of Buddhism."

My Luoyang experience convinced me that communist China is changing in two fundamental ways. On the one hand, it is achieving prosperity at a blinding speed, unparalleled in human history. On the other hand, not only the common people but even the best minds in modern China are also rediscovering the value of their own ancient civilization. In this process of rediscovery, many of them are also realising the greatness of civilizational India. Incidentally, India has built, with Chinese cooperation, a beautiful new Buddhist temple adjoining the White Horse Temple. It was inaugurated by President Pratibha Patil, during her visit to China in May 2010. Wen Jiabao expressed happiness over this unique milestone in the civilizational links between India and China by describing it "as yet another effort by our two countries to promote friendly relations."

Wen Jiabao and India

A few months before Vajpayee's visit, defence minister George Fernandes had paid an official visit to China. As is well known, Fernandes was, for many years, a strong critic of the communist China. The highlight of his visit was his meeting with Wen Jiabao, who, as reported by the press, told him: "Friendliness accounts for 99.99 per cent of the 2,200-year-old Sino-Indian exchanges and misunderstanding merely 0.01 per cent. It is high time we buried that 0.01 per cent and re-established the 99.9 per cent." I later asked Fernandes if he trusted Wen Jiabao. He replied: "The Chinese Prime Minister was exceptionally warm and sounded genuine. I felt that we should now leave our misunderstandings behind and build a new relationship."

Heads of state and government are known to make friendly-sounding statements about other countries, on official occasions. However, China watchers in India have noted that Wen Jiabao's public remarks about India have been particularly effusive. During his visit to India's IT hub of Bangalore in 2005, young Indian professionals were pleasantly surprised to hear him say that India and China should put aside their historic rivalries and instead strengthen mutual cooperation to create a "New Asian century". Likening India-China cooperation to "two pagodas, one hardware and one software", he remarked that the two countries should work together to dominate the world's tech industry, bringing together Chinese hardware with Indian software. "Combined, we can take the leadership position in the world. When the particular day comes, it will signify the coming of the Asian century of the IT industry."

During the same visit, while attending the commemoration ceremony of the 55th anniversary of the establishment of diplomatic ties between India and China held in New Delhi, Wen Jiabao recalled Mahatma Gandhi's words that "China and India are real friends in need" and Rabindranath Tagore's affirmation that "China and India are old and close brothers". Echoing the thoughts of well-meaning people in both countries, he said, "China and India are the two biggest developing nations in the world. The development of friendly relations and close cooperation between China and India not only accord with the fundamental interests and common aspirations of the two peoples but also exert great influence on the peace and development in Asia and the world at large."

Wen Jiabao's most recent friendly gesture towards India came during his annual press conference in March this year. (Notably, it lasted nearly two-and-a-half hours.) PTI's Beijing correspondent asked him if India and China can be "good friends and good neighbours". After a lengthy reply, replete with facts and figures about the growing economic ties between Delhi and Beijing, Wen Jiabao said, "I wish to ask this reporter to send my message back to the Indian people that China and India are not competitors, we are friends. I wish to conclude by quoting from an ancient Indian scripture, probably written more than 3,000 years ago in Sanskrit, that is in the title of 'Upanishad'. It is to the effect: 'May He protect us both together. May He nourish us both together. May we conjointly work with great energy. May our study be vigorous and effective. May we not hate anyone. Let there be peace, let there be peace, let there be peace.'"

The immortal Shanti mantra being invoked by the Chinese premier! Clearly, here is a leader whose personality is cut from a different cloth of communism. After reading this report, I couldn't help wonder, "How many Indian leaders have paid similar heartfelt tribute to the pearls of wisdom in Chinese history?"

Wen Jiabao's Strong Emphasis on Morality

What is remarkable about Wen Jiabao is that he sounds so different from a typical communist leader. He makes no efforts to gloss over the enormous problems and challenges being faced by China as it modernises at breakneck speed. Not everything is hunky-dory in that country. As in India, the illegitimate marriage of power and money has corrupted governance and distorted China's development. There is widening rich-poor gap, labour-peasant unrest, environmental degradation and a growing spiritual vacuum in society due to one-sided emphasis on material development. Thanks to the internet's spread at blinding speed (China aims to have 100 crore netizens by 2014, up from 41 crore today), the youth, in spite of tight government censoring, is debating issues with a critical openness that was unthinkable just a decade ago. China is clearly a society in ferment.

Wen Jiabao's speeches, before domestic or foreign audiences, are never propagandistic. He candidly refers to the huge and widening, rich-poor and urban-rural divide in the Chinese society. Nor does he hide the problem of corruption in government. He repeatedly warns his party men that "unfair wealth gap and corruption" could endanger the Communist party's rule. Economic growth, he exhorts, must not conflict with the highest ethical and moral standards. In his speech at Cambridge University in early 2009, when the famous university commemorated its 800th anniversary, he drew attention to a very important aspect of the global financial crisis. As is well known, China's export-intensive economy suffered due to the crisis, which was then at its peak. Wen Jiabao said, "The international financial crisis once again shows how dangerous a market economy without regulation can be. Since the 1990s, some profit-driven financial institutions in economies lacking effective regulation have raised massive capital with a leverage of dozens of times. While they reaped huge profits, the world was exposed to enormous risks. This fully demonstrates that a totally unregulated market economy cannot work. We must strike a balance between financial innovation and regulation, between the financial sector and real economy, and between savings and consumption."

He then went on to emphasise the role of morality in economic growth. "To effectively meet the crisis, we must fully recognise the role of morality. Nothing is greater than morality. It shines even more brightly than the sun. True economic theories will never come into conflict with the highest moral and ethical standards. Instead, they should stand for justice and integrity, and contribute in an equal way to the well-being of all people, including the most vulnerable ones. Adam Smith, known as the father of modern economics, held the view in 'The Theory of Moral Sentiments' that if the fruits of a society's economic development cannot be shared by all, it is morally unsound and risky, as it is bound to jeopardise social stability. *The loss of morality is an underlying cause for the current crisis. Some people have sacrificed principle and sought profits at the expense of public interests. They have crossed the moral baseline. We should call on all enterprises to take up their social responsibilities. Within the body of every businessman should flow the blood of morality.*" (Emphasis added.)

The subject of morality figured prominently in Wen Jiabao's widely appreciated hour-long interview on CNN in 2008, conducted by the Indian-born journalist and scholar, Fareed Zakaria.

> Zakaria: Let me ask you, Premier, finally a couple of questions that are personal. You've said that you've read the works of Marcus Aurelius a hundred times. (Marcus Aurelius, a Roman emperor, was a stoic philosopher.) My reading of him says that one should not be involved with the self, and in any kind of pursuits that are self oriented but should be more for the community as a whole. When I go to China these days, I am struck by how much individualism there is, how much consumerism there is. Are you trying to send a signal to the Chinese people to think less about themselves and more about the community?
>
> Wen Jiabao: It is true I did read the *Meditations* written by Marcus Aurelius Antonio on many occasions, and I was very deeply impressed by the words that he wrote in the book. I very much value morality, and I do believe that entrepreneurs, economists and statesmen alike should pay much more attention to morality and ethics. In my mind, the highest standard to measure the ethics and morality is justice.

When we think about economy, we think more about the real elements concerning the company, the capital, the market, the technology, so on and so forth. And we might forget about the other sort of elements that work behind the scene, and these factors are also affected by the visible factors like conviction and morality. Only when we combine these two kinds of factors, can we put in place a full picture of the DNA of the economy.

It is true in the course of China's economic development, some companies have actually pursued their profits at the expense of morality and we will never allow such things to happen. We will not allow economic growth at the expense of the loss of morality because such an approach simply cannot sustain.

In a recent free-wheeling Q&A session with law students in Beijing, he said, "We should have a high moral standard and an understanding of truth, law and morality. Morality is the basis of legal consciousness and observance of law. It is higher and more powerful."

Wen Jiabao's emotional tribute to Hu Yaobang

My admiration for Wen Jiabao grew manifold after I read a lengthy and emotional tribute to the former communist party chief Hu Yaobang, which he wrote in People's Daily in April this year. I regard this article, which surprised China-watchers around the world, as one of the most significant political writings in the world, in our times. For it holds a mirror to the interesting, and heartening, ways in which China's communist party is changing. Hu Yaobang, General Secretary of the party (1982-87), was removed from his post by hardliners because of his tolerant attitude towards demands for political freedom and reform. He was replaced by Zhao Ziyang (1987-89), who also took a liberal and accommodative approach when China was rocked by pro-democracy student protests in many cities, most notably at Beijing's Tiananmen Square in May-June 1989. (The protest demonstrations actually began in the form of mourning for Hu Yaobang, who died during a politburo meeting on April 15, 1989.) Zhao Ziyang too was sacked, and the protests were violently suppressed.

Notably, Wen Jiabao had worked closely under both Hu Yaobang and Zhao Ziyang, but he survived the turmoil in the Communist Party. He not only survived but went on to become vice-premier and later premier of China. His heartfelt tribute to Hu Yaobang is significant because it clearly shows that his survival was not secured by selling his soul. After all, Hu Yaobang's name had been almost erased from the Chinese media after the Tiananmen Square massacre. And now a serving premier is penning a eulogy for him, and that too in the Communist Party's own official newspaper! This is the clearest indication that mild winds of glasnost are blowing in China.

The article is significant for another reason. It portrays both Wen Jiabao and Hu Yaobang as sensitive leaders, deeply committed to serving the common man. Recalling how, during Hu Yaobang's fortnight-long survey of a drought-hit province in 1985, he was asked by his leader to go incognito to villages and gather correct information, Wen Jiabao writes: "He said to me that leading cadres (of the communist party) definitely must personally go to the lowest rungs of society to investigate; to experience and observe the people's suffering, listen to their voices, and understand the situation firsthand. As far as the work of a leader was concerned, Yaobang said that the greatest danger was separating oneself from reality. Years later, Yaobang's gravely earnest words often still echo in my ears."

Remarkably, Wen Jiabao has used the essay to inform the Chinese people that "after his (Hu Yaobang's) passing, I have visited his home every year for the new (lunar) year, and it is always with a deep feeling of love that I look on his portraits in the living room there. His long gaze and firm expression always give me strength, give me encouragement, and drive me to be more diligent in my work of serving the people."

Is Wen Jiabao sincere? Is all that he says, believable? The answer to this question, in my opinion, lies in what he told Fareed Zakaria at the beginning of the CNN interview. "Before we begin," he said, "I would like to let you know that I will use the words from the bottom of my heart to answer your questions, which means that I will tell the truth to all your questions. I always tell people that sometimes I may not tell what is on my mind, that as long as I speak out what is on my mind, the words are true."

Wen Jiabao has two more years left as China's premier, after which he will have to retire. However, one can be certain that the distinct imprint he has already left on Chinese politics will become wider and more decisive in the time to come.

Cheng Ruisheng

Experiences and Enlightenments: The Sixty Years of Diplomatic Relations between China and India

On April 1, 1950, India became the first country among non-socialist countries to establish diplomatic relations with New China, thus leaving behind a thick stroke of writing in the annals of friendly relations between China and India. Since then, relations between China and India, the two big countries in Asia, entered a new era. From 1950 to 1958, China-India relations witnessed a very friendly period of "honey-moon", with the slogan of "Hindi-Chini Bhai-Bhai" resounding across the land of both countries. However, it was indeed very unfortunate that China-India relations sharply deteriorated after 1959, owing to their differences on the Tibet question and China-India boundary question, and under the influence of a number of complicated factors, both international and internal, leading to the border conflict in 1962 and confrontation between the two countries for more than ten years. Since 1976, China-India relations gradually improved. In 1988, the visit of Indian Prime Minister Rajiv Gandhi to China became a major turning point for China-India relations, which entered a new period of overall restoration and development after that, with only a short setback in 1998, after India's nuclear tests. With the beginning of the new century, a rapid development of China-India relations was achieved and a Strategic and Cooperative Partnership was established in 2005.

In general, India is one of China's neighbours whose relations with China witnessed big ups and downs after the founding of New China. It will be very beneficial to sum up some experiences and enlightenments from the tortuous course of China-India relations. Especially at present, while the general trend of China-India relations is good, there still exist some unstable factors in the relations, due to the fact that the China-India boundary question remains unresolved and mutual trust between the two countries is insufficient. Therefore, to conduct some summing up and reflecting on the past can play an important role for both countries to march towards the future in a better way.

Cherishing Historical Friendship

There has been a history of friendship between China and India lasting more than two thousand years. During his meeting with Indian Defence Minister, George Fernandes in April 2003, Premier Wen Jiabao said that during the past 2200 years, China and India had devoted 99.9 percent of the time to friendly cooperation between the two countries. These remarks made by Premier Wen Jiabao indicated how much he cherished the historical friendship between China and India.

Reviewing the history of China-India relations, people can see many moving events such as visits paid by Indian reverend monks to China and visits paid by Chinese reverend monks, including Xuan Zhuang, to India, taking back Buddhist scriptures from India. Among China's neighbours, India was one of the very few countries which did not have a war with China in the past. Especially in their struggle against imperialism and colonialism, people of both China and India sympathised with each other and supported each other, with fraternal friendship established. The heroic deeds of the Indian Medical Mission to China, including Dr Kotnis, dedicating themselves to the cause of liberation of the Chinese people, are still well remembered and highly praised by people of both countries.

By cherishing the historical friendship between the Chinese and Indian people and regarding it as a kind of common wealth of the two people and the foundation for developing friendly relations, both sides could have stronger determination and greater initiative to promote their friendship, so that new milestones could be set up one after another in the history of China-India friendship and the process of this history of friendship could be continued, generation after generation. At the same time, it could also make both sides more sober-minded and more prudent in dealing with some major differences emerging between them, so that confrontation could be avoided and conflict prevented, without leaving behind any historical legacy of regret for the descendants of both peoples. In order to enhance friendly sentiments of both people, it is necessary for governments, friendship organisations and media of both countries to attach more importance to widely publicising and commemorating the major events and prominent figures in the history of friendship of the two countries and building essential sites of historical moments, so that the historical friendship of both countries could strike deeper root in the heart of both people.

Harmony Being Precious

Through reviewing the history of sixty years of diplomatic relations between China and India and making comparisons of those different periods of friendship, confrontation and renewal of friendship, a conclusion of incomparable importance for both governments and peoples could be obtained, i.e. harmony is precious.

Friendly relations between China and India from 1950 to 1958 brought out great gains, either from the angle of peaceful construction of both countries or from the angle of safeguarding peace in Asia and the world.

(1) During Premier Chou En-lai's visit to India in 1954, both sides fixed the Five Principles of Peaceful Coexistence as guiding principles for China-India relations. At the end of that year, Indian Prime Minister Nehru paid a visit to China, holding very good talks with Chairman Mao Tse- and Premier Chou En-lai. In 1956, Premier Chou En-lai paid another visit to India. All these events led to a high tide of friendship between China and India which had been unprecedented in history. It was during this period that India gave up its special privileges in Tibet.

(2) China-India friendly relations were conducive to creating a peaceful environment necessary for the peaceful construction of both countries, which had won independence not long before.

(3) Maintaining friendly relations with both India and Pakistan, China adopted a neutral stand on the Kashmir question. It was shown that China-India relations were helpful to safeguarding peace and stability in South Asia.

(4) China and India had very good cooperations in international affairs. Take the Bandung Conference in 1955 as an example. Before the conference, both India and Burma (now Myanmar) took a firm stand that China should take part in the conference. And at the

conference, Nehru made a number of efforts to support Chou En-lai, giving a helping hand to New China which had just ascended the international stage.

In sharp contrast to the above period, the deterioration of China-India relations and the confrontation between the two countries from 1959 to 1976 caused enormous losses.

(1) The China-India border conflict in 1962 brought about serious damage to the friendship between the Chinese and Indian people and a long-term suspension of friendly exchanges between the two countries. The shadow of this conflict has not fully vanished even today.

(2) The long-term confrontation between the two countries caused great drain on the resources of both countries, negatively affecting peaceful development of both countries.

(3) Along with the deterioration of China-India relations, relations between China and Pakistan were rapidly improved and strengthened, with the result that India had to face a two-front unfavourable strategic environment. And due to the continued improvement of relations between India and the Soviet Union and the formation of an alliance between them, China, whose relations with the Soviet Union deteriorated at that time, also had to face a two-front disadvantageous strategic environment. After the U.S. President Nixon's visit to China in 1972, there emerged in South Asia, the confrontation involving China, Pakistan and the United States on the one side and Soviet Union and India on the other side, giving rise to a serious threat to peace in Asia and the world.

Since 1976, China-India relations were gradually restored and improved and witnessed greater development in this new century, producing very encouraging "bonus".

(1) Both China and India are two neighbouring countries on a fast rise among newly emerging countries. The friendly cooperation between the two countries would offer an indispensable and important guarantee to their peaceful rise.

(2) With the swift development of trade and economic relations between China and India, China has become one of the biggest trade partners of India. Since both China and India have quite similar national conditions, they could learn from each other's strong points to offset their own weaknesses in the fields of economic and social development. It is well known that China's hardware and India's software have mutual complementarity.

(3) China has developed friendly relations with both India and Pakistan separately, while trilateral relations between China, India and the United States have maintained a general balance. These are conducive to stability in South Asia.

(4) Both China and India have common stands on a number of major international questions. With both countries taking part in more and more regional and international regimes, they support each other on many important questions, such as the climate change.

It can be seen from the above comparisons that it is not any empty talk that China-India friendly relations are in conformity with the fundamental interests of the two people. That harmony is precious, has more and more become a common understanding of both governments and people.

Correctly Handling Differences

It can be seen from the history of international relations that it is somewhat a rule that differences of one kind or another would emerge between countries, especially between major powers. In order to safeguard relations between the two sides, it would be of the utmost importance to handle these differences in a correct way. Since the differences between China and India have been related to such questions as Tibet and China-India boundary which involve sovereignty and territorial integrity, the above point has become even more conspicuous.

While facing differences, it is necessary, first of all, for both sides to deal with the relationship between the partial interest and the overall interest very carefully. Reviewing the developments since the establishment of diplomatic relations between China and India, one can see that relations were quite smooth when both sides could handle their differences calmly, attaching importance to the overall interest. For instance, both sides dealt with the Tibet question quite well in the initial period after the establishment of the diplomatic relations between them, with the result that this question did not affect the development of their friendly relations in the 1950s.

However, after the Tibet rebellion in 1959, both sides over-estimated the seriousness of their differences on the Tibet question and later on the China-India boundary question and failed to give first priority to the overall interest of safeguarding their friendly relations, leading to the conflict and confrontation between the two sides. Today, when people re-examine China-India relations in that period, it is not difficult for them to see that despite the fact that the differences between China and India involved core interest of both sides, they constituted only questions of partial interest after all, while safeguarding China-India friendly relations were related to their fundamental and overall interest on the question whether a peaceful environment could be maintained for both countries. So it is not difficult to differentiate what is primary from what is secondary. Again, the situation from 1988 up to now has indicated that despite the fact that the differences between both sides on the China-India boundary question have not been resolved, yet both sides have reached a common understanding that while seeking the ways and means to settle the boundary question, both sides should develop their relations in other fields and make efforts to create atmosphere and conditions conducive to the final settlement of the boundary question in a fair and reasonable way. Due to this understanding reached by both sides with the overall interest of China-India relations in view, China-India relations witnessed quite fast development during this period.

Another question related to the above is that it is imperative that both sides should avoid making their policy in an emotional way. It could be seen from the situation during the period of confrontation that emotional approaches appeared to bedevil both sides with the result that calm and objective judgments could not be made and a few wrong decisions were taken with serious consequences. On the contrary, judging from the situation of a short setback in China-India relations in 1998 after India's nuclear tests, both sides tried hard to avoid emotional approaches, so that China-India relations could come out of the low quickly and were restored and developed again.

It is also important that both sides should offer greater guidance and education to the masses of the two countries, in view of the sentiments of narrow nationalism among them. Since both the Chinese and the Indian people suffered for a long period, the oppression by imperialism and colonialism in the history, quite strong sentiments of nationalism could be found among the masses of both countries. This is understandable. However, under these conditions, it is even more necessary for both sides to guard against the sentiments of narrow nationalism and defend the overall interest of maintaining the friendly relations between the two countries. Otherwise some very radical remarks and actions might emerge, leading to unwarranted damage to the relations between the two countries. The demarcation between patriotism and narrow nationalism is whether overall interest has been put in the foremost or not. Besides the two governments, the media of both countries has also great responsibility in correctly guiding the public opinion.

Policy Being the Key Factor

Since its reform and opening to the outside world, China has kept a quite high speed of development, while India's development has also been quite fast since its economic reform in 1990s. With the continuous strengthening of their comprehensive national strength, people have often heard such argument from world media that rivalry will certainly arise between China and India as two big powers, leading to sharp competition and conflict between them. Since China's speed of development has been a little higher than that of India for a number of years, this has become one of the grounds for some people in India to propagate the "China threat" theory.

Reviewing the history of international relations, people can see that though the balance of power forms an important factor affecting relations between different countries, the decisive role is played by the policy of relevant countries.

In Europe, France and Germany were "arch enemies" in the past, with many wars between them. However, since the end of the Second World War, both countries have maintained friendly relations all along, forming the core for promoting the integration of Europe. While answering a question raised by the author about the reasons for such change, a French ambassador to China said that the reason was very simple: both France and

Germany, summing up historical experiences, were determined to adopt a policy of mutual friendly cooperation and promotion of the integration of Europe, with the result that relations between the two countries had been developed continuously.

Take the relations between the United States and Japan as another example. In the Second World War, they were the major rivals fighting the Pacific War that ended through the surrender of Japan. However, after the war, due to the rise of the Soviet Union and the triumph of the Chinese Revolution, the United States swiftly readjusted its policy towards Japan to prop up Japan and the two countries formed an alliance.

After the founding of New China, both China and the United States were locked in confrontation with each other for a long time, owing to the policy adopted by the United States to contain and encircle China and the policy adopted by China to form an anti-U.S. united front. However, after 1971, along with the change in the international situation, both China and the United States drastically readjusted their policy towards each other, leading to a fast thaw of their relations and the establishment of diplomatic relations between them later.

Analysing the China-India relations, one can see that from 1959 to 1976, it was mainly due to some major mistakes committed by both sides in their policies, that their relations were deteriorated and confrontation followed, while their comprehensive national strength was not strong at all at that time. On the contrary, the situation since 1988 has shown that despite the fact that the comprehensive national strength of both countries has greatly increased than before, their friendly relations have been continuously developing. The major reason for this is that both countries have adopted a policy of good-neighbourliness and friendship towards each other. History has proved incontrovertibly that policy is the key factor.

The policy of good-neighbourliness and friendship adopted by both China and India towards each other at present has its rich and important connotation.

Both sides, viewing China-India relations as one of their most important bilateral relations, have raised the level of their relations higher and higher. In 2005, both sides announced that they agreed to establish a China-India Strategic and Cooperative Partnership for Peace and Prosperity on the basis of the Five Principles of Peaceful Coexistence. This should be the fundamental starting point for both sides to deal with various specific questions between the two countries.

Both sides have reaffirmed in official documents that the common interests of both countries outweigh their differences and the two countries are not a threat to each other. Both sides have decided to settle their differences through peaceful and friendly consultations, without using or threatening to use force against each other. In view of the armed conflict between the two countries in 1962, this policy adopted by both sides has very important significance.

On the China-India boundary question, both sides have agreed to a policy of seeking a political settlement and have undertaken that while seeking ways and means to settle the boundary question, both sides would develop their relations actively in other fields. Both sides have also agreed that pending an ultimate settlement of the boundary question, the two sides should strictly respect and observe the line of actual control and work together to maintain peace and tranquility in the border areas.

India has readjusted its original stand of recognising Tibet as an "autonomous region" of China to the present stand of recognising that "the Tibet Autonomous Region is part of the territory of the People's Republic of China" and has undertaken that it does not allow Tibetans to engage in anti-China political activities in India. China has recognised Sikkim to be part of India's territory.

Both sides have adopted a policy of actively promoting friendly exchanges in all fields, so that friendly exchanges between the governments, political parties, parliaments, armed forces, industrial and commercial circles, cultural circles, youth and civil organisations of the two countries have continuously increased. Both sides have attached much importance to their trade and economic cooperation, with the result that trade and economic relations have witnessed a swift development.

China has adopted a policy of developing friendly relations with India on the one hand, and with Pakistan and other South Asian countries on the other in a separate way and has expressed its desire that South Asian countries could be friendly with each other. China has tried hard to persuade the relevant parties to become reconciled when conflicts occur between

India and Pakistan or between India and other South Asian countries. This policy of China is conducive to peace and stability in South Asia. However, up to now, a small number of people in India still consider that it is for "encircling" and "containing" India that China has been developing its relations with Pakistan and other South Asian countries. What is the truth? It has already been more than twenty years since China adopted the above policy. What people can see is that China-India relations have been greatly improved and developed in this period and cannot find any kind of "encircling" and "containing" India by China. Perhaps some friends in India are still worried. Then the best way is to continue their watching on this question.

In recent years, India's diplomatic strategy has shown a certain degree of inclination towards the United States. However, India has still adhered to its policy of friendship with China, with the result that a general balance has been maintained in the trilateral relations between China, India and the United States.

The above are some important aspects of the policy of good neighbourliness and friendship adopted by both China and India towards each other. These are achievements obtained by the two countries through their summing up of both positive and negative experiences in the past and would constitute forceful guarantees for the future development of China-India relations. It has not been easy to gain these fruits, which need to be highly cherished by both governments and people.

Energetically Enhancing Mutual Trust

With the common efforts of both sides, the main trend of China-India relations has been quite good in recent years. However, the inadequacy of mutual trust between the two sides has still been a major factor with certain negative impact on their relations. The inadequacy of mutual trust between China and India has been mainly revealed through the fact that the "China threat" theory has been on rise again in India in recent years. There are a number of factors leading to the inadequacy of mutual trust between China and India. Some are the questions left over from the history while some are related to real politics. Thus the situation has been quite complicated.

The first factor is that no major breakthrough has been achieved on the China-India boundary question. Since 2003, a number of rounds of talks have already been held by the Special Representatives of the two governments. During Chinese Premier Wen Jiabao's visit to India in April 2005, both governments signed the Agreement on the Political Parameters and Guiding Principles for the Settlement of the China-India Boundary Question, thus laying a good foundation for both sides to realise the final solution of the boundary question. However, owing to the complicated nature of this question, it seems that there is still some difficulty in reaching the final settlement. Since the impact of the 1962 border conflict between the two countries has not fully vanished, the Indian side still has considerable apprehension about China on the boundary question.

The second factor is that the economic gap between China and India has been widening. In recent years, both China and India have achieved quite fast economic growth, but China's rate of growth has been higher than that of India, with the result that the economic gap between the two countries has been widening to some extent. Since India has, all along, had a quite strong motive of competing with China, it seems India has some worry over this question.

The third factor is the influence of geopolitics. Along with the development of China-India relations, the impact of geopolitical factors on China-India relations has been reduced gradually. However, these factors still play a role to some degree. As stated above, India still has some apprehension on China's relations with India's neighbours, while China has also its concern on India's military and security cooperation with countries like the United States and Japan.

The above factors are interwoven together instead of being isolated from each other, leading to a rather complicated situation and considerable difficulty in solving them. Therefore, time and patience are needed and both sides should refrain from getting a wrong conclusion on the overall relations between the two countries. At the same time it is advisable that both sides should attach much importance to this question and make more efforts to enhance their mutual trust in an active way.

In accordance with the situation of China-India relations and with reference to historical experiences of China's relations with some other countries, if both sides could make greater efforts in the following three areas, it would play an important role in enhancing mutual trust between the two sides.

Judging from the situation in recent years, mutual visits and meetings in third countries between leaders of China and India could play an especially vital role in promoting the mutual trust between the two countries. Leaders at the highest level of both countries have cherished very much, these opportunities of personal contacts and conducted in-depth exchange of views, from a strategic altitude, on ways and means to further develop relations between the two countries, offering some new thoughts and proposals and publishing some very important documents which have much significance in guiding the relations between the two countries, so that greater impetus has been given to the development of relations between the two countries. These mutual visits and meetings have also shown outstanding effects in dispelling the dark clouds which might appear sometimes in the sky of China-India friendship and promoting the confidence of both people in the future of their friendly relations.

The final settlement of China-India boundary question will be the most important key to greatly enhancing mutual trust between the two countries. Judging from the present situation of China-India relations, it seems conditions are already mature for the final settlement. (a) The overall relations between China and India have been good with Strategic and Cooperative Partnership already established. This is very conducive to the final settlement. (b) This century will witness the great event of simultaneous rise of both China and India. Both countries need a peaceful environment, which will be in conformity with the supreme national interest of both countries. The final settlement of the boundary question will be a very important factor for this purpose. (c) The Agreement on the Political Parameters and Guiding Principles for the Settlement of the China-India Boundary Question has laid a good foundation for the final settlement. (d) Since so many rounds of talks have already been held between the Special Representatives of the two governments on the boundary question, both sides are already quite aware of each other's stand on the question. If there is still a gap, it will not work for either side to press for unilateral concession by the other and the only right way is to explore a framework of compromise in the spirit of mutual respect and mutual understanding. There is no reason why this can not be realised.

Both sides could also take more active steps to support each other on major questions involving core interests of the other side. This would fully reflect the practical significance of their Strategic and Cooperative Partnership and play an important role in promoting mutual trust.

The situation in recent years has indicated that both sides have taken a number of steps in this respect, with good effects. The main steps taken by the Indian side in support of China are: recognising Tibet as part of China's territory; taking resolute measures so that the Olympic torch passed through New Delhi successfully in April 2008. The main steps taken by the Chinese side in support of India are : recognising Sikkim as part of India's territory; making positive remarks on India's desire to become a permanent member of the United Nations Security Council; taking a flexible attitude so that the resolution to lift nuclear embargo against India could be passed by the Nuclear Suppliers Group. On the major question of climate change which involves fundamental national interest of both nations, China and India have had very close cooperation to make a joint approach, which has won great attention of the international community. Since both China and India are large countries, very active in international arena, both sides could find a number of problems on which mutual support is needed in the future. If both sides could give more and more support to each other, the mutual trust between the two sides would certainly be greatly enhanced.

In general, China-India relations have become mature gradually, after passing through a tortuous course in the past sixty years. This is very precious. In the future, with the continuous development of friendly relations between the two countries, it can be expected that those unstable factors in their relations would be further removed so that mutual trust between the two countries would be steadily enhanced. It is believed that people could take a quite optimistic view on the future prospect of China-India relations.

B R DEEPAK

Sino-Indian Border Mismanagement: An outcome of China's 'victim's psychology' and India's 'tough posture'?

This chapter looks into the misjudgments and miscalculations, both from India and China before the outbreak of a brief border war in 1962. The Chinese perception that Nehru wanted to make Tibet as a 'protectorate' or 'buffer' between India and China by accepting the British legacy in Tibet and the Indian perception that China showed mistrust for India from day one have been found holding no grounds after siphoning through vast Chinese, Indian and western sources. The author maintains that these perceptions were wrongly perceived as both India and China, prior to 1959, tried hard to avoid the conflict and attempted to resolve the crisis; however, China's 'victim's psychology' was brought into full play in the backdrop of India's 'tough posture' on border on the one hand and macro and micro environments outside and inside China on the other when it decided in favour of a punitive action against India. Besides, various plausible solutions to the border resolution have been weighed and have suggested that the 'package deal' still remains the best possible solution to the problem.

India and China had a glorious history of cultural and material exchanges, which developed into friendship and subsequently into camaraderie during first half of the twentieth century when both India and China fought western imperialism, shoulder to shoulder. The fraternity and camaraderie rendered borders meaningless, even if they existed in some shape or form throughout the history of India and China. Faxian (342-424), Kumarajiva (343-413), Bodhidharma (6th Century), Xuanzang (600-

664) Yijing (635-713) and innumerable cultural ambassadors from China to India and vice versa moved freely across the Himalayas and represented the spirit of Chindia in true sense. It was the same spirit when the Indian soldiers serving the British in China turned their daggers towards their masters and sympathised with the Taiping cause during the second half of the 19th Century.[1] Yet it was the same spirit and synergy between the cultures of India and China that the nationalists and revolutionaries of India and China could develop deep mutual contacts, forge unity and render support and sympathy for each other's national cause during the early 20th century.[2]

But why did this spirit dampen then and dampen to the extent that India and China had to fight a war in 1962? The reason lies in the expansionist policies of the British and the Qing dynasty (1644-1912), the last Chinese dynasty that resulted in the territorial dispute between India and China. After having taken most of the Himalayan states under its wings, the British Indian borders were extended to the Chinese borders of Xinjiang and those touching its tributary, Tibet. Ever since, the issue has been of protracted contest between the British India and the Qing dynasty on the one hand and the Republic of India and the respective Chinese governments after the fall of the Qing dynasty, on the other.

The sources

The analyses, arguments and conclusions in this paper have been constructed on the basis of Chinese, Western and Indian sources. The official Chinese version of the boundary problem has been derived from *Zhongyin bianjing ziwei fanji zhangzhengshi* (*History of China's counter attack in self-defence along the Sino-Indian borders*) compiled by the Chinese Academy of Military Sciences (1994) and *The Sino- Indian Boundary Question* (1962, 1965). Li, Jian's (1992) *Xinzhongguo liuci fanqinlue zhanzheng shilu* (*A Veritable Record of New China's Resistance to Six Wars of Invasion*), Shi, Bo's (1993)

---

[1] For more details see Deepak (2005) *The 1857 Rebellion and the Indian Involvement in the Taiping Uprising of China*. In *India and China in the Colonial World*, pp. 139-149. Social Science Press, New Delhi (2005).

[2] For details please refer to Chapter 2 and 3 of Deepak (2001) *India-China relations during first half of the 20th century*, APH Publishers, New Delhi 2001.

1962 Zhongyin dazhan jishi (*1962: Records of Sino-Indian War*) also reflects the Chinese version of the Sino-Indian border conflict. Besides, other secondary sources such as Lu, Zhaoyi's (1996) *Yingshu yindu yu zhongguo xinan bianjiang 1774-1911 (British India and China's South-western Border: 1774-1911)* published by the Chinese Academy of Social Sciences Publication, Beijing; Yang Gongsu's (1992) *Zhongguo fandui waiguo qinlue ganshe xizang defang douzhengshi* (*History of China's Struggle and Resistance to the Foreign Invasion and interference in Tibet*) by China's Tibetology Publications, also draw heavily from the Qing dynasty and Republican official histories have been extremely helpful and reflects the ROC and PRC perspectives on Tibet question. More recent Chinese works by Wang Hongwei (1998) and Zhao, Weiwen (2000) etc. scholars, give a bird's eye view of the border conflict and ensuing developments in the Sino-Indian relations from a military, geo-strategic and economic point of view.

On the other hand, the Indian official viewpoint is reflected in the heaps of documents published by the Ministry of External affairs from time to time, including the voluminous *Officials Report* (1961), nine volumes of White Papers (1959-1963) and more recently published *History of the Conflict with China, 1962* by S. N. Prasad and others. There are scores of other works by Indian Army officers and researchers that give invaluable information about the government and military approaches of the conflict. References from various Indian newspapers and journals would be obvious to the readers in this study.

The western works such as Alastair Lamb's two volumes on the Sino-Indian border and McMahon Line (1964, 66), Neville Maxwell's *India's China War* (1970), and a recent study by John Garver (2001) on Sino-Indian relations has been very handy and helpful. However, none of the above works have tried to look into the misperceptions and miscalculations by India and China during the 1962 conflict. The present study attempts to look into the border issue from a Chindia viewpoint and tries to locate the misjudgments and miscalculations of either side.

What went wrong between the two?

Was Nehru indeed a victim of the British legacies in Tibet?

At the outset, it could be argued that India injured the Chinese sensitivities in Tibet by informing the Kuomintang (KMT) government in 1948 that the British obligations and rights under existing treaties with Tibet have been devolved to the present government, for it sent wrong signals to the KMT as well as its successor, the People's Republic of China (PRC) founded on October 1, 1949. As posited by Wang, India exhibited that it wanted to inherit one and all privileges of the British imperialism in Tibet. Not only this, the Indian government also attempted to force illegal Simla [Shimla] Convention of 1914 on China that was not even recognised by the British imperialists themselves. Primarily, this wrong attitude and thinking [of the Indian government on Tibet issue] led to the border conflict in the following years."[3] This author is of the view that India could have refused to inherit the privileges in Tibet by citing article 6 of the Anglo-Chinese trade regulations of Tibet (1908) which specifically stipulated that *Great Britain would relinquish her rights of extra-territoriality in Tibet whenever such rights are relinquished in China.* Since Great Britain did not relinquish its treaty obligation in China until 1997 in the case of Hong Kong, it could have done the same in Tibet. The fact remains that the Britain simply wanted to wash its hands of Tibet, as it was no longer a profitable proposition to it after the loss of India. Nevertheless, the wrong signals had been sent and most of the Chinese perceptions veered around these signals after the relations deteriorated. However, China's perceptions that India attempted to turn Tibet into a 'buffer zone' and a 'protectorate' or to 'cut off Tibet from the motherland' or to 'overthrow China's sovereignty in Tibet' in this author's views were or if they still exist, are miscalculations and misunderstandings. It was these assertions and perceptions of the Chinese leadership and scholarship alike, that turned Nehru into a villain in the Chinese eyes, and the very belief that since Nehru was a villain he should be punished underpins China's punitive action against India in 1962 border conflict. It was China's misperception about Nehru and his

[3] Wang, Hongwei (1998). *Ximalayashan qingjie: zhongyin guanxi yanjiu* (The Himalayan Sentiments: A Study of Sino-Indian Relations) Beijing: Tibetology Press, p. 64.

Tibetan policies that made her to conclude that India was hell bent to 'slice Tibet out of China.'

However, if we analyse Nehru's attitude towards China, be it the pre-1949 Republic of China or the post 1949 People's Republic, he attached utmost importance to China as could be gleaned from his relentless writings about China. No other leader in India has perhaps ever attached such an importance to China as Nehru did. As early as in 1927, while reflecting on KMT and Communist Party of China's campaign against the warlords, Nehru, in an article entitled "The situation in China and India's Duty" wrote "Hope it will be possible for the [Seva] Dal to send to China an ambulance corps of trained volunteers, carrying the message of goodwill to our Chinese comrades and rendering such help as they can for the relief of pain and suffering. China is holding out her hand of comradeship to India. It's for us to grasp it and renew our ancient and honourable association and thereby ensure the freedom and progress of both these great countries which have so much in common."[4] In other words, this was the Chindia spirit that Nehru wanted to resurrect and envisioned it as a natural course for post 1947 and 1949 Sino-Indian relationship. Chinese people on the other hand responded to Nehru's overtures with equal enthusiasm and considered his as a close friend of China.

Though India inherited the British duties and responsibilities in Tibet after the British withdrawal from India, Nehru, however, was clear in his approach as to what policy India should follow as regards Tibet and China. In early 1947, during the Asiatic Conference in Delhi when Tibetan delegates told Nehru that they would like to discuss the border issue with India, Nehru told them that "no political decisions were going to be made [at the Conference] and asked them not to raise any issue regarding borders or political status [of Tibet]." When Chinese delegates protested to the Tibetan map being shown outside China, correction was undertaken when the matter was brought to the notice of Nehru.[5] In later half of 1949, when Tibetans initiated mass expulsion of the Chinese from Tibet, Nehru

[4] Gopal, Sarvepalli (1976). *Jawaharlal Nehru: A Biography*, volume 1, Delhi: Oxford University Press, p327.

[5] Li, Tieh Tseng (1956). *The Historical Status of Tibet*, New York: King Crown Press, Columbia University, p 195.

showed concern and wrote, "We are concerned over the Tibetan government's decision to turn out all Chinese officials in Lhasa. These officials were appointed by the National Government of China; their wholesale expulsion would naturally be regarded as an anti-Chinese rather than anti-Communist move."[6] In 1950 when People's Liberation Army entered Tibet, Nehru was greatly disturbed. In this backdrop when the United States expressed its desire to supply arms to Tibet, provided India would be willing to allow them pass in transit across Indian territory, Nehru categorically told Henderson, the US ambassador in India that "US could be most helpful by doing nothing and saving little just now. Series of announcements by the US Government condemning China or supporting Tibet might lend certain amount [of] credence to Peking's charges that great powers had been intriguing in Tibet and had been exercising influence over India's Tibet policy." Nehru also requested the US to stop Formosa [Taiwan] from bringing Tibet to the UN, according to Nehru, "since Peking charges KMT of intriguing in Tibet, Taiwan raking Tibetan issue at UN would give fresh ammunition to Peking. Henderson also reported to Acheson that the invasion of Tibet by China did not lose *Nehru's enthusiasm for Peking regime*, for *Nehru was still convinced that communist China should be admitted to UN* (emphasis added)."[7] On the eve of the 17-point agreement between Tibet and China when Tibetans asked Nehru whether India could mediate between Tibet and China, Nehru made no comment but instead advised them that since China would insist on Tibet being an integral part of China; Tibetans would have to accept this point. However, Tibet must not agree to the stationing of Chinese troops in Tibet, as it would have serious repercussions on India.[8] In 1953, negotiations started between India and China on Tibet that resulted in the signing of "Agreement between the Republic of India and the People's Republic of China on Trade and Intercourse between Tibet Region of China and India" on 29 April 1954. Nehru came under scathing criticism for his enthusiasm for China and the Panchsheel. Nehru

---

[6] Gopal, Sarvepalli, ed. (1975). *Selected Works of Jawaharlal Nehru* , Vol.2, New Delhi: Orient Longman, p. 411

[7] *Foreign Relations of United States [FRUS]* (*1950*: vol. VI) Washington: United State Government Printing Office, pp. 550-51

[8] Shakya, Tsering (1999). *The Dragon in the Land of Snow: A History of Modern Tibet Since 1947*, London: Pamlico, p. 64

remained undeterred and silenced his critics by asserting that "in international affairs, we can never be dead certain and the friends of today might be enemies of tomorrow. That may be so. Are we then to begin with enmity and suspicion, and not give any other approach a chance?"[9] In December 1956 when the Dalai Lama expressed his desire to stay on in India and not to go back to Tibet in the wake of Chinese democratic reform in Kham and confrontation arising out of it between the Tibetans and the Chinese, Nehru advised the Dalai Lama to cooperate with the Chinese within the 17-point agreement, as there was nothing India could do to help Tibet.[10] It appears that Nehru had also tacitly accepted the Chinese compromise proposal for the Western Sector and Eastern Sector exchange until 1959. To this effect we see him making statements about non-delimitation and no actual administrative jurisdiction of India in Western Sector.

Therefore, China's perception of Nehru as a villain is unfounded. However, what went wrong in between? This author believes that Nehru wanted China to show an understanding towards Indian cultural and security sensitivities in Tibet within the framework of Chinese sovereignty, so as the fraternity between the two could be maintained and sustained. Zhou Enlai seems to have responded to these sensitivities initially; however, in the wake of the Tibetan revolt, Beijing viewed Nehru's Tibet policy with suspicion and framed her viewpoints about Nehru surrounding these misperceptions. Granting the Dalai Lama refuge and accepting large numbers of Tibetan refugees in India; not punishing the Tibetan émigré for engaging in anti-China campaign from India; Nehru discussing the Tibet issue in Indian Parliament; not curbing on anti-China reportage of the Indian press etc. "acts" of the Indian government were treated as anti-China policies of Nehru and treated as an unwarranted interference in China's internal affairs. As a result, Nehru's Tibet policy if viewed from the Chinese prism attempted to create a buffer or denying China to exercise her sovereignty over Tibet.

---

[9] Appadorai, A and Rajan, M. S (1985). *India's Foreign Policy and Relations*, New Delhi: South Asian Publishers, p. 116

[10] Gopal, Sarvepalli (1984) *Jawaharlal Nehru, A Biography*, Vol. 3, London: Jonathan Cape, p. 36.

Nehru's policies, however, were not derived from converting Tibet as an "Indian protectorate", but from a desire to uphold Tibet's autonomy under Chinese sovereignty as part of Chindia fraternity and camaraderie, which would make a real cooperative and strategic partnership between India and China possible at the world stage. In other words, it was autonomy and sovereignty swap compromise; by virtue of which China would show an understanding towards the Indian interests in Tibet by granting her autonomy as incorporated in the 17-point agreement, and in lieu India would respect Chinese sovereignty over Tibet. Even after the Dalai Lama's flight to India in 1959, when the Dalai expressed his desire to establish a government in exile, on 24 April 1959, during his first meeting with Nehru in Mussoorie, Nehru rejected the idea outright, and said that it would not be recognised by the Government of India.[11] The manifestation of Nehru's approach is reflected in India being the first non-socialist country to recognise the People's Republic; accepting Tibet as a part of China; voting against the UN resolution that declared China as an aggressor in Korea; meditating in the Korean crisis; univocally and relentlessly supporting China's place in the UN; adhering to one China policy by supporting transfer of Taiwan to China; confirming China's role in the Afro-Asian movement and so forth.

However, his Chindia spirit went for a nosedive especially after the flight of the Dalai Lama to India. The mounting pressure from the opposition in Parliament and press; and the vitriolic and vituperative attack from China forced Nehru to take a tougher posture to China. Nehru was dismayed when China dissolved the Tibetan government and its powers and functions were transferred to the Preparatory Committee for the Tibet Autonomous Region (PCART), as it was a death knell to the Tibetan autonomy, and the militarization of the Tibetan borders by a powerful army would send the feelings of an uneasy calm across the Himalayas. Non-militarization of Tibet is not tantamount to turning Tibet into a "protectorate" at all. China's tough military measures in Tibet, and huge domestic pressure forced Nehru to adopt an equally tough border policy that ultimately culminated into a unilateral approach and finally into the formulation of ill conceived Forward Policy in November 1961.

---

[11] Ibid, 90

This "tough approach" toward China was again envisioned under the premise that China would withdraw rather than use force. The Indian attitude that China would not involve in large scale offensive could also be gleaned from the absence of Nehru from India prior to the Chinese assault. Nehru had embarked on his Colombo visit on 12 October 1962. However, Indian approach was considered as territorial encroachment by China and could not have been sustained for long. In such a situation, an appraisal of the Forward policy should have been carried out, but was left to fall pray to yet another miscalculation. Meanwhile, China also fell a victim to the "victim's psychology", especially after the Tibetan revolt.

Was Zhou Enlai a victim of China's "psychology of a victim"?

It could be argued that besides the macro environment surrounding China in the form of imperialistic wars, the encirclement of China by the US; the Sino-Soviet split; Taiwan's attempt to assert independence or win back China, and the micro environment inside China manifested in the form of international isolation, the economic crisis in the aftermath of Great Leap Forward; Tibetan revolt and the three year's famine resulted in China developing a "victim's psychology" as depicted in Figure 1. And, such a psychology made China to formulate "ultra leftist" policies that at times were away from the reality and full of vengeance.

Figure 1. China: Formation of "Victim's psychology" and policies formulation

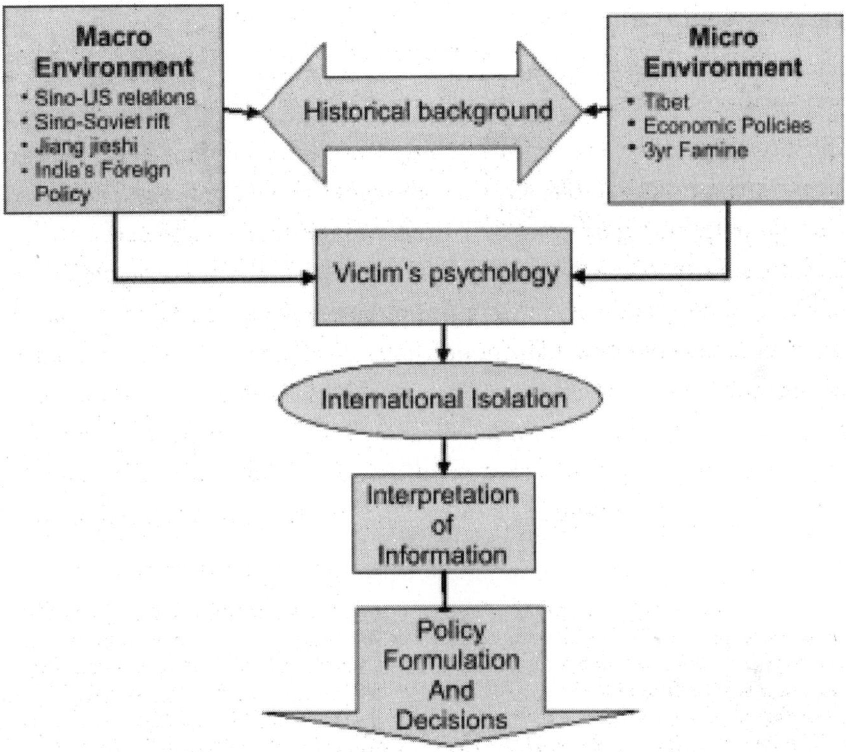

But, does it imply that Zhou did not respond to Chindia enunciated in the policies of Nehru? If we analyse Zhou's attitude and pronouncements before, during and after his India visits, one can surmise that Zhou was an equal enthusiast for India-China fraternity. Let's examine the following facts: Knowing that India had a Mission in Lhasa, Zhou met Panikar, Indian ambassador to China on 14 June 1952, and proposed that the Chinese Government was in favour of re-establishing the Indo-Tibetan relations through consultations and since the resolution of Tibet problem would require considerable time and measures, the Chinese government is of the view that the Indian Mission at Lhasa may be converted into Indian consulate."[12] From 26 April to 21 July 1954, when Indo-China and Korean

[12] Deepak, B. R (2005). *India and China 1904-2004: A Century of Peace and Conflict*, New Delhi: Manak Publishers.

crises were being discussed in Geneva, Zhou wanted the participation of India; expressed his dissatisfaction when India was not invited to the conference.[13] Nehru still dispatched Krishna Menon to Geneva, where he had five meetings with Zhou. After the conclusion of Geneva Conference, Zhou thanked Nehru for his contribution when he wrote to him on 14 August, 1954 in a telegram, "Here, I would like to point out that you have not only expressed your desire for an armistice in Indo-China much before the convocation of Geneva Conference, but also the common efforts by you and other prime ministers of Colombo powers greatly contributed to the progress of Geneva Conference. During the convocation period, the dispatch of Mr. Menon to Geneva by you provided invaluable help to our work. Undoubtedly, your efforts were one of the important elements that contributed to the success of Geneva Conference."[14]

The Chindia spirit was restored to some extent when India and China jointly propounded the *Panchsheel* during the conclusion of the "Agreement between the Republic of India and the People's Republic of China on Trade and Intercourse between Tibet Region of China and India" in 1954. The spirit was carried to the Afro-Asian Conference in Bandung too. In the words of Shi, the success of the Bandung Conference for China was a "victory in smashing the international blockade," and the credit for this victory goes to the "close cooperation between Zhou and Nehru."[15] During his second visit to India while addressing both Houses of the Indian Parliament, Zhou said, "The Chinese Government and people will always remember the unequivocal support rendered by the Government of India and its people to us in our struggle of complete reunification of our motherland and the restoration of our rightful place in the United Nations. Likewise, we assure the Government of India and its people that you will always get all-out support from the Chinese Government and its people in your struggle to safeguard sovereignty, territorial integrity and promote world

---

[13] Zhao, Weiwen (2004). *Yinzhong guanxi fengyunlu: 1949-1999* (*Records of Turbulences in Sino-Indian Relations: 1949-1999*), Beijing: Current Affairs (shishi) Publishers, p. 42.

[14] Ibid. 46

[15] Shi, Bo (1993). (1993). *1962 ÿZhongyin dazhan jishi* (*1962: Records of Sino-Indian War*), Beijing: Chinese Earth (Zhongguo Dadi) Publishers, p. 52.

peace."[16] As regards the border problem, Zhou's attitude was similar to Nehru, i.e. the border should not become a hindrance in developing friendly relations between the two countries. Zhou further expressed that through necessary preparations the problem that has been left over by the history could be resolved through friendly negotiations. It could be reasonably resolved on the basis of Five Principles of Peaceful Coexistence, asserted Zhou.[17]

During his third visit to India in 1957, Zhou assured Nehru that China would maintain the autonomy of Tibet under the Dalai Lama's leadership. This is what Nehru had been advocating and what I have called the "autonomy and sovereignty" swap for Tibet between India and China in the preceding sections. In this respect, Nehru and Zhou had reached an understanding and the border issue according to both the leaders would also be best resolved through an East-West swap. This could also be ascertained from Nehru's minutes of a meeting with Zhou in 1954 during Nehru's China visit. According to Nehru's minutes of the meeting, "Premier Zhou referred to the McMahon Line and again said that he had never heard this before though of course the then Chinese government had dealt with this matter and not accepted that line. He had gone into this matter in connection with the border dispute with Burma. Although he thought that this line, established by the British imperialists, was not fair, nevertheless, because it was an accomplished fact and because of the friendly relations which existed between China and the countries concerned, namely India and Burma, the Chinese government were of the opinion that they should give recognition to this McMahan [sic] line."[18] Even after the breakout of war Zhou wrote to Nehru that China looks upon its south-western border as a border of peace and friendship. The dispatch of Chinese border guards to south-eastern part of Tibet was undertaken merely to prevent remnant armed Tibetan rebels from crossing the border back and forth and in no way constituted a threat to India.[19]

[16] Zhao, Weiwen (2004).p. 64.

[17] Shi, Bo (1993). (1993), p. 62.

[18] Ministry of External Affaira (1959). *Notes, memoranda and letters exchanged and agreement signed between the Governments of India and China* [White Paper I], New Delhi: Government of India Press, pp. 49-50

[19] White Paper II (1959), p. 27-33

From these assertions of Zhou Enlai, it could be ascertained that both Nehru and Zhou tried hard to keep a balance between friendship and the border dispute. The procrastinations on border issues by both the sides, initially aimed at not letting the issue be an irritant in friendly relations, became so hypersensitive amidst the international and domestic events in India and China that it dragged the two friendly nations to a war in 1962. These events together with the toughening stance of Nehru on border after 1959 brought China's "victim's psychology" into full play and made China skeptical and suspicious of India's actions. India's mediation in the Korean crisis; Nehru sending Krishna Menon to Geneva in 1954; India's initiative in the Bandung Conference and so forth were now treated by China as "Nehru wanting India to play an important role at the international stage in the capacity of a big Asian Power."[20] The vicious attack even went to the extent that People's Daily accused "ambitious Nehru" of establishing an India centric empire unprecedented in Indian history! It said that once India is established "as the center of economic and political activity" or when "the great empire conceived by Nehru comes into existence," the small states would be doomed and become vassals of Nehru's empire.[21]

Negative role of the press and opposition

The negative role of the press in both the countries cannot be denied during the conflict. In India, as the press is not controlled by the government, the views on Sino-Indian boundary conflict were mostly cacophonous. Instead of playing a positive role, the Indian press exerted undue pressure on government to see reason in the crisis that was not there. For example, when Nehru invited Zhou for a summit in New Delhi, the *Indian Express* wrote on 16 February 1960 that before entering any negotiations, China must accept two prerequisites set by New Delhi [accept McMahon Line and evacuate the Aksai Chin]. The entire opposition criticised Nehru in the Parliament and declared that if the Government was prepared to treat Chou En-lai as an honoured guest, the country was not, because "he is a murderer with the blood of Indian soldiers on his hands," reported the *New Leader* on 21 March 1960. Praja Socialist Party and Jan Sangh decided

[20] Shi, Bo (1993), p. 31

[21] People's Daily (27 October 1962) "cong zhongyin bianjie wenti zailun nihelu de zhexue" (Analyzing Nehru's Philosophy from Sino-Indian boundary question).

to stage anti-Chinese demonstrations. Vajpayee, the former Prime Minister of India ironically was at the forefront of organising anti-China demonstrations. *Hindustan Times* wrote on 12 April 1960 that there was "little ground for negotiations." The pressure on Nehru continued to build before the start of the negotiations. The divergent and hostile views in the Indian press and Parliament about China and its leaders, and sympathy shown to the Tibetans by the Indian press enraged China to the extent that on 30 April 1959 *Renmin Ribao* warned the "imperialists and Indian expansionists" in the following words: "You must stop at once; otherwise you will be crushed to pieces under the iron fist of 650 million Chinese people," another extremist approach!

Possible solutions

It was not until Chinese Foreign Minister, Huang Hua's India visit in 1980 that India and China agreed to hold talks on the border issue. Between 1981 and 1987, eight rounds of talks were held in Beijing and New Delhi alternatively. After Rajiv Gandhi's path breaking China visit in 1988, a Joint Working Group (JWG) was especially established for the resolution of border issue. Between 1989 and 2006, fifteen round of talks had been held. Besides, Special Representatives of the two countries appointed to look into the boundary issue during Vajpayee's China visit in 2003 have held 15 rounds of talks. Furthermore, during Wen Jiabao's 2005 India visit, an Agreement on Political Parameters and Guiding Principles for the Settlement of the India-China Boundary was signed. Irrespective of all these mechanisms and the parleys of 25 years, the border issue is still awaiting resolution. Nevertheless, the signing of the Agreements on the maintenance of peace and tranquillity along the Line of Actual Control (LAC) in 1993 and building confidence building measures (CBMs) in 1996 has created an atmosphere that is conducive for the final resolution of border problem.

Could there be a military solution? Is it advisable to go to the war and at what price? Three full wars and a mini-war with Pakistan, failed to solve the Kashmir issue with Pakistan, can a second war solve the much larger boundary issue with China? And, when both the countries desperately need to improve the living standard of their people, can they afford it?

More importantly, for India, can she afford to open another front in the east? No, military solution will not solve the problem. It will aggravate the situation and the fruits of 25 years of parleys will go in vain.

Can there be a solution in tradition and history? In fact this is the solution both sides have been seeking ever since the unfolding of the border issue. Both sides submitted heaps of documents and maps in support of their claims and counterclaims as regards the territory in all the sectors. India argued that the Western Sector was defined by the Tibet-Ladakh Treaty of 1684, 1842 Treaty between Kashmir and Ladakh on one the one hand and Tibet and China on the other, and the Chinese response to the note of British India in 1899.[22] Since the treaty of 1684 was found in Ladakhi Chronicles only, China questioned the existence of such a treaty. China also rejected the 1842 treaty by saying that it was an exchange of notes ensuring mutual non-aggression, nothing beyond that. As regards the British note of 1899, China argued that the proposal put forward by the British to "delimit" boundary was not accepted by the Chinese government.[23] Various boundary lines such as Johanson Boundary (1865), John Ardagh Boundary (1896), and Macartney-Macdonald Line (1899 are not acceptable to China as these have been drawn as a result of unilateral British surveys in the western sector and are not delimited on the ground. As regards McMahon Line in the Eastern Sector, it is again not acceptable to China as the entire Simla Agreement was repudiated by China.

As regards the traditional and customary boundary lines claimed by India and China, they are like two parallel lines that will never converge. If the Indian side asserts that the official Chinese maps of 1893, 1917 and 1919 showed the customary boundary exactly as depicted in official Indian maps of India today, China is quick to add that the Indian maps of 1938 published by the Survey of India and even 1951 edition of Nehru's *Discovery of India* did not show the McMahon Line.[24]

---

[22] Ministry of External Affairs (1961). *Report of the Officials of the Government of India and the People's Republic of China on the Boundary Question*, New Delhi: Government of India Press, pp. 52-54

[23] Ibid, pp. 12-17

[24] Prasad, S. N ed. (1992). *History of the Conflict with China, 1962*, New Delhi: History Division, Ministry of Defence, Government of India, p.2; also refer to Deepak (2005), p. 226.

It could be discerned that no solution could be found if both India and China stuck to their customary lines and treaties. Therefore, it is time that both India and China talked less about history and try to find a solution that is acceptable to both the parties.

Can the issue be resolved on the basis of watershed principles? The watershed principle of delimiting boundaries has so far remained the best one. Most of the boundaries have been demarcated on the basis of this principle. China has resolved its border dispute with Myanmar and Nepal on the basis of watershed. For that matter most of the boundaries drawn by the British in the subcontinent, whether the Durand Line or the so-called McMahon Line of 1914 all follows the watershed principle. The Sino-Indian boundary could be negotiated afresh on the watershed principle and it would not be difficult to locate the watersheds from the tri junction of the India, China, Myanmar boundaries till the tri junction of India China and Pakistan in Kashmir and solve the problem.

But, will it be acceptable to both the parties in the face of actual position on the ground? It could be, if both the parties wish to do so; the area falling here and there after joint survey could be sorted out by negotiating the problem of their jurisdiction. However, going by the 26 December 1959 note of China to India, China might have reservations in accepting such an arrangement, for she has clearly said in the note that the watershed is not the sole or main international principle for delimitation of boundaries.[25] Other geographical principles, such as river valleys and mountain passes should be equally applicable to all sectors of the boundary.[26]

Could LAC be the border? For the last four decades or so, the LAC has remained a de facto border between India and China. Meanwhile, both sides have initiated a number of confidence building measures (CBMs) along the border area. Two of the CBMs that are often treated as no war pacts between India and China and possible parameters for future resolution of the boundary issue are: the agreements signed during the visit of Indian

---

[25] *The Sino- Indian Boundary Question* (1962). Peking: Foreign Language Press, pp. 51-52

[26] Ministry of External Affairs (1961). *Report of the Officials of the Government of India and the People's Republic of China on the Boundary Question*, New Delhi: Government of India Press, pp. CR 188 89.

Prime Minister Narsimha Rao in 1993 and that during Chinese President Jiang Zemin's India visit in 1996. The Agreement on Maintenance of Peace and Tranquility along the LAC in the Sino-Indian Border Areas of 1993 stipulated that the border issue should be resolved through peaceful and friendly negotiations; neither side should use force or threaten to use force against the other; the two sides should strictly respect and observe the LAC before the border issue is settled and each side should keep its military forces in the areas along LAC to a minimum level; effective confidence building measures (CBMs) in the area along LAC should be worked out through consultations; any contingency that might arise along the LAC should be dealt through consultations between border personnel of two countries. The agreement on confidence building measures (CBMs) in the military field along the LAC in India China border areas of 1996 stipulated that both sides would exchange data on the military forces and armament to be reduced along the LAC, and give prior notice to the opposite side in the event of military exercises involving a brigade (approximately 5000 troops) and avoid holding large scale military exercises, involving a division (approximately 15000 troops). The flight of combat aircrafts would not fly within 10 kilometers from the LAC, in case they are required to take a flight, the other side should be informed. In short the 12-point agreement further elaborated the 1993 peace and tranquility agreement except the fact that 1996 agreement specified some of the CBMs on paper.

What about the East-West swap as a solution? The problem with the LAC as border could be problematic from Indian point of view as the LAC prior to 1962 was different in the Western Sector, whereas it remained unchanged in the Eastern Sector. Initially, China had suggested a line on the basis of its 1956 map, but later added the Galwan Valley in the maps produced in 1960 and enforced its 1960 claim line. As regards Eastern Sector, it was only during the 7th rounds of talks held in Beijing from July 21-24 1994 that China's stand on package deal went under a change. China no longer pointed to East-West swap. China rather told India that only if India made some adjustments in the Eastern Sector, then only could China agree to some concessions in Western Sector.[27] This author is of the view that China was forced to alter its position as India insisted on a

[27] Wang, Hongwei (1998), p. 317.

sector to sector resolution of the border, contrary to China's package deal that applied to all sectors of the border. By agreeing to a sector-to-sector approach China lost the bargaining power and it laid larger claims, including Tawang, in the Eastern Sector. At present some of the Chinese scholars feel that Tawang is the only irritant in the resolution of boundary problem. If India hand over Tawang, China would be willing to make greater compromises in the western sector. This was explicitly expressed by the Chinese scholarship recently in Beijing, prior to Hu Jintao's India visit in November 2006, at the sidelines of a seminar organised by the Institute of Asia Pacific Studies, the Chinese Academy of Social Sciences. This author also presented a paper and enunciated the perspective discussed in this paper.

Half a century later, if China is making claim to Tawang, it is contradicting its Chindia approach of Zhou Enlai. India at present has gone back to the Chindia approach of Nehru and has expressed its willingness to accept the package deal proposed by Zhou. If present leadership in China is willing to respect the deal proposed by its leaders, I believe the LAC as a border with minor compromises and accommodations from both the sides in all the sectors could be an option for a resolution. It would not be purely on the principle of watershed and neither on history and customary lines. This in other words is finding the solution on the basis of the "package deal" offered by Zhou Enlai to India in 1960. As revealed by a former Chinese ambassador to India, "Zhou's proposal called for mutual understanding and mutual accommodation, by way of which China agreed to accept Himalayas as border between India and China in the Eastern Sector by way of accepting the McMahon Line, which was never accepted by the respective central governments of China. China agreed to hand over 90,000 square kilometers of disputed land to India and make major compromise. On the other hand, India would have agreed to Karakoram as a border between India and China in the Western Sector and would have compromised on handing over 33,000 square kilometer of land to China."[28] This was the best possible solution to bury the crises and

---

[28] Zhang,Minqiu (2006) *Kuayue ximalaya zhangai: zhongguo xunqiu liaojie yindu* (*Across the Himalayan gap: A Chinese quest for understanding India*) Chongqing: Chongqing Publishing House, pp. 380.81.

resurrect India-China fraternity. If agreed, both countries need to conduct joint surveys and demarcate the entire border on the ground. Once it is done, further discussions on the CBMs, such as deployment of forces or even demilitarisation of the area could be taken.

In conclusion, the 1962 war was an outcome of miscalculations and misjudgements from both India and China. However, now, when both the countries have expressed their desire to develop and strengthen relations in various domains, it is high time that India and China resolve its long pending issue of border with strong political will, for Chindia and border conflict cannot coexist. Therefore, the procrastinations in the resolution of border issue would continue to eclipse the realisation of a real friendliness and good neighbourliness between India and China.

DP Tripathi

China Through Indian Eyes

What this brief retrospective essay strives to do is to trace the origins and evolution of Chinese Studies in India. Keeping in mind the constraints of space and the readership that is targeted, no attempt is made to be comprehensive. Our purpose, it is felt, will be served if on a broad canvas, a few bold strokes can paint the main contours. The main concern is to raise some important questions.

China has intrigued Europe for centuries. The fantastic travelogues of Marco Polo fired the imagination of generations and intrepid explorers, Jesuit priests, adventurers; traders lured by tales of fabulous riches have headed eastward from time immemorial. India hasn't remained untouched by its mystique. Travellers like Hiuen Tsang and Fa Hien have left behind detailed chronicles of their journeys in the 'Western World' and these eyewitness accounts fill up many a gap in our historical knowledge. This has never been a one way traffic. Mystics and teachers of esoteric *tantra* doctrine who crossed the high Himalayan passes have been no less frequent and numerous. Names of Dipankar Atisa and Guru Rimpoche Padmasambhava are well known, both in India and China.

Sinology, strictly speaking, is the study of China - including its society and culture in broadest sense - usually confined to scholarship focussing on classics. And this is how it had started in India in the 1920s when China Bhawan was established in Shantiniketan-Vishwabharati

In 1913, Rabindra Nath Tagore became the first Asian to be awarded a Nobel Prize. His achievement became a matter of shared pride, in some measure a restoration of Asian self-esteem. Within a few years his name became household word in China and Japan. The mystic poet undertook a journey to China in 1924 and delivered a series of public lectures. It was during this visit that he made acquaintance with Tan Yun Shan, in Singapore and the idea of establishing an institute of Chinese studies began to take an embryonic shape. Cheena Bhawan was founded in 1937 and this may be marked as the beginning of a systematic study of China, Buddhism, Chinese language and literature in contemporary India. The credit for this pioneering effort should be given primarily to that visionary Chinese Scholar who was the moving spirit behind this ambitious venture to start this 'civilizational dialogue'. Not only did he keep goading Gurudev into persisting when irritating obstacles were encountered, but also devoted himself to fund raising. Others like Lin Yutang too did their bit but Prof. Tan was uniquely placed as he strode with equal ease, the two contending worlds of pre-revolutionary and post- revolutionary China. He had, as a young scholar, interacted with Maoists and spent years of his life in 'Third China'- in South-East Asia. With him at the helm, Cheena Bhawan busied itself with study of classics, reverse translations of lost Sanskrit and Pali texts and attracted scholars like P C Bagchi and Kshitindra Mohan Sen. Years later, his son served with great distinction in University of Delhi and JNU. It is a matter of more than little regret that this stream of traditional Sinology dried out during the 1950s and 1960s as the arid wasteland of strategically motivated (US prompted, Ford Foundation and Asian Foundation sponsored) area studies expanded. Policy relevant research undertaken and guided by compulsions of the Cold War affected Chinese Studies more than others. Increasing misunderstanding between India and China, regarding the disputed Himalayan border and 'liberation of Tibet', aggravated the matter. The changing domestic milieu and the international environment influx, shifted not only the focus but shook the basic foundations of the scholarly edifice[1].

In 1947, when India attained Independence, China was engulfed in a civil war. The Communists, led by Mao Tse-tung were on the verge of registering a decisive victory and Nehru was optimistic about charting a New Course in Asia partnering China. He had been sympathetic to the Chinese cause and the Indian National Congress had dispatched a Medical

[1] Tan Chung, *Across the Himalayan Gap - An Indian Quest for Understanding China* (New Delhi: Gyan Publishing House, 1998)

Mission[2], Dr. Kotnis being one of the members, to provide succour to the 8th Route Army[3] after the Long March. Though Nehru had friendly relations with the Soong sisters, one of them married to Chiang Kai- sheik, the Maoist Chinese did not look upon him with suspicion. Nehru sent the scholarly Sardar KM Panikkar as India's envoy to China and expected the accomplished historian with a specialist's interest in resurgent Asia, to keep him abreast of latest developments. Ironically, in In Two Chinas[3], he provides more interesting insights into India of that vintage than the new born People's Republic of China.

1950 was marked by the 'liberation' of Tibet and the Korean War. Both these events shocked India. It became impossible to sustain illusions about a China that would be guided by India in conduct of its international relations. The signing of the Panchsheel Agreement and the Bandung Conference brought India a brief respite but by the end of 1950s, the simmering differences had surfaced as an explosive conflict. 1962 is the watershed when the cartographic war turned into the nightmare of a real military conflict that changed the course of Sino-Indian relations. Indian perceptions of China, both popular and scholarly, could not remain unchanged.

Before proceeding further it would be useful to review briefly the growth of this area of scholarship in India.

---

[2] The decision to send a medical mission to China was adopted by the Indian National Congress (INC) at its 52nd session by passing a resolution. Soon after, a special committee was also set up to collect funds and select personnel for the mission. By the end of August, a team of five doctors namely Dr. M. Atal from Allahabad, leader of the mission, Dr. M. Cholkar from Nagpur, Dr. Debesh Mukherjee and Dr. Bijoy Basu both from Calcutta; and Dr. D.S. Kotnis from Sholapur was selected, which left Bombay for China carrying with them the friendship of the Indian people on September 1, 1938; the mission arrived in China on September 17, 1938.

[3] On September 1937, CCP issued a manifesto entitled "Together We Confront the National Crisis" (gongfu guonan) and explained its stand on the war of resistance against Japan. It declared that the CCP would reorganise the Red Army and put it under the control of military commission of the government. Consequently, 30,000 strong Red Army was reorganised as the 8th Route Army was later renamed the 18th Route Army under the command of Zhu De and Peng Dehuai. The Army was sent to fight the Japanese in northern Shanxi.

[4] K.N. Panikkar, *In Two Chinas: Memoirs of a Diplomat* (California: G. Allen and U Win Publisher, 1955)

The Indian School of International Studies (ISIS) was started by the Indian Council of World Affairs in 1955 and soon after its birth became the premier institution in the field of area studies. The mother institution was founded in 1943 by Pt. Hridayanath Kunzru and his associates like the brilliant lawyer Sir Tej Bahadur Sapru, a fellow Kashmiri, a public spirited veteran freedom fighter, a serious member of the Indian National Congress and a close associate of senior leaders of that party. It was inspired by the idea to prepare Indians to take an active and responsible part in the international arena after the country attained independence. Although an NGO, it worked closely, often in tandem with the Government of India and had played an important role in the organisation of the historic Asian Relations Conference in 1947. Affiliated to the Delhi University initially, the school was soon granted the status of a deemed university and started awarding Ph. D degrees[5].

Prof. V P Dutt, who had earlier worked for the ICWA headed the department of East Asian Studies at ISIS. Like many others of his peers, he had been sent abroad by the Council to gain expertise in the field of his interest. He had studied in the USA and specialised in Chinese history. He was hand-picked by Dr. A Appadorai, the then Secretary General of the ICWA and first Director of the ISIS, to pioneer study of contemporary China - a subject quite different from traditional Sinology. However, it should be hastily added that competence in Mandarin is essential for any meaningful expertise in the subject. It is curious that after this generation the split between students of Chinese language and Chinese politics-foreign policy, etc kept getting wider and the breach has, by now, in India, become glaring as a major fault-line.

Some diplomats of an earlier vintage, when posted in China or sent to Hong Kong, have far greater fluency in the language than most academic specialists. From Jagat Mehta and Mira Sinha to Kishan Mehta and Vinod Khanna, there have been many Indian Foreign Service officers who have combined linguistic fluency with abiding interest in China. Others, without the language apparatus, kept themselves up-to-date about China. Brijesh

[5] M. S. Rajan, *International and Area Studies in India*, International Studies, Vol. 31, April 1994, pp. 207-214. Also see other articles of M. S. Rajan on birth and growth of area studies in the same journal and in volumes of collected essays.

Mishra and A K Damodaran can be put in this category. However, the only person who could qualify as an undisputed Sinologist was V K Paranjape who had started his career as an interpreter.[6]

V P Dutt's wife Gargi Dutt too was a member of the faculty of the school. The school shifted from the congested rented premises in Connaught Place to its own campus in Sapru House and became the hub of Chinese studies in India. The ISIS attracted young Indian scholars like a magnet as it offered unprecedented opportunities to enter and explore an exciting emerging discipline. From the beginning, the focus was on contemporary China and strategic affairs, particularly on Sino-Indian relations and the border dispute. This was the time in mid-1960s when funding was generously made available for study of China.

After the 'Himalayan Blunder' or the 'Chinese Blunder' there was general agreement that there was an urgent need to build an expertise in the field of Chinese Studies. The department of Chinese Studies was set up at the Delhi University and Dr. Dutt moved over to head it. Mrs. Dutt continued with the ISIS as an associate professor.

It would not be out of place to mention that the ideological divide among the Indian Sinologists can be traced back to this period and is entwined with the personalities. Prof. Dutt was a member of the Congress Party's think-tank and had easy access to the higher echelons of its leadership. His views were respected and lent weight to the exertions of officials of the ministry of external affairs. He was nominated to the Rajya Sabha and also served as the pro-Vice Chancellor of the Delhi University. He frequently travelled abroad as a member of official Indian delegations and articulated with exceptional brilliance, the stand of his country.

These two departments have accounted for almost all the Indian Sinologists who have been active for the past half century or more. The Department of Chinese Studies at the Delhi University, like the Department of East Asian Studies was conceived, and has functioned, as an inter-disciplinary centre. It has drawn postgraduate students from the

[6] Details of the fascinating career of this exceptional scholar were recapitulated in the obituary published by *The Hindu*.

Departments of History and Political Science and the faculty has comprised, in addition to its core staff, members of the teachers of Sociology and Political Science Departments, with an abiding interest in China. At one time it could boast of young experts who had specialised in Chinese society, polity and economy. (K R Sharma, K P Gupta, Manoranjan Mohanty were all in late 1960s part of a stellar constellation). Prof. K N Raj, who was, for some years, the Vice Chancellor of the Delhi University and was identified as a Marxist intellectual, had delivered a series of stimulating lectures comparing the economic performance of China and India and encouraged studies and research projects that went beyond the run of the mill justifications - historical and legal -of the Indian case on the disputed border with China.

This was also the time when the Institute of Chinese Studies was set up at the Centre for Study of Developing Societies. The CSDS was headed by the eminent political scientist Rajani Kothari, a critic of authoritarian regimes and enthusiastic proponent of World Order Project. His theoretical contributions are considered seminal and his affinities with Gandhian and other outsiders projected his institution as a 'rival pole' to the centres aligned with the establishment. Nor can it be denied that China Scholars of all shades found breathing space at the Institute of Chinese Studies (ICS). The working group was an eclectic mix of academics, diplomats, journalists and scholars, young and old, representing different subject streams. Giri Deshingkar, Mira Sinha and Patricia Oberoi provided the critical mass that could start a chain reaction, involving younger persons working in the field. Ideological differences were recognised but none was excluded on sectarian basis. Giri Deshingkar and Mira Sinha - neither of them an alumnus or member of the faculty of ISIS-JNU, Delhi University or Vishwa Bharati-Shantiniketan - brought exceptional language skills and refreshingly different expertise to the Institute. Self confident and free from the burden of running departments as fiefdoms or building powerful empires, they concentrated on topics of research that engaged them. They did participate and contribute to seminars and workshops at home and abroad but remained focussed on long-term serious academic pursuits. It is a pity that neither published a substantial book that could be reckoned as a fitting legacy.[7]

[7] Both edited several useful volumes, see, G. Deshingkar, Manoranjan Mohanty and M. Sinha (eds), *Security and Sciences in China and India* (New Delhi: Samskriti, 2005) and M. Sinha, China, the World and India (New Delhi: Samskriti, 2001).

By mid-1960s some dissenting voices had started emerging and the old 'patriotic' China hands were challenged by youngsters who weren't burdened by the baggage of unpleasant past and were enthusiastic supporters of the resurgent People's Republic of China. G P Deshpande at the ISIS and Manoranjan Mohanty at the Delhi University represented the 'Young Turks'. G P Deshpande had joined the ISIS in 1962 and after finishing a preparatory pre-Ph.D course, was sent for language training to Hong Kong, on a scholarship. He returned in 1965 and was appointed a research fellow at the Department of East Asian Studies. Manoranjan Mohanty had, after completing his masters in Political Science from Delhi University and teaching for a short while, proceeded to Berkeley to acquire a Ph.D in Chinese Studies. He returned by the end of the decade and joined the Department of Political Science in the Delhi University.[8]

This wasn't just a clash of generations or a conflict between individuals with patrician and plebian temperaments. Ideological partisanship lay at its core. Tensions were inevitable. Careers could be made or marred by reputation of belonging to one camp or the other. It was difficult to stand on unclaimed ground. One either eulogised or demonised China. There were numerous comparisons between Mao and Gandhi - flattering or otherwise. (Prof. Jayantanuja Bandyopadhyaya at Jadavpur University who had resigned from the Indian Foreign Service to take up teaching and research contributed a volume on this subject).

By 1969, the Sino-Soviet Schism had surfaced and China was engulfed in the throes of the Great Proletarian Cultural Revolution. India was confronted with the challenge of coping with the Maoist uprising in Naxalbari of West Bengal. After a brief lull, the People's Republic of China again seemed to be working overtime to destabilise democratic India. Passions reigned high and 'sympathies' with China were considered 'unpatriotic'.

---

[8] However, most of these contributions were in the nature of seminar papers and topical commentary. Other scholarly interests seem to distract these fine minds away from the arid vastness of Chinese Studies, Some of his work includes Manoranjan Mohanty (ed), Class, Caste, Gender (New Delhi: Sage Publication, 2004), Manoranjan Mohanty (ed), Chinese Revolution: Comparative Perspective on Transformation of Non-Western Societies (New Delhi: Ajanta Publications, 1992) M. Mohanty, P.N. Mukerji, & O. Tornquist,, People's Rights: Social Movement and State in the Third World (New Delhi: Sage Publication, 1998).

Indian experts on China were once again arrayed against one another in dubious battle.[9]

Ever since the war with Pakistan in 1965, the government of India had been apprehensive about Chinese machinations to forge an anti-India Pindi-Jakarta-Beijing Axis. Chou En-lai, once lauded as a friend of India, now seemed completely under the spell of mercurial diplomats Zulfiqar Ali Bhutto and Subandrio. The emergence of New Emerging Forces reinforcing the solidarity of Afro-Asians and Africans, appeared to challenge Indian leadership of the Old Established Forces, represented in the Non-Aligned Movement. It was the People's Republic of China once again at work, destabilising India's position in Nepal. In brief, 1960 through 1975 was a period marked by suspicion and simmering hostility between India and China. This was reflected in the work of Indian scholars specialising on China. Priority was accorded to strategic threats from China, its military strength and diplomatic relations. Society and culture, economy and polity were considered 'soft' subjects that could wait fraternal friendship.

The battle lines were sharply drawn and shades of the Oedipal conflict weren't missing. Honour of the first family of Indian Sinologists seemed at times, to interfere with objectivity. G P Deshpande's travails at the SIS (renamed, after it was merged with the Jawaharlal Nehru University in 1969) are illustrative of the malady. Not only was it made difficult for him to clear the Ph.D hurdle but his elevation to the professor's post was delayed inexplicably. G P, as he was popularly known, was associated with the CPI (M) and wrote scintillating anti-establishment columns with his wide ranging interest and biting satire. An eminent Marathi playwright and gifted stage artiste, G P was the recipient of the national award of the Sangeet Natak Acedamy. All this was held against him when the time came to judge him. What had he done as a Sinologist? Were his views on China not insensitive to national interest? How many Ph.D candidates had he guided and how many MA students had he taught? Quantity of published papers, it appeared, was more significant than their quality. The students and research scholars working with 'dissenters' too were stigmatised

---

[9] *Jayatanuja Bandyopadhyaya, Mao Tse-tung and Gandhi: Perspective on Social Transformation* (Bombay: Allied Publishers, 1973).

and suffered. Those in favour, were rewarded with accelerated academic elevation, and were included in prestigious committees and advisory bodies. The patronage network extended to universities - central and others - outside Delhi.

The Institute of Chinese Studies relied mostly on honorary visiting guests and adjunct faculty. Many retired diplomats and some Army officers joined it.

The China Study Centre in Chennai started, it appears, as a think-tank that would be a parking lot for superannuated civil servants and academics, who found it bothersome to travel to Delhi, to give decision makers and media, the benefit of their expertise.

The Institute of Defence Studies and Analyses, set up in the wake of Sino-Indian Border War, drew (from its inception) from the pool of talent at the ISIS/SIS and Delhi University. The resident China Expert for years at the IDSA was K R Ramachandran, a student of the East Asian Studies Centre at the ISIS. He was later joined by Sujit Dutta, who belonged to the first batch of MA, International Relations at the SIS-JNU. Subsequently he joined the Chinese Studies department at SIS but dropped out of the Ph.D programme to join the news agency, PTI. Posted in Beijing for some time, he served for many years at the IDSA and at present, occupies the Nelson Mandela Chair at the Institute of Third World Studies at Jamia Millia University. A regular participant in seminars and symposia, Professor Dutta is reckoned today among the senior China hands in the country. Prof. Srikant Kondapalli, at present with SIS, also started as a graduate student at the SIS before serving for some years at the IDSA. The research priorities of the IDSA are understandably very different from that of a University Department. Scholars are working assiduously and have produced commendable work, both qualitatively and quantitatively.

Far Eastern History continues to be a popular option in the History Honours courses and China understandably occupies the pride of place in this paper. Some students retain this interest at the post- graduate level and quite a few opt for China when doctoral research is contemplated. The list of Indians who have obtained Ph.Ds in Chinese Studies is quite impressive which augers well for the future of Sinology in India.

Ma Jiali

The Development and Issues in Sino-India Security Relations

The security issue between China and India is a very sensitive topic. It involves each and every general judgment on the other's security strategy, and also the direction of mutual political relations. Presently, we must be serious and calm in observing the military and security relations between the two countries; find out fundamental problems and put forward creative suggestions; carry out effective confidence building measures; and try our best to provide richer content and more solid bases for a India-China Relation, towards peace and prosperity.

The first step towards security dialogue between China and India was started by way of setting up of a Joint Working Group for the resolution of border issue in the wake of Indian Prime Minister Rajiv Gandhi's China visit in December 1988. Between December 1988 and June 1993, there was a visible progress in our security environment as various Confidence Building Measures (CBMs) were initiated, including mutual troop reductions, regular meetings of local military commanders and advance notifications of military exercises etc. During Indian Defence Minister Sharad Pawar's visit to Beijing in July 1992, the first ever by an Indian Defence Minister, it was agreed to develop academic, military, scientific and technological exchanges. A senior level Chinese military delegation, aimed at fostering CBMs between the Defence forces of the two countries, made a six day goodwill visit to India in December 1993. The visit was reciprocated by the Indian Army Chief Gen B C Joshi's visit to China in July 1994. All these exchanges culminated into signing of the agreement on CBMs in the military field along the LAC during President Jiang Zemin's India visit. Since then, regular exchanges have been taking place at various levels. The agreement stipulated that both sides would exchange data on the military forces and reduce armaments along the LAC; give prior notice to the opposite side in the event of military exercises involving a brigade (approximately 5000 troops) and avoid holding large scale military exercises involving a division (approximately 15000 troops); combat aircrafts would not fly within 10 kilometres from the LAC, in case they are required to take a flight, the other side should be informed. The 1996 CBMs in fact further elaborated the peace and tranquility agreement signed during the Indian Prime Minister Narasimha Rao's China visit in 1993. Since then there have been an increased and higher level of cooperation between the three forces of the two countries.

I would like to make three broad propositions and some suggestion as regards the security issue between China and India as following:

Owing to joint efforts from both sides, there is an obvious improvement in the security relations between China and India in the last few decades. The improvement has been demonstrated in the following areas:

1. The governments of the two countries have expressed their political will not to pose a threat to each other:

   In 2000, during the Indian President's visit to China, both China and India clearly expressed their wish to not threaten each other in the official documents and communications. During dialogues and conferences between leaders of the two countries and senior officials, both sides expressed similar opinions. Judging from the high strategic vantages, such expressions fundamentally define the security relations between the two countries. In terms of security threat to China, China has always insisted and maintained that India is not a threat to it. Viewing from the Indian side, it not only wants to develop good bilateral relations with China, but also wants to strengthen cooperation and coordination with China.

2. Close high level contacts between the armies of the two nations: In the early years of the 21st century, Defence Ministries of the two countries have carried out several high level visits. In 2003, Indian

Defence Minister George Fernandes[1] visited China, resulting in a 180 degree turn in his attitude towards China. In the same year, Chinese Deputy Chief of Staff and another two Army delegations visited India. In 2004, Chinese Defence Minister, Cao Gangchuan paid a return visit to India and Indian Army Deputy Chief of Staff visited China, while Chinese Military Academy and Defence University delegations visited India. In February 2005, Chinese Central Military Committee member and Chief, General Liang Guanglie visited India and met with the top ranking officers of the Indian military. In May 2006, Indian Defence Minister, Pranab Mukherji visited China; during his visit, Mukherji also visited highly sensitive Chinese Centre of Space Conduct and Control, and signed the "Memorandum of Understanding for Reinforcing Communication and Cooperation in Defence Areas" with his Chinese counterpart, Cao Gangchuan. The memorandum put forward the ideas, including institutionalising and expanding long term cooperation in military training, military exercises, counter terrorism, fight against sea pirates, joint search and rescue, and personnel communications etc. In early November 2008, the General Wu Shengli, Chinese Central Military Committee member and Naval Commander-in-Chief, visited India. And in December, Deputy Chief of Staff, Ma Xiaotian visited India, carrying out the second Defence dialogue. Not long ago, China also invited several Generals-in-charge of 'China-India Border Area Defence' to visit Beijing, Chengdu and Lhasa, allowing them to visit relatively sensitive military installations, to signal good will and relieve their suspicion, clearly showing that Chinese military presence in Southwest is not intended to target India as an enemy.

3. The two militaries have been carrying out Confidence Building

---

[1] Fernandes paid a week-long official visit to China from 21-28 April 2003 at the invitation of Chinese Defence Minister, General Cao Gangchuan. During his visit, Fernandes, besides calling on General Cao, also met Chinese Premier, Wen Jiabao, Vice-Chairman of Central Military Commission (CMC), General Guo Boxiong, and Chairman of the CMC and former President, Jiang Zemin. Both sides decided to step-up military-to-military exchanges, hold a counter-terrorism dialogue and increase CBMs to maintain peace along the LAC, paving the way for the final resolution of the boundary dispute - Editor.

Measures at various levels: Since 1996, when the governments of China and India signed the Agreements on Building Confidence Measures along the Line of Actual Control on China-India borders: The two militaries have carried out a series of confidence building measures. For example, in November 2003, China and India's Naval forces conducted joint search and rescue exercises in the East China Sea. In 2004, the border troops conducted joint mountaineering exercises.

The First Joint Training Exercise between the PLA and the Indian Army, 'Hand in Hand 2007', was conducted in Kunming, China. One company each, from the PLA and the Indian Army, participated in the counter terrorism exercises. Lt Gen Ma Xiaotian, Deputy CGS PLA and Lt Gen Susheel Gupta, DCOAS, represented China and India respectively, as observers.

In 2008, the Indian Air Force's aero display team, the Suryakiran Aerobatic Team (SKAT), participated in the 7th International Aviation and Aerospace Exhibition in Zhuhai, China. The performance of the SKAT was extensively covered in the Chinese media and marked a new beginning for cooperation between the Air Forces.

Second Joint Training Exercise between the Indian Army and the PLA "Hand in Hand 2008" was conducted at Belgaum, India, between December 4 and 14, 2008. The theme of the exercise was Counter Terrorism again. Lt Gen Ma Xiaotian, Deputy CGS of the PLA and Lt Gen Nobel Thamburaj, GOC-in-C, Southern Command were the senior most observers from the Indian and Chinese sides, respectively.

Following the high level of bilateral defence cooperation in 2008, the Chief of Naval Staff, Admiral Suresh Mehta visited China from 18 - 25 April 2009 on a bilateral visit and also participated in the International Fleet Review (IFR) in Qingdao from 20-23 April 2009. Two Indian Naval ships, INS MUMBAI and INS RANVIR participated in the IFR from 19 - 23 April 2009.

We should also notice that due to historical reasons, China and India have been suffering huge security deficit.

1. Border dispute is the fundamental cause for changing the security relations:

   China and India Border has never been demarcated, and the areas of disputes are huge. Due to both subjective and objective reasons, it is still very hard for either side to solve the problems in the near future. The border issue is related to the core national interests of each country, to the mass media and national feelings, therefore, cannot be excluded from the important contents of mutual concerns. Judging from the current situation, India is increasing troops to occupy the disputed areas; increasing numbers of immigrants in the disputed areas shows that it is trying to consolidate its actual control of the disputed areas. Especially, in last two years, some senior Indian officials have paid visits to the disputed areas, attracting high attention from China.

2. Lack of confidence is one of the important factors influencing the security relations:

   The security environment on both sides is full of suspicion, resulting in the loss of strategic mutual confidence. The Indian side is apprehensive about China's rise to becoming a big power and the impact it would have on its national security. It is also apprehensive about China's relations with Pakistan and other Asian countries, which has also cast a shadow on China's relations with India.

3. Sea navigation escorting is a new factor influencing the security relations:

   Since 2008, new developments in sea lanes have increased Indian suspicions as regards China's naval intentions. China needs to protect its commercial ships from attacks by sea pirates, according to international laws. India mistakenly believed China's entry into Indian Ocean, as an encroachment on its sphere of influence or the Chinese intention to contain India, with the so called 'String of Pearls.' This is obviously a misunderstanding of the Chinese lawful actions.

Concrete suggestions are as follows.

It could be discerned that irrespective of the border issue, bilateral Defence exchanges have been brisk. Peace and tranquility along the LAC in the border areas is being largely maintained by both sides, as stipulated in the 1993 and 1996 agreements. The MoU signed on Defence Exchanges between the Armed Forces of India and China during the Indian Defence Minister A K Antony's 2006 visit of China, further boosted the cooperation. Visits and return visits by the highest ranks of Armed Forces Officers have proved conducive to better understanding and confidence building between the forces of these two countries. However, since security is a sensitive issue, owing to various above mentioned reasons; both China and India need to consider the following suggestions for a better security environment:

1. Keep the momentum of mutual visits of high ranking officials ;
2. Continue the existing confidence building measures, and search for new measures;
3. Promote dialogue between forward troops of both the sides in actually controlled areas;
4. The two Governments and Defence Ministries must carry out their responsibilities to manage and monitor their media, avoiding excessive stir-up coverage.

Both sides need to create a congenial atmosphere, and steadily improve the comprehensive strategic partnership, with added emphasis on security relations.

Amitabh Mattoo

Imagining China

On the 175th anniversary of the French Revolution, the former Chinese Premier Chou En-lai is reported to have declared that it was too early to judge the impact of the revolutionary events of 1789. By Chou's reckoning, assessing Sino-Indian relations (which go back at least 2000 years) on the basis of the history of the last fifty years, is exceedingly premature. Nor is it easy to speculate about the bilateral ties in the new century.

And yet there are few countries that have had and will continue to have as much an impact on India and its future, as China. Moreover, China fascinates, intrigues, and challenges the intellectual imagination and traditional categories of analysis like few other states in the international system do. Will China be able to surmount its internal problems and emerge as an economic and military superpower? Or will the Chinese "empire" too, like the Soviet Union, crumble under the weight of the manifold contradictions that continue to beset it? Will China, as superpower, turn revisionist and challenge the hegemony of the western-dominated international order? Or will it, with increasing stakes in the status quo and the stability of the international system, defy the historical record of emerging great powers and continue to collaborate and cooperate with the Unite States and its allies? Will economic reform lead to political change and will the forces of western style democracy transform it into yet another capitalist democracy? Or will China continue to confound the votaries of the "end of history" and emerge as an alternative model of governance? What will China's attitude be towards South Asia and particularly India? Will India and China, the two Asian giants and civilizational states, become partners in stability or will they fall into the historical stereotype of two powerful, but belligerent neighbours? And what will China's policy be on vital issues affecting India's security and in areas that have cast a shadow on bilateral relations? This essay seeks to answer a basic, but often neglected, question: How does India and Indians view China?

Through much of the 20th century China has been constructed in multi-faceted ways by the Indian imagination. The complex of emotions, ideas and policies that defines India's engagement with China was in evidence again in the very first days of the 21st century. On 4 January 2000, the arrival of the 14-year-old Ugyen Thinley Dorjey, the 17th Karmapa of the Kagyupa sect of Tibetan Buddhism from his monastery in Tsurphu near Lhasa in Tibet to the capital-in-exile of the Dalai Lama at Mcleodganj in Himachal Pradesh once again proved how difficult it is to force Sino-Indian relations into a Manichean straitjacket of friendship or enmity.

Consider a sample of the response of India's leading English newspapers to the most dramatic flight out of Tibet since the Dalai Lama's in 1959. An editorial guardedly warned a possible Chinese trap and suggested that India need not be in "a hurry to grant political asylum" to the Karmapa[1]. In a signed piece in The Hindustan Times titled, "The Dragon Game", a regular columnist Bramha Chelleney was more explicit: "While it is possible that the Karmapa teddy got fed up with his life in a glided Chinese crib and vamoose, one cannot at this stage discount the possibility that Beijing gave him the nod to go, for compelling reasons."[2] What compelled the flight, according to the writer, was the need to get hold of the "black hat", located in the Rumtek monastery in Sikkim, without which Dorje could not have sustained, in the long term, his spiritual claim, and to "aid Chinese designs to divide the Tibetan exile community…[3]" In another piece in the same vein, Chellaney argued : "Preliminary official investigations do not show that the boy-lama and his entourage slipped through the heavy Chinese security cover. On the contrary, the investigations suggest the they had a fairly smooth passage out of their Chinese-occupied homeland, indicating that Beijing may at least have acquiesced in the departure."

Contrast this with an editorial of *The Indian Express* titled, "As welcome as ever: India lives up to its image by sheltering the boy Lama", which suggested that by granting Dorje sanctuary, India would live up to its "image built over the millennia, as a refuge for the persecuted." And added:

---

[1] *The Hindustan Times,*13 January 2000

[2] *The Hindustan Times,*12 January 2000

[3] Ibid.

> "that the hospitality rendered to the Tibetan Buddhists, all these 40 years has not been at the cost of the abiding and good neighbourly relations India has with China. Many Chinese leaders, including the Head of State, have visited India during this period.
> India has been steadfast in its belief that Tibet is an internal affair of China and what kind of autonomy should be granted to Tibet is a matter to be sorted out between the Tibetans and the Chinese. The arrival of Karmapa does not, therefore, signify any change in India's time-tested policy. He is as welcome as the senior Lama was 40 years ago."[4]

Less than a week later, however, the newspaper was more circumspect:

> "...the government needs to study carefully whether India can afford to host a powerful Buddhist sect with deep internal conflicts and powerful links in the West or whether it would be better to help the Karmapa find refuge elsewhere. In any case, it is high time that the West, which has actively espoused the Tibetan cause thus far, steps in to help the Karmapa Lama"[5]

The Times of India, which sees itself as speaking for the nation, and where the country's most distinguished security analyst K. Subrahmanyam often wrote the editorials on foreign policy issues, described Dorje as a "Pilgrim of Peace" and focussed also on Chinese repressive policies:

> "For all the supposed change in Beijing's traditionally hostile policy towards Tibetans religious and cultural practices, the Karmapa's flight is proof of the fact that Chinese authorities still feel profoundly threatened by the region's autonomous temper. The excesses of the Cultural Revolution where monasteries were desecrated and ransacked by Maoist zealots may have given way to greater tolerance and faux mass produced Buddhist relics for sale to international tourists, but Tibet remains a tightly controlled zone of unfreedom. The political intolerance of State Socialism and excessive freedom of the market economy have come together to undermine the spiritual plenitude

---

[4] *The Indian Express*, 13 January 2000.

[5] *The Indian Express*, 17 January 2000.

and tranquility of the land."[6]

The Karmapa issue is not isolated. It is reflected in the multiple ways in which India has responded to the idea of China and to its manifestation as a civilization and a nation-state. This essay is an initial exploration into the plurality of ways in which contemporary public imagination in India has constructed China. Four images of China are briefly discussed: ancient friend and modern ally; role model; unpredictable adversary and dangerous rival; inscrutable and mysterious. As will become obvious, many of these images overlap, some are exaggerated for heuristic purposes and indeed all can be made more weighty and nuanced, by more scholarly China-specialists. In this sense, this essay must be read as a deliberately provocative, almost polemical essay which will, hopefully, generate a real debate on India's China policy - a debate, which will not reduce itself, as so often, to a slanging match between the apologists for China and the so-called China-baiters.

Ancient Friend and Modern Ally: Hindi-Chini Bhai-Bhai!

The view of India and China as two ancient civilizations, with strong past links, in partnership together in the modern world, has been articulated all across India. It is essentially a normative idealised view, rooted in the desire to see India and China emerging as strong allies in the contemporary international system. Understandably, therefore, this image of China often exaggerates both the historical links as well as the space for contemporary cooperation. In this sense, some critics may find this image distinctly antediluvian in the first years of the 21st century.

This view of China was most powerfully advanced by India's first Prime Minister Jawaharlal Nehru, in his writings and speeches in the 1940s and early 1950s. For instance, in a speech broadcast from New Delhi, on 7 September 1946, Nehru said:

> "China, that mighty country with a mighty past, our neighbour, has been our friend through the ages and that friendship will grow. We earnestly hope that her present troubles will end soon and a united

[6] *The Times of India*, 11 January 2000.

> and democratic China will emerge, playing a great part in the furtherance of world peace and progress".[7]

This was some time before the Communist Revolution of 1949. In 1951, in a broadcast from London, he was, with minor caveats, equally enthusiastic:

> "China has taken a new shape and new form. But whether we link that shape and form or not, we have to recognise that a great nation has been reborn and is conscious of her new strength, has acted sometimes in a manner which I deeply regret. But we have to remember the background of China as of other Asian countries, the long period of struggle and frustration, the insolent treatment that they received from imperialist powers and the latter's refusal to deal with them in terms of equality. It is neither right nor practical to ignore the feelings of hundreds of millions of people. It is no longer safe to do so. We, in India, have had two thousand years of friendship with China. We have differences of opinion and even small conflicts, but when we hark back to that long past, something of the wisdom of the past also helps us to understand each other. And so, we endeavour to maintain friendly relation with this great neighbour of ours, for the peace of Asia depends on these relations".[8]

While Nehru is seen as the most important champion of this view, other distinguished public figures like President Radhakrishnan, during the same period, articulated similar views. In 1955, while proposing a toast to Madame Soong Ching-ling, Vice-Chairman of China, Radhakrishnan said:

> "One of the most remarkable things in the world's history is the relationship between our two countries, of peaceful co-operation across the centuries. We have traces of the influences we have exerted on each other in the literature and art of our two peoples. Our cultures intermixed, our trade flourished, mutual appreciation grew and there

[7] Jawaharlal Nehru, *Future Taking Shape*, in *India's Foreign Policy: Selected Speeches, September 1946-April 1961* (New Delhi: Publications Division, 1961), p. 3.

[8] Nehru, "Drift Towards Catastrophe", in ibid, p.186.

> has not been a single instance of military conflict. Something precious and unique has been built up over a long past. Though intercourse between our two peoples was interrupted for some centuries it has now been revived. We passed through trials and tribulations and have now achieved the power to shape our future and are facing similar problems."[9]

There are three strands to this image that need to be spelt out. First, it is an image that is rooted principally in an "anti-colonial" and "anti-western" discourse. It is a view of China in which Beijing and New Delhi, having been subjected to years of similar western humiliation and re-entering the world stage more or less at the same time as independent actors, will seek together to change the status-quo to create a more humane and just world order. The fight against colonialism and the desire for Afro-Asian unity were policy expressions of this view in the 1950s. In its current avatar, issues such as the struggle against American hegemony, the western discourse on human rights and in support of a multi polar world, foster this image. Given also what were perceived to be their common problems and common strengths, it was assumed that a "united front" of the two, on a diversity of issues was sine qua non, as was cooperation in a number of areas. Consider a contemporary statement to this effect, by two well known China-watchers:

> For a whole range of issues the only country whose experience is really relevant to Indian conditions is China, and vice versa, because of the sheer scale involved. It is therefore important to appreciate that when we say that India and China have to cooperate, and to learn from each other, this is no mere diplomatic jargon."[10]

It is an image that seems to believe that the so-called glorious past of friendly India-China relations will continue to shape contemporary relations. Even if there are phases of tension and bitterness, ultimately a bond rooted

---

[9] S.Radhakrishnan, *India and China, Occasional Speeches and Writings*, October 1952-January 1956 (New Delhi: Publication Division, 1956).

[10] C.V. Ranganathan and Vinod C. Khanna, *India and China : The Way Ahead After Mao's India War* (New Delhi, Har-Anand, 2000), p.180.

in ancient friendship will prevail. Thus, in this view, the border war of 1962 and China's nuclear cooperation with Pakistan should be viewed as aberrations that must not be allowed to impact on current relations. Second, this image quite clearly takes a rather benign view of China's future role, both within the international system and in the neighbourhood. According to this view, there is no real threat to India from China. Not only because China is satisfied with the status quo, with respect to the Sino-Indian border, but also because India does not figure in China's threat cosmology. "Thus, for instance, the co-editor of this volume, Kanti Bajpai argues elsewhere:

> "...while the border dispute is unresolved in a formal sense, Beijing has got what it wanted out of the issue. If its primary aim was to secure the route from Xinjiang to Tibet, it long established the goal."[11]

Similarly, he asserts:

> "...it doesn't take an expert on China to know that India has never figured in China's threat cosmology in any serious fashion - unlike the Russian expansionist, the American imperialist and the Japanese Upstart".[12]

China's future role in the international system is also seen as being stabilising and largely defensive rather than subversive and offensive. Three different trends, which seem to justify such a conclusion, are often identified. First, China's foreign policy, it is argued, has increasingly become de-radicalised. Ideology, it is suggested, no longer plays, if it ever did, a decisive role in China's policy towards the outside world. China is no longer seeking to export a revolution, nor are its relations with other countries determined by the nature of their political systems. In this view, China has accepted the basic parameters of the international system as it operates today. Second, China has gradually become a shareholder in the world economic system. It has a stake in global economic stability and the prudent, responsible manner in which Beijing responded to the economic crisis is just one example

[11] Kranti Bajpai, *The Fallacy of an Indian Deterrent*, in Amitabh Mattoo (ed.), *Pokhran II and Beyond: India's Nuclear Deterrent* (New Delhi: Har-Anand, 1999), p.156.
[12] Ibid.p157.

of China's maturity. In short, China is well integrated into the international economic system. Third, it is argued, that there are increasingly external constraints on China's behaviour. Beijing has willingly accepted constraints by signing up for the NPT and CTBT, accepted, by and large, the tenets of the MTCR, is increasingly associating with regional institutions and has gradually been "socialised" into accepting the principal norms of contemporary international relations.

Ideationally, the liberal-institutionalist view sees Chinese strategy as a product of Confucian-Mencian paradigm. In this paradigm, accomodationist grand strategies are preferred over violent defensive or offensive ones. And, it is suggested, that the Chinese view military force is "inauspicious", to be used only under "unavoidable circumstances", and prefer the submission of the enemy without resort to force[13].

Role Model

Closely related to the image of China as both an ancient friend and a contemporary ally, is the view of China as a role model. There are at least three aspects of this image that merit attention. First is the image of China as the near ideal Communist state and society. This image of China, although much eroded, inspired a whole generation of communists as well as activists of the Naxalite movement and even middle class radicals in Delhi colleges. As the Tibetan scholar, Dawa Norbu recollects:

> "When in 1969 I joined the St Stephen's College (Delhi), to my surprise, I found the very people from whom we had escaped a decade ago right next door. In fact my college proved to be the centre of the Naxalite activities. They used the same jargon, had the same convictions, and held identical views to the Chinese communists. One of their popular slogans was: "China's way is our way; and China's Chairman Mao, our Chairman.[14]"

While revelations about the excesses of the Cultural Revolution have done much to erode this image, it continues to find takers within sections

[13] See Alastair Iain Johnston, *Cultural Realism : Strategic Culture and Grand Strategy in Chinese History*(Princeton: Princeton University Press,1995).

[14] See Dawa Norbu, *Tibet: The Road Ahead* (New Delhi: Harper Collins, 1997), pp.xii-xiii.

of opinion, within the Left.

Second, it is China's ability to take hard internal decisions as well as endure pressure from the West that has been lionised by sections within virtually the whole spectrum of public opinion in India: from the extreme Left to the extreme Right. Why can we not do a Tibet in Kashmir? Would China have capitulated before the hijackers in Kandahar? Would China sign the CTBT under pressure? These are only some of the questions that are being rhetorically posed in public debates in India.

Third, China's emergence as an economic and military power of significance and the manner in which it has been able to reform its economy without compromising on its security posture, is also viewed with awe and admiration. For instance, Sujit Dutta and C. Raja Mohan argue:

> "The difference in the asymmetrical attainments in power, wealth and autonomy between India and China therefore significantly lie in the time lag between the two states in reforming closed door and ideologically oriented economic and foreign policies. The ability of the leadership to grasp international strategic changes and consciously adopt cooperative ties with principal global powers and the advanced nations is a fundamental dimension of the route to power and relative autonomy. China grasped this reality and changed itself earlier than India with immense gains."[15]

Analysts compare India's adhocism to China's systematic strategic planning. As Giri Deshingkar argues, India has

> "never showed any inclination to formulate a strategic doctrine and consistently displayed panic reactions and ad hoc responses. In contrast China formulated a strategic doctrine right at the beginning and changed it drastically in the light of changes in the wider situations

[15] Sujit Dutta and C. Raja Mohan, *In Search of Power and Autonomy: The Indian and Chinese Experiences in Dealing with the Global Powers,* unpublished paper presented at the conference on *Fifty Years of India and China: A Comparative Perspective*, New Delhi,7-9 October,1999.

and China's own experiences."[16]

Unpredictable Adversary and Dangerous Rival

It is China that is consistently identified as the most likely source of insecurity to India, and the greatest potential threat to Indian interests in the medium-and long-term future, in any survey of the opinion of the strategic elite in the country. In the popular imagination, it is Lata Mangeshkar's patriotic song: *Ae Mere Watan Ke Logo,* composed and sung after the 1962 war, that captures, most effectively, the public perception of China as a dangerous and unpredictable adversary.

Not surprisingly most strategic analysts believe that the principal strategic rationale for the construction of a credible and effective Indian nuclear weapon posture is to provide a hedge - an insurance policy -against the possibility of a belligerent China in an uncertain anarchic world[17]. Many, even within Left, admit the possibility of a future clash of interests between India and China over trade and influence in Asia. This view has found strength through the recent re-reading of Chinese strategic culture. The best known, the most incisive and the most quoted is the one provided by Alastair Iain Johnston. Based on his close reading of Chinese history and the classic texts of Chinese strategy, Johnston argues that China has historically exhibited a relatively consistent hard realpolitik or parabellum strategic culture that has persisted across different structural contexts into the Maoist period and beyond. The Confucian Paradigm, according to Johnston, only existed as an idealised strategic discourse and had rarely been practised. On the contrary, Chinese decision-makers have internalised the parabellum strategic culture so that Chinese strategic behaviour exhibits a preference for offensive use of force, mediated by a keen sensitivity to relative capabilities. This paradigm views the external environment "as dangerous, adversaries as dispositionally threatening and conflict as zero-sum, in which the application of violence is ultimately required to deal

---

[16] Giri Deshingkar, "Strategic Doctrines: India and China", unpublished paper presented at the conference on *Fifty Years of India and China: A Comparative Perspective,* New Delhi,7-9 October ,1999.

[17] See, for instance ,the collection of essays edited by this author, *Pokhran II and Beyond: India's Nuclear Deterrent* (New Delhi: Har-Anand, 1999)

with threats." Most importantly, this paradigm explicitly embodies a key decision axiom, the notion of 'quan bian' which stresses absolute flexibility and conscious sensitivity to changing relative capabilities. The more this balance is favourable, the more advantageous it is to adopt offensive coercive strategies; the less favourable, the more advantageous to adopt defensive or accommodationist strategies to buy time until the balance shifts again. If one accepts this view, and indeed the empirical evidence that Johnston garners is very impressive, then China's present posture cannot be viewed in benign terms. If China was being accomodationist, it is only because the balance does not seem to be in its favour. Indeed, as Johnston points out, "in comparison with other major powers, China was far more likely to use violence in a dispute over military-security questions such as territory."[18] China used violence as a key conflict-management technique in 80 percent of the crisis in which the primary issue was territory or related to territorial security. For the United States, the figure was 0 percent; for the Soviet Union, 20 percent; for Britain, 8.3 percent; for France, 27.3 percent; and for India, 33.3 percent.

From the perspective of India's strategic elite however, there are at least a few warning signs already. They view with serious concern, the help provided by Beijing to Pakistan's nuclear programme. The true extent of Beijing-Islamabad nuclear collusion may never be revealed, but it is clear that Pakistan's nuclear weapons programme has relied enormously on China's help and Chinese nuclear engineers may even have designed Islamabad's nuclear weapons. Nuclear cooperation of this kind, it is often asserted, is unprecedented in the history of international relations since 1945; indeed, not even the United States and Britain shared such a relationship. Why would China want to help Pakistan to become a nuclear weapon state? India's elite feel that Beijing consistently regarded a nuclear-armed Pakistan as a crucial regional ally and as a vital counterweight to India's growing military capabilities.

---

[18] See Alastair Iain Johnston, "Cultural Realism and Strategy in Maoist China", in J. Katzenstein, ed., *The Culture of National Security: Norms and Identity in World Politics*(New York: Columbia University Press,1996) pp.216-268.See also: Alastair Iain Johnston, *China's Militarised Inter-State Dispute Behaviour 1949-92:A First Cut at the Data,* China Quarterly, No 153,March 1998, pp.1-30

No less serious is the Chinese unwillingness to settle any of the bilateral irritants to which India attaches importance. Despite repeated promises, Beijing has still not recognised Arunachal Pradesh as a part of India and in 1997-98, violated the letter and spirit of the bilateral Confidence Building Measures (CBMs), on more than a dozen occasions. Chinese inroads into Myanmar, including the reported construction of a Chinese naval facility on the Coco islands is of deep strategic concern to the Indian elite. Additionally, the presence of thousands of Tibetans refugees is an irritant that is likely to worsen as the scale of Chinese atrocities in the region, deepens. Much less written about is the direct threat from Chinese nuclear weapons. China has deployed nuclear missiles in Tibet that clearly have one target: India. Admittedly, Chinese inter-continental ballistic missiles elsewhere could also target India, but the potential political and psychological impact of these missiles, literally a few miles from India's border during a future conflict, cannot be underestimated.

This image is widely supported within the Armed Forces also because India suffered a humiliating and traumatic defeat in the war against China in 1962. The defeat deeply embedded itself in the psyche of the nation, and especially in the morale of India's Armed Forces. In 1986-87, India and China nearly went to war again after Indian Army units established a presence in the Sumdurong Chu Valley. According to one top Indian source, the Chinese even threatened to use tactical nuclear weapons during that encounter.

Inscrutable and Mysterious

The image of the mysterious, unfathomable, inscrutable Chinese is probably the one which strikes a cord with most sections of public opinion. The positive image in this context is that of exotica, of fine silks and beautiful princesses in secret gardens. The negative image, at its most extreme, is a monochromatic one of teeming millions in Mao jackets deeply involved in hatching dangerous conspiracies.

Take the positive image first. In Kashmir, children still grow up on a diet of stories about the princesses from "Cheen Ma Cheen" and Chinese brocade and Shanghai silk are still watermarks of the highest quality, even though the only commodity found on the "silk route" is heavy armour.

China, in the popular imagination, is still the land of a hundred treasures and a thousand well kept secrets, ranging from the elixir of youth to the most potent aphrodisiacs. College students continue to be fascinated by the "stoic" Chinese of Pearl S. Buck's *Good Earth*.

But the negatives are no less overwhelming. An anecdote, probably apocryphal, about a well known Indian political leader, is illustrative. Arriving at an airport in the North East, the leader, just before stepping on the tarmac and seeing the reception committee, asked his aide nervously where all these Chinese had come from! The incident not only speaks of the extent to which "north" Indian politicians are ignorant of the North East, but also of the underlying fear that the Chinese may be insidiously creeping in. In popular imagination, it was Joy Mukherjee, as a Chinese agent, in the controversial 1960s' film, *Hamsaya,* who reflected this deviousness on part of the Chinese.

It is this inscrutability which has led to frustration among intelligence agents in India and abroad. As one former intelligence agent once revealed to this author, it is extremely difficult to identify Chinese agents in the country, though the place is probably teeming with them, because the Chinese follow such a sophisticated modus operandi. "If they have to debrief an informer, they will invite ten others to the embassy as well. Unless one interrogates all the ten, it is very difficult to find out which one is the agent." Moreover, the Chinese do not believe in one "master" spy and prefer to rely on putting together facts, based on small pieces of information. This was, of course, revealed most recently also in the United States after the arrest of Wen Ho Lee, a Chinese American scientist at Los Alamos National Laboratory, on charges of "mishandling nuclear secrets". The FBI's former chief analyst for Chinese counter-intelligence said that it doubts if the agency will find a master spy because the Chinese collect secrets "grain by grain."[19]

In sum, an average Indian, in the 20th century, reacted to China in multiple ways: as an old friend, as a model to be copied and as a potential adversary. But, at the end of the century, Indians are still not sure what to make of China and its people.

[19] See *Washington Post*, 12 December 1999.

An Shuanghong

Development of Education in China and India - A View from China

The People's Republic of China and the Republic of India have been on the course of steady development ever since the establishment of the diplomatic relations between the two countries some sixty years back. Sixty years ago, the foundation of Indian educational development was better amongst the developing countries; ever since then the Indian educational achievements have been outstanding, especially in higher education. At present, the development of education in China and India are facing serious, albeit different challenges. Looking forward to the next 60 years, there is a heavy responsibility and a long way to go for both the countries.

Introduction

Both China and India recently celebrated their 60th birthdays, China in 2009 and India in 2010. 2010 also marks the 60th anniversary of the establishment of diplomatic relations between the People's Republic of China and the Republic of India. As the two largest developing countries in the world, China and India are not only neighbouring countries, but also share many commonalities and similar challenges that have attracted the attention of academics and researchers across the globe. In accordance with the Chinese tradition, 60 years is a cycle of *Jiazi*.[1] Both China and India have opened a new chapter of growth and progress in their respective developmental history, and undoubtedly, education has made a vital contribution to the development, through these years. During the next

---

[1] The Chinese system of time keeping is based on Tian Gan and Di Zhi which means Heavenly Stems and Earthly Branches. There are 10 Heavenly Stems and 12 Earthly Branches and carries either yin or yang properties. They also carry the properties of the Five Elements. The stems combine with the branches in a sequence to form a cycle of 60 combinations known as the "60 Jiazi". This 60 Jiazi is mapped to the year, month and day and repeated infinitely.

cycle of sixty years, the developments in education will be even far more crucial, for both have pinned their hopes on education for a better future.

The basis for the development of education in India was better among developing countries

Britain's colonial rule in India was undoubtedly an evil. Although the British colonists brought advanced scientific technologies and liberal democracy with them that had an enormous impact on the Indian education, religion and culture, it also seriously damaged India's self-sufficient economy and the closed social system and hindered India's political, economic, and educational development. The guiding principle of the colonisers for running schools in India was enslavement of the intelligentsia. The school curricula put emphasis more on arts rather than science; the medium of instruction was only English, which resulted in the lower quality of education.[2]

Although the level of education was very low in the country when the Republic of India was established, it was still higher at all levels compared to the level of education in most of the developing countries, including that of China. In 1949, enrollment rate was 40% in Indian primary schools (6-11 age group population); 10% in secondary school (11-17 age group population); and the enrollment rate at university level (17-23 age group population) was 0.9%. The national literacy rate was 17.2%[3]. In the same year, enrollment rate of China's primary school was only 20%, junior middle school, higher middle school and university enrollment rates were 2.7%, 1.9% and 0.3% respectively[4]; At that time, China's national literacy rate was no more than 15%.

India's achievements in education are prominent amongst developing countries

As the first generation leaders of the Republic of India and the successive ones were well educated, they fully recognised the role played by education

---

[2] Ma Jiali, Introduction to Present Indian Education, published by He'nan Educational Publishing House, 1994, pp.97-102.

[3] Planning Commission, Government of India. India 1st Five Year Plan, p.68.

[4] Exhibition of Educational Achievements in China in 60 Years. http://www.stats.edu.cn/tjdt/60/

in promoting national economic and social development; therefore, they adopted a series of measures to develop various types of education at all levels.

First, the Constitution of the Republic of India which came into effect on the 26th January, 1950, set a goal to popularize 8-year compulsory education within 10 years. The agenda of popularizing 8-year primary education under the condition when much was needed to be done in other sectors, indicates the amount of importance that the Indian leadership attached to primary education to improve the overall quality of the people. In India's first Five-Year Plan period, 56% of the state education funding was allocated to primary education[5]. With the rapid population growth and the adjustment in policies, India has not achieved universal 8-year compulsory education, but the goal is within its reach. More recently, the Indian constitution has made the 8-year compulsory education a fundamental right. It is believed that this new amendment will pave way for millions of children to go to school.

Second, in as early as 1960s, India raised the idea of an appropriate diversion in secondary general education and vocational education. The Education Commission (1964-66) and the "National Policy on Education" in 1968 emphasised that the secondary vocational education should be closely linked with economic development. This emphasis on vocational education in Indian society is bound to gradually reverse the trend where mental work was stressed while physical work was ignored, where learning was valued while attaining skill was overlooked.

Third, the Indian government attaches great importance to protecting the right of the disadvantaged groups to be educated. After independence, Government of India implemented the Reservation Policy; 15% and 7.5% of enrollment quota in institutions of higher learning were reserved for "Scheduled Castes" and "Scheduled Tribes", and later 27% enrollment quota was reserved for "Other Backward Castes". According to this policy, these vulnerable groups, while participating in college entrance exams will be given priority in admission, even if their grades are very low. The Reservation Policy has played an active role in maintaining education equality in India.

---

[5] A.Gnanam, A. Stella. Emerging Trends in Higher Education and Their Implications for Future [J]. Journal of Educational Planning and Administration, 1999(2), p.191.

Fourth, India has made a commitment to popularise secondary education by 2020. In January 2009, after five years of deliberation and preparation, the Cabinet Committee on Economic Affairs of India formally approved the "Universal Secondary Education Programme (Rashtriya Madhyamik Shiksha Abhiyan)". The plan was officially launched in March 2009. This ambition to develop education is truly admirable.

Fifth, India has made remarkable achievements in higher education. Indian higher education system has cultivated the world's second largest professional contingent after the United States who is able to use English, and the world's third largest pool of engineering and technical personnel. In particular, it was only 40 years or so after independence that India developed the Indian Institutes of Technology into a world-class university. Indian software development industry and personnel training have made remarkable achievements, and its experience is worth emulating and is already spreading to other developing countries.

Challenges faced by China and India in the development of education

Successive governments in India have had well-educated leaders, who always put emphasis on education and have developed a number of ambitious schemes and the corresponding measures. However, these objectives were largely not achieved on schedule, and the reasons are worth pondering. For instance, the universalisation of 8-year compulsory education provided for by the Indian Constitution has been delayed and still not achieved; proper segregation of secondary general education and vocational education in India is progressing very slowly; although the Indian Institutes of Technology stand out, the ordinary quality of higher education is worrisome; the realisation of a unified school system is still like "Christians have their table."

Today, China has fully realised the universal 9-year compulsory education; higher secondary school enrollment rate has reached 74%, higher education gross enrollment rate has arrived at 23.3%, and the illiteracy rate has dropped to less than 4%. Needless to say, the development of education in China has made tremendous progress. However, educational development in China also faces many serious challenges, such as the goal of investment in education has been delayed for more than 10 years and there is a serious imbalance in the development of general elementary and secondary education, and the contradictions between educational equity and the quality of education is worrisome; moreover, the bureaucratic management system of higher education has serious flaws. Educational Reform in China is still a very arduous task!

One of China's leading academic giants, Prof. Ji Xianlin had made original research and great comments on cultural exchanges between China and India. In the preamble of his own book *Sino-Indian Cultural Exchange History*, he posits, "China and India are neighbours; at least for over two thousand years, the two countries have been good neighbours. We have had uninterrupted exchanges in the field of philosophy, religion, art and even natural sciences and technology, which enriched both Chinese and Indian cultures. We can even say that had there been no cultural exchanges between China and India, the cultural development of the two could have been totally different." He further points out, "Today's world is at a new historical juncture; China and India are in a new stage of development. China has developed rapidly and the achievements are recognised all over the world; India has also been rapidly changing in high-tech development with each passing day, which has drawn world attention. In the new situation, it is even more important for China and India to learn from each other, communicate with each other in order to build better tomorrow."[6]

Because of its special geopolitical and national situation, India tends to compete with China. In particular, a number of countries including the United States also encourage India to compete with China, even encourages an overt or covert confrontation with China. As the world's major ancient civilizations, the friendship and cooperation between China and India have been the mainstay in their long history. In the 1950s, India and China even had the common slogan "Indians and Chinese are brothers!" In fact, China and India each has sufficient space for development, and they don't necessarily strive to know who is stronger and who is weaker; and, even if there is competition, it should also be rooted in cooperation and they should not change competition into confrontation.

Many scholars in India and China have contemplated over the question of an alliance between these two countries. If the two most populous countries in the world could join hands and move in tandem, imagine the impact it will have on contemporary world order.

---

[6] Ji Xianlin. *Sino-India Cultural Exchange History*, published by China Social Sciences Publishing House, 2008, the preamble, pp.1-3.

P. Stobdan

India-China Relations

For over half a century, China had indubitably entertained an absolute psychological superiority vis-à-vis India and also perhaps decided to tack on the idea that India can be politically, diplomatically and militarily contained - though the issue of Tibet and India's involvement in it was never overlooked by Beijing. The popular perceptions in China about India, particularly in the recent times, were characterised by many observers as that of benign or benign neglect with fewer and select number of Chinese strategic elite circles paying attention to India as an issue of prime importance.[1] This was perhaps based on the assumption that China had to focus primarily on the US and the issues relating to Asia-Pacific. For decades, Beijing remained preoccupied with Taiwan and with its strategic entanglement with Japan. India, a psychologically defeated nation for China caught little attention except in the context of a strategy to facilitate and boost the military capabilities of Pakistan. Many Chinese scholars articulated that India had never been China's security priority.

The frosty relations between India and China lasting for over half a century have witnessed a thaw in the recent decades that had allowed the perplexed border issue not to hold up other aspects of their relationship. The experiment worked as the bilateral trade crossed $50 billion in 2008.[2] The two countries later decided to forge a landmark agreement for Strategic and Cooperative Partnership in 2005 and had instituted fresh political parameters to seek a peaceful resolution of the pending boundary issue. A landmark change had included China's entry into the South Asian

---

[1] Mohan Malik, *War Talk: Perceptual Gaps in 'Chindia' Relations*, Publication: China Brief Volume: 9 Issue: 20 October 7, 2009 http://www.jamestown.org/single/?no_cache=1&txttnews%5Btt_news%5D=35589

[2] The bilateral trade is now nearing $70 billions.

Association for Regional Cooperation (SAARC) with an observer status in 2005. This was viewed on the one hand as a sign of a greater maturity and a balance in India's attitude; on the other hand, many skeptics saw the development with slight ominous tones, for India's continuing inability to learn lessons from the past.

However, growing economic relationship has not been able to overshadow the geopolitical rivalry as the dark clouds of mistrust were once again gathering over a host of issues at bilateral, regional and international arena. The growing surge of a new brand of nationalistic feelings, both in China and India, owing perhaps to the growing economic strength and confidence, had raised new questions, challenging the respective governments for their fervour to seek a compromised solution to the territorial issue. It did seem that if Indian leadership faced the constraints of electoral politics, China's Communist leadership too has faced the risk of finger-pointing and charges of deceit by Party members. The differences that came on the surface were hyped by the media to the point of acute misunderstanding. The situation in 2009 had compelled the Indian National Security Advisor to suggest that if rhetorical expression of media continued, "Someone somewhere might lose his cool and something might go wrong."

A number of developments in the recent years seemed to have changed the Chinese perception of India. Although China's concerns related to India were heightened after India's nuclear test in May 1998, the subsequent turnaround in India's economic and foreign policy may have come as a rude shock to China for it would have thought that India will never alter its rather antediluvian foreign policy and its military will never give up obsession with Pakistan and shift the focus away to pay attention to China.

The Chinese may have noticed several key transformations in India's policy outlook that are to impinge on China's strategic calculus. Though there have always been stray write ups in the Chinese media, negatively reprimanding India and its hegemonic role in South Asia, it was always easy for Beijing to counter India bilaterally, regionally and also in the international arena. For India, China's growing influence in India's neighbourhood (Pakistan, Nepal, Bangladesh, Sri Lanka and Myanmar) suggested by western observers as China's 'string of pearls' strategy was a matter of concern.

However, the recent surge in Chinese rhetoric against India, especially from the informed Chinese circles, tended to suggest that Beijing was reassessing its traditional understanding of India, so assiduously built in the earlier decades. Clearly, Beijing had become wary of India's hard hitting policy under the UPA government as compared to relatively soft-piddling adopted by the National Democratic Alliance (NDA), towards China.

Until recently, Beijing was comfortable and had continued to harp on India maintaining its autonomy in foreign policy as a legacy of the Cold War era, that suited the Chinese the most in terms of keeping at bay the influence of major powers, in its neighbourhood. However, China has noticed a fundamental shift in India's foreign policy when India and the US forged a landmark agreement on a nuclear deal in 2005, which was ostensibly meant to boost India's global strategic aspirations. The July 18, 2005 Indo-US nuclear deal and a serious strategic partnership meant to China that India would significantly benefit from the US transfer of state-of-art technology and will have access to sophisticated US, European, and Israeli weapon systems as against continued Western arms embargo against Beijing. This would also mean the US will be able to grow more influence in South Asia. China's Premier Wen Jiabao rushed to New Delhi to sign a treaty, laying out the political parameters and guiding principles to guide the future course of India-China relationship particularly to resolve the boundary question. For China, the Sino-Indian Strategic and Cooperative Partnership for Peace and Prosperity Agreement, signed in April 2005, was to take this into consideration if not fully preempt the shift in strategic constellation. China had never hidden its apprehensions about closer Indo-US ties. In more than one way, Beijing tried to show concerns and even contested India's great-power aspirations which China thought would seriously challenge the existing Asian power structure. Some Western scholars have argued that the deepening of Indo-US partnership had caused Beijing's four-decade-old India policy to go haywire[3]. It was evidently proved when China made attempts to scuttle the agreement at the September 2008 Nuclear Suppliers Group (NSG) at Vienna, that Beijing was loath to accept India's rise and its assertion on the world stage. India's bitterness over the role China played at the Nuclear Suppliers Group meeting was reflected throughout in the Indian media, as it created a sense of hysteria about it and as it happened that there was no forward movement in the subsequent boundary discussions. India also remained wary as to whether China was going to sign a nuclear agreement with Pakistan on the line of the Indo-US nuclear deal. It was hard to find a reasonable Chinese explanation about what they did in Vienna but most Chinese experts had explained that China had to be careful before taking a position on an issue that was to change the existing international order and their representatives had to behave in the manner as they did and that India should have appreciated it. There were enough diplomatic moves made by China in connivance with Pakistan, to block the expansion of the United Nations Security Council, where India would have a chance for membership.

Undoubtedly, Beijing was also getting seemingly edgy over India's rising global profile and its growing comfort level with other powers. The Japanese inspired the "axis of democracy" that included India, Japan, US and Australia for greater strategic partnership, including frequent military exercises with the American, Japanese and Australian counterparts, thus enraging China's anxiety further. These developments, in addition to India's greater outreach within Asia, were viewed by Beijing with displeasure and as a means to counter China's influence in South Asia. Instead of creating a favourable environment for closer cooperation, Beijing started using every lever in its growing global reach, to off-balance India.

This paper does not intend to deal with the traditional aspects of India-China relations but focusses on certain key areas where India and

---

[3] In a panel discussion on "China 2025" by the Council on Foreign Relations, Evan Feigenbaum, an expert on South Asian affairs said "Since 1962, the Chinese strategists have basically decided that they can deal with India on their own terms. But when you introduce the United States into that equation, it introduces all kinds of uncertainties into Chinese planning." China 2025: Panel II: China Goes Global, Council on Foreign Relations, 19 October 2009.http://www.cfr.org/publication/20662/china_2025.html?breadcrumb=%2Fbios%2F5263%2Fevan_a_feigenbaum

China tend to clash. It covers the developments evolving particularly after the 2005 India-China Strategic Partnership Cooperation. Among other things, the important findings of my analysis include that while on the surface, the ties between India and China have grown leaps and bounds, over the years (trade increasing manifold to over $50 billions in the last few years) suspicion between the two countries began to increase more due to changes in several strategic arenas. China once again upped the ante against India and had started reasserting on several fronts, including the claims on Arunachal Pradesh. Simultaneously, China had also taken several strategic steps to consolidate its hold over Tibet. The upgradation and modernisation of infrastructure on the Tibetan plateau had deepened and renewed fear among Indians.

Significantly, New Delhi also finally woke up since 2005 and had decided firmly to shed some of its outmoded mindsets, pertaining to national security. The sustained rise in India's economic growth meant that India was able to devote more resources for the defence of the country. India was more diligently trying to widen its foreign policy options, refined its diplomacy and most importantly narrowed down the deficiencies it had to live with, for a long time vis-à-vis China. With these changes being placed on priority, the fissures and frictions along the over 4,000 kilometers long India-China border, have become starker in the recent years.

A careful analysis of the events in the last few years, suggests that Beijing's inability to handle the Tibetan issue has caused massive apprehensions inside China. Political instability in Tibet, especially the riots in 2008 in the run up to the Beijing Olympics, had rattled the Chinese who were unprepared to face embarrassment on such a huge scale caused by the display of protests by the Tibetans and their sympathisers worldwide during the torch rallies. The popular impression among the Chinese, which is actually unfounded, was that the riots in Tibet were instigated by India - a reason why there had been a spurt in anti-India rhetoric in China recently. Even though India had long held a position on Tibet explicitly prohibiting the Dalai Lama and his people from conducting anti-China political activities, the sporadic unrest inside, had put India in a difficult position. The politics around Tibet and the role of the Dalai Lama has certainly complicated the India-China relations.

Consequently, a stream of opinion makers and media write ups had whipped up a scenario of India-China conflict. The Chinese have issued a stern warning to India through the official think tanks not to "misjudge the situation as it did in 1962," and to "stay away from a path of confrontation."[4] The Chinese have been articulating the case that the government of India is deliberately playing the Tibet card by manipulating the Dalai Lama's activities and at times at the direction of the Americans. Research reports and surveys conducted by several institutions and the media have found that majority of Chinese have viewed India as an enemy country that posed a threat to China's security. The situation turned ugly and people from both sides made scathing attacks against each other through the media, during 2008-2009.

Notwithstanding the improvement in bilateral relations, there has been little or no progress in the boundary issue. This is despite having placed several high-level mechanisms to fasten and regularise the border discussions. It appeared that the negotiators from the two sides were talking more on trade and other issues than on the boundary issue. The Special Representative-level talks remained shrouded in mystery with both sides unwilling to disclose the details of their discussions, merely stating that they are committed to find a "fair and reasonable" solution according to the political principles laid downed in the 2005 SCP. Officially, 13 rounds of talks held so far had made progress but no deadline was suggested for a final resolution.

Importantly, China has retracted from the Article VII of the 2005 agreement that had said that in reaching a settlement, the two sides would duly "safeguard the interests of their settled populations". This was construed by most Indians as a sign of China's willingness to give up claims to Arunachal Pradesh. But shockingly, the Chinese Foreign Minister, Yang Jiechi later told India's External Affairs Minister Pranab Mukherjee on the sidelines of a meeting in Hamburg, that according to China, the settled populations did not mean that it had given up its claim over Arunachal

[4] Website of the General Staff Department's 2nd Department owned Institute of International Strategic Studies posted an article "Zhenggao Indu zhengfu: Buyao yiyuan baode," ("A Warning to the Indian Government: Don't Return Evil for Good"), March 26 2008, str.chinaiiss.org/content/2008-3-26/26211952.shtml.

Pradesh.

Over the years, the Chinese, in a more nuanced way, have hardened their position on Arunachal Pradesh, claiming it to be its territory. It has laid claim to the town of Tawang and contradicted the guiding principle laid down by both sides in 2005. Further, Beijing firmly objected to even the visits by Indian leaders to the State. In fact, the Chinese retracted from the earlier agreed position that the settled populations would be excluded from the boundary settlement. Beijing has also continued to make symbolic but forceful policy stand over Arunachal Pradesh by refusing entry visa to an officer from Arunachal Pradesh in May 2007, compelling New Delhi to cancel the visit of the entire delegation to China[5]. Similarly, Beijing had enthused controversy in 2009 by blocking an Indian application for a loan from the Asian Development Bank (ADB) to fund a water management project in Arunachal Pradesh. The differences over Arunachal Pradesh has stayed on the boil hitherto despite upswing in the bilateral trade that has been doubling annually over the past few years.

On its part, New Delhi had time and again reassured China that there is no dilution of its position on Tibet as the "Tibetan Autonomous Region is part of China". However, it does seem that Chinese position for example on Sikkim as part of India had still appeared ambiguous. There were attempts made by China to reintroduce Sikkim as a part of boundary dispute in 2008. Not just Sikkim, China has also tried to open a new front against India on the status of Jammu & Kashmir by issuing Chinese visa to those hailing from J&K on a separate sheet. Such actions by Beijing have inevitably enraged the Indians about China's intentions.

There has been gradual but subtle change in the Indian mind-set towards China in the recent years. It is being noticed that the usual hawkish pronouncement vis-à-vis China, in the military circles cherished for the past few decades is now being replaced by a more nuanced and calibrated policy approach. New Delhi no longer sulks about China's rapid military capabilities and modernisation and instead views its giant neighbour as an important player in global affairs and moving firmly along its well chartered

[5] Surjit Mansingh, *Rising China and Emergent India in the 21st Century: Friends or Rivals? The Korean Journal of Defence Analysis*, Vol. XIX, No. 4 (Winter 2007), p. 133.

out goals[6]. It essentially meant that India has decided to gear up firmly to meet the challenges posed by China instead of just talking about it. India's defence planning and implementation undertaken over the years have indicated that China and not Pakistan is the centre of its thinking.

It needs to be underlined that India, since 2005, has adopted a firm policy to strengthen its military deployment and invested on infrastructure along the border. In fact, one of the most remarkable changes that was noticed in India included a complete reversal of its strategy in the past, to keep its border areas in a state of underdevelopment. Primarily, the policy driven by the military for decades was a part of its deceitful strategy to create physical obstacles for the enemy to advance. While the Chinese went on a faster drive for infrastructure development, India had remained cautious. India's decision to go in for road construction along the border regions was part of its larger plans to develop 94 districts that lie along India's borders with other neighbours: China, Bangladesh, Myanmar, Bhutan and Nepal. It was also part of the objective to boost socio-economic development of the far-flung districts by linking them with the major economic centres of the country. India has tried to rebuff China's tough stance by initiating a wide variety of infrastructure schemes for Arunachal Pradesh. During his visit to Arunachal Pradesh in January 2009, Prime Minister Manmohan Singh's had flagged off several infrastructure projects which were to give a firm signal to China that India does not accept China's claim. The visit came after China went back from its earlier commitment not to transfer the populated areas in the boundary negotiation that was enshrined in the 2005 agreement. These underlined India's non-negotiable position on Arunachal Pradesh as an integral part of India and a reality that China would have to live with.

However, India's sudden decision to go on high gear in developing the border infrastructure since 2006 seems to have caught the Chinese by surprise. It was perhaps inconceivable for them that India too could embark on modernisation. China was seemingly worried that improved infrastructure would lead to possible infiltration of Tibetan activists as saboteurs into China. China had closed all the entry points along the border

---

[6] Ministry of Defence, Annual Report 2007-2008 http://mod.nic.in/reports/welcome.html

for border trade throughout 2009. The PLA installed a metal-gate at Nathula Pass as a preventive measure against such infiltration. China had agreed to open the Nathula Pass for border trade in 2005, after a gap of 44 years, to boost trade ties. Despite the euphoria created then for increasing the prospects for trade, nothing very great is happening across the pass[7].

India had also adopted a punitive response to China's assertion by reinforcing military deployment along the vulnerable points in the eastern sector. It had decided to relocate its 27th Mountain Division hitherto stationed in Jammu and Kashmir to the Eastern sector while also adding two new military divisions in the sector. By 2008, India had also decided to deploy additional squadron of combat aircraft along the border with China, apart from upgradation of several airbases in Ladakh sector for operation readiness. However, China reacted to Indian activism by calling it a hegemonic act[8].

In response to growing military facilities on the Indian side, the Chinese have once again tried a fresh muscularity by increasing ground as well as air incursions into the Indian territory, while also resorting to trivial acts like painting rocks in Mandarin, air dropping outdated foodstuff on the Indian side, etc. These incursions have increased over the years, numbering for example in 2008 at 230 times. It was reported to be higher in 2009. An air incursion in the Ladakh sector during the summer of 2009 had received hysterical reaction from the Indian media even though the

---

[7] Impression gathered when the author had visited Nathula in January 2010.

[8] An editorial of the People's Daily said "In recent years, Indians have become more narrow minded and intolerable of outside criticism as nationalist sentiment rises, with some of them even turning to hegemony. In a hard hitting article, the daily said India's hegemony "is a hundred per cent result of British colonialism…when the country covered a vast territory including present-day India, Pakistan, Myanmar, Bangladesh as well as Nepal….a previous victim of colonialism and hegemony, India started dreaming about developing its own hegemony after the British left. Obsessed with such mentality, India turned a blind eye to the concessions China had repeatedly made over the disputed border issues and refused to drop the pretentious airs when dealing with neighbours like Pakistan." It called India's dream of being a superpower as impetuous, "the dream of superpower is mingled with the thought of hegemony, which places the South Asian giant in an awkward situation and results in repeated failure." It suggested that "If India wants to be a superpower; it needs to have its eyes on relations with neighbours and abandon the recklessness and arrogance as the world is undergoing earthshaking changes." People's Daily Online 14 October 2009.

officials on both sides had downplayed the issue. Tension along the border in 2009 had reminded people in India of the days of 1962. The agreements on maintaining peace and tranquility signed in 1993 and 1996 were out of question.

Several well-informed commentators went to the extent of cautioning the government not to repeat the mistakes committed in 1962 when India similarly downplayed the reports of the construction of road by the Chinese in the Aksai Chin in the late 1950s.[9] The Army, however, rubbished the chances of a repeat of 1962 and confidently claimed that it holds capability to ward off any Chinese aggression. The Army also suggested that the incursions take place due to the lack of clarity of LAC and the transgressions, made by the PLA in 2009, remained at the same level as in 2008.

At the diplomatic level, desperate attempts were made to keep the border calm. The Armies of both sides have strictly avoided direct skirmishes since 1996, when confidence-building measures were enforced to maintain peace and tranquillity along the Line of Actual Control. India's restrained approach was guided by the Border Management Postures (BMP) along the border. Officials, both in India and China maintained that the boundary has been one of the most peaceful[10]. However, the reports of frequent Chinese incursions had ignited nationalistic sentiments in India, though largely played up by the media. The Indian government's position was that its relations with China were not weak and the ties between the two countries would not be allowed to be guided by emotions. Finally the governments both in China and India found the incessant media reports completely baseless. Every effort was made to temper down the reactions. Possibly as a result of its economic muscle, the Chinese society has turned more assertive and nationalistic, according to Indian understanding. The public opinion

---

[9] B. Raman, "Our PM's Visit to China: Core Concerns Persist," Chennai Centre for China Studies, C3S Paper No. 99, January 15, 2008.

[10] Indian Defence Ministry followed a non-confrontationist approach with regards China irrespective of frequent provocation witnessed along the border. Defence Minister A K Antony had said in a conference of the top commanders of the Integrated Defence Staff in June 2008 "We (India) are not ignoring (these incidents). To a maximum extent, we will try to avoid confrontation." He said this after controversy over Finger Area in North Sikkim, which was assumed settled by the Indian side. 'Despite issues, confrontation with China to be avoided' PTI, 10 June 2008,

in both countries have become sharper than before; especially in China the government seemed to have allowed its media to speak in a more nuanced tongue with nationalistic streak than the cautious line usually taken by the Foreign Ministry. This has become more pronounced in the aftermath of the Beijing Olympics, after the Chinese had felt humiliated by the Tibetan uprising and street demonstration against the Olympic torch relay. After the March 2008 riots in Lhasa, the Chinese seemed to have interpreted problems emanating from Indian soil as a matter of core issue of China's national sovereignty. This may also be symbolic and aimed more at China's domestic audience, especially to quell the party cadres.

In India, an assertive middle-class has found the Chinese assertion against India not incomprehensible. Moreover the media and people outside the government find the official Indian response to Chinese bullying, somewhat weak. The media has particularly shown restlessness over India's inability to counter the Chinese. This may partly be explained by the government's unwillingness to share worthwhile information with the public. There is obviously a systemic problem in India.

As the boundary issue faces a serious deadlock, there is a growing constituency on both sides for the need to break the impasse while adopting a pragmatic approach which factors in ground realities. While India seems quite willing to accept the reality on the ground acknowledging Aksai Chin remaining under China's control, Beijing seems unwilling to forgo its claim by accepting Arunachal Pradesh as an integral part of India.

The most controversial visit by the Dalai Lama to Tawang in November 2009 and the manner in which Beijing had furiously denounced it, it is clear that as the fierce People's Daily editorial had proved, the Tibet problem very much remains a part of India-China boundary imbroglio. China had almost warned India against playing the Tibet card. As China has gone overboard over its claim on Arunachal Pradesh, India has shown more self-confidence in protecting its turf in the Himalayan borderland. It was, for the first time, proving that it is neither weak nor defenceless to China's continuous assertion. By playing the Dalai Lama card, New Delhi has indicated to Beijing that India still holds a reasonable stance by acknowledging the Tibetan leader only as an "honoured guest" and that any future compromise between India and China on the boundary issue should take this into consideration. However, given China's sensitivity about its claim over Tibet, the issue will remain ambiguous for years to come.

It has to be more than the Tibet issue and the massive uprising in Lhasa in March 2008 to cause the bilateral trust deficit to sink quite so low. Today, India and China differ strongly on many issues including over energy competition to tap energy at source. China has consistently outbid India in this competition. This issue also gets reflected in the assertion of the two countries in the sphere of naval power. Water is also fast becoming a potential divisive issue if not a threat multiplier. India has shown greater concerns in the recent years over the reports of China's plan to divert the Brahmaputra water. In the coming years, this issue will assume critical importance for bilateral relations between India and China.

Until 2008, India's ability to leverage from the situation in Tibet seemed to have had diminished. On the other hand, China appeared determined to get back Tawang one day. As mentioned earlier, the Chinese may have earlier correctly assessed that governments in India were always soft, with its foreign office not willing to take a confrontationist line, its military not in a mood to fight, a large section of its political class, across party lines, are amenable for concession to China, and most importantly Indian intellectuals, including the think-tanks have become ardent aficionados or acolytes of China. However, these assumptions of the Chinese may have undergone a change because of India's willingness to stand up against China on all fronts. And, most importantly, India's hard unwillingness to relent on the boundary issue and going all out to strengthen infrastructure along the border may have paid off finally. Remember, China believes in taking advantage of others weaknesses. If India concedes, it will corner India further.

In this regard, a cue from the Sino-Russian negotiations was noteworthy for India. Moscow avoided the euphoria of interdependence, conceded where it saw benefits, rejected where it saw potential threats, sought conformity on terrorism, curbed energy supplies after having entered a fast track economic partnership, insisted boundary demarcation as a pre-condition to promote strategic partnership with China and rejected

Beijing's proposal for a free-trade zone in Eurasia. China had to concede to the Russian on the boundary issue in the interest of securing energy needs, while also upholding to proceed on its campaign for a 'peaceful rise of China'.

It looked rather appropriate that India by now should have raised other territorial issues such as China's holding on to a 5,180 square kilometre area of Skasgyam Valley that was ceded to China by Pakistan. And, if the Chinese continue making diversionary moves on the boundary issue, say on Tawang, Sikkim and Jammu & Kashmir, India should start thinking about reclaiming ownership of the hitherto forgotten Minser Enclave, composed of several villages, that lies deep inside the Tibetan territory on the bank of Mount Kailash. Minser was a sovereign part of India and the revenue authority of Jammu & Kashmir collected annual taxes from Minser until mid-1960s, which New Delhi forgot due to apathy and it deserves a revisit before the final boundary settlement.

It is fundamental that negotiating with China requires art and not policy. Dealing with China does not require supporters or critics, but a set of complex internal deliberations derived through various tracks. The style and tactics require a corresponding understanding that is often missing from the Indian side.

One of the key aspects of the India-China spat was the role media had played in sensitising the public about the mischief being played by the Chinese at the border. To a large extent, the media, this time did play a crucial role in influencing India's response to China's threat[11]. Several Indian commentators thought it was unfair to blame the media as some of the facts on Chinese incursions were circulated by the government authorities. Besides, some of the sensational views had been aired by the top defence officials, both serving and retired ones. For many observers, it looked unfair for the government to have played down the Chinese assertion.

India is going to face a long-term dilemma to deal with China. China is viewed as an inscrutable entity by most Indians. There have been many

---

[11] T.P. Sreenivasan, "Media under attack: No harm in playing up China threat", *The Tribune*, 24 September 2009 http://www.tribuneindia.com/2009/20090924/edit.htm#6

blow hot, blow cold from both sides on a number of issues. Some say dealing with assertive China will be difficult especially when the country will assume the superpower status in the coming decades. Others would say India has no option but to learn to live with China. The problem comes when some Indians fancy themselves as emerging as the next superpower. However, the points of differences have no fundamental bases for a major conflict. The Indian and Chinese civilizations are essentially not contradictory in terms. Both have lived together and learnt from each other for centuries. The Chinese have always appreciated Indian wisdom and the Indians have prudently dealt with the Chinese. The greatest foreign policy challenge for India, therefore, will be to find a steady and robust course to get a state of equilibrium in its dealing with China. But as of now, relationship between the two countries is going to be profoundly mixed with the elements of both competition and cooperation. In 2008 alone, India has encouraged Chinese companies with contracts worth $11 billion. In many areas, things are ratcheting up between the two countries, but in several areas there is firm resoluteness on both the sides to work together. It appears that there is no other solution but for the two countries to continue to walk this path. For the time being the two sides should strengthen the confidence-building efforts little more so that miscalculation and risk for a direct face-off in the Himalayas can be avoided.

Sheng Rong

India's Land system, A Revelation to China's Land System Reform*

Both India and China are countries with huge rural population but meager rural income; in India it is manifested as poverty issue, and in China an issue of farmers' income. India's system of private ownership of land has many pitfalls, as even after 60 years of continuous reforms in different fields, the phenomenon of poverty has gone unchecked; China though having a different political system, is nevertheless apprehensive of the outcome of a the private ownership of land system. "State owned but permanent rent system" is in sync with the system that is to say the state owns the land but the farmer enjoys the right of permanent tenancy. The core objectives of "right to permanent land use" are to reduce the number of people renting the land, and at the same time provide and enhance the agricultural income of those who engage in agriculture.

Augmenting farmer's income Vs. poverty issue

The issue of enhancing farmers' income in China is a major national issue which worries the central as well as provincial governments. Unexpectedly enough, India doesn't have this issue; the issue in India is poverty alleviation. While China's poverty rate has declined to less than 5%, India's poverty rate is still above 26%; so much so that in some states, two thirds of the total population is poor. So, why is poverty not a serious issue in China? And why is enhancing farmers' income not an issue in India?

---

* Translated from chinese by Madhurender Kumar Jh, Assistant Proffesor of Chinese School of Languages, Doon University, Dehradun.

The farmer income issue after all, is the conflict between agricultural output and high proportion of working population; presently the proportion of agricultural output in China does not reach 14%, whereas the proportion of labour force in this sector is still at 48%. If we compare it with high-end science and technology service industries like software, finance etc, then their average labour output is perhaps more than ten times the average labour output in the agricultural industry, thus it is quite obvious that they don't face the risk of lower per capita income. This is applicable to India as well, for the agricultural output of 23% is produced by 60% of the labour force, and therefore, the average labour income is very low; as a result farmers' income issue has become a major national issue. The system of private ownership of land does not allow equal distribution of agricultural income among the agricultural labour force (farmers); it is distributed by the market on the basis of land ownership.

There is no uniformity in the classification of Indian farmers; they can be divided into four different categories on the basis of the amount of land they own: 1) the farmers who own the land but do not till themselves; 2) the farmers who own small amount of land and till themselves, 3) the farmers who primarily till the land of others; and 4) the contractual agricultural workers. India's system of private land ownership has an upper limit so that an average household land should not cross a certain area limit, but there are still many families who, through methods like getting the land separately registered in the name of different family members, own a lot of land. Presently, 43% of the peasant families own no land or own less than half an acre of land, and all along there have been one fourth of the peasant families who have no land at all (almost corresponding to the poverty rate).

This style of land ownership has formed the following characteristics of the urban and rural India: 1) Indian villages still have many wealthy farmers; they own land, their education level is quite high and so is the quality of life; they are the middle bourgeoisie living in the villages; they have thrown-over the issue of farmers' income. 2) The landless farmers are pouring into the cities in large numbers; they are the main reason for the slums in the cities. Actually, they are just another manifestation of the farmers' income issue. Therefore, in India, a lawyer who graduates from a reputed university will give up his work and go back to his village for farming, because his income from an apple orchard will be double of the annual salary of a university professor, and why? Because he owns the land. The most fertile area of the Ganges river basin is also the poorest area in present India, as the high density of population has led to scarce per capita land resource, and as a result of the system of private ownership, more than half of the population cannot depend on land for living. Although, if there is an equal distribution of land, the issue of adequate food and clothing for everyone can be solved. It is because of the pyramid-like system of ownership of land that India does not have farmers' income issue; therefore, the dominating issue is the issue of poverty.

Contrary to the Indian situation, the issue of serious poverty is non-existent in China, because the 14% of the agricultural output is almost equally distributed among the 48% of farmers. Therefore, the food and clothing issue has been resolved. However, moderately well-off society and harmonious society cannot be simply achieved by the right to equality. The basic nature of farmers' income issue is that a weak industry cannot sustain a huge population. Hence, the root of solving this issue is to improve the science and technology element in agriculture and reduce the proportion of agricultural employment; the land reforms may be able to solve the issue of large scale benefits, but it can certainly not solve the farmers' income issue. On the contrary, it might produce a serious poverty issue, as there will be no food and clothing assurance. One of the logics that people use to advocate private land ownership is that "the tiller owns his land", but the Indian experience tells us that the private ownership of the land has created a phenomenon of rendering the tiller landless in India. Obviously modern agriculture inevitably demands the existence of large land owners and agricultural employees; if the land is not privately owned, then in a similar fashion, large scale land management can be implemented and a portion of the farmers will become agricultural employees, who will only be concerned with manual work and not management; the crux is how to protect the land loss of farmers willing to cultivate the land. It is estimated that the private land ownership system in China will render more than 20% of farmers landless, and the farmers' income issue will transform into the poverty issue.

Land being an essential factor in production, if privatised, will be able to utilise the market mechanism to carry out the distribution of resources; it is said that the distribution efficiency will improve a lot. But in order to see if a system will succeed or not, other specific conditions have also to be looked into. Turning to India again, the density of population in Himachal Pradesh in the north is 109 people per square kilometer (2001), but in the Ganges river basin of Bihar it is 881. In Himachal, because the population is less, there is less pressure on land. The Government has come out with a law ensuring at least one bigha of land to every labourer. (However, people are not allowed to sell the agricultural land to people from other parts of India). Since this state started cultivating apples from the eighties, the agricultural benefits have been good all along; it became a relatively wealthy region of India. Whereas in Bihar, where the man and land ratio is quite strained, the Government could not force equal distribution of land, and it also could not find any land that was not developed and owned to distribute among the poor people. Therefore, the landless people unlike Himachal have remained landless in Bihar. With the struggle of subsistence becoming grim, and also the fact that consecutive elected Governments have failed to ensure basic law and order in Bihar, migration of large number of people to the city slums became inevitable. The condition of man and land ratio in China is also pitiful; the per capita cultivable land is far less than that of India. However, whether this type of strained land resource will be able to shoulder the burden of private land ownership system, is an issue.

Since the last 60 years India has continuously been carrying out land system reforms (India has been carrying out land reforms with states as the units). Over the last fifty years, sixteen main states of India have promulgated over eighty laws related to land reforms; among them Bihar alone has carried land reforms eight times between 1950 and 1986 (Besley and Burgess, 1998). These reforms mainly touch upon four aspects, thirty six laws for tenancy system reform, twenty five laws for getting rid of the middle men, fifteen laws for controlling an upper limit of land ownership and seven laws for systemising land rights. Among these, the tenancy system reform includes eliminating practices which are not beneficial to the poor, guarantee the distribution of agricultural output and permanent tenancy right at the minimum amount of land, etc. As for the upper limit of land ownership, the highest upper limit since 1972 has normally been about twenty hectares. Bihar has the highest limit of 18.21 hectares, and the density of population in this state is almost nine people per hectare. Thus, it can be seen that this upper limit is still very high. Many land laws do not really guarantee that the tiller will have his land, "tilling other's land" is still a common phenomenon. If China wants privatisation of land, perhaps she will also need to continuously make laws to protect the interest of small farmers, to control big landlords, to eliminate middle men, and to control the large scale benefits as a result of amassing of land.

The demand of land hinges on direction of land reform

The system requirements are the basic prerequisites for establishing as well as reforming the system. Then, what kind of requirements does the present land system have in China? Few people assume that the Chinese farmers are welcoming the privatisation of land. Indeed, if a survey is done, then a majority of farmers will probably choose the immediate transformation of the Contract Responsibility System into their property right. However, try to think of it, if the land is equally distributed among the people of these 60% agricultural households, we can also say that these 60% people will occupy the means of production such as land, but this means of production will only provide 14% output and income. What will happen in that case then? One section of people, owing to thorough urbanisation will gradually sell land; the other section owing to capability to generate non-agricultural income will rent their land to others. Then what about the last section? Braving the enormous risks involved in cultivation, they will engage in agriculture; where after, they will handover a large portion of their meager agricultural income to the former two sections in the form of land price and land rent. Thus without any doubt, the burden of agricultural workers will further increase; it will again enable those in non-agricultural sector to scrounge on agriculture. The farmers certainly do not need this type of a prospect; it also does not conform to the idea of justice of the Chinese people.

Which type of land system is highly desired by the farmers? In order to answer this question, at the outset, it is necessary to classify the farmers. Farmers at different places with different condition have different demands towards the land system. In the view of this, in how many categories can the farmers of present China be classified? If we classify them according to the degree of their agricultural involvement, which is to say "the degree of agricultural correlation", farmers can be divided in three broad categories: real farmers, semi-farmers and zero farmers (who engage in farm work in negligible degrees). The term 'real farmers' includes all those farmers whose immediate nuclear family is completely engaged in crop farming , their non-agricultural income does not exceed the income from farming. The term 'semi-farmers' includes all those farmers whose immediate nuclear family is partly engaged in farming and partly engaged in non-agricultural industries, the income from the non agricultural employment is higher than the earnings from farming. The 'zero-farmers' belong to a category of farmers whose immediate nuclear family is mainly employed in non-agricultural pursuits; more than 90% of their household income comes from non-agricultural employment. Out of these three categories, the third category of farmers essentially doesn't require land; they desire that current land rights and interests be capitalised or materialised. The semi-farmers are also a potentially urbanised force, they may presently require land, however, this requirement may not exist forever; some time in the future, they too will desire that their land may be capitalised or benefitted from. What about the real-farmers? Laws of economies of scale will require them to cultivate more land. This variation in the degree of agricultural correlation illustrates that China's land system must guarantee that the land is stable in the hands of the real cultivators. At the same time, agricultural land must be smoothly transferred; additionally, those who have left the agricultural sector no longer should continue to enjoy any little amount of income from agricultural land or farming.

We can still further segment the beneficiaries of the agricultural land reform: large farming households, agricultural enterprises, and employees, migrant workers and non-agricultural workers from the villages. The large farming households hope to get even more land, they will of course engage in leasing the land; only thing that has to be taken care of is the appropriateness between the land rent and profit ratio. The agricultural enterprises hope to directly obtain land rights; they will not negotiate the land transfer contract with the numerous scattered farmers, and allow them to become the "second landlords". The agricultural employees lack the technical skill of grasping market information, they are willing to strive for labour wages, but they are not concerned with affairs related to production. The migrant workers hope to get rid of the land and all related tax burdens, but they do not want to lose the security that comes with land. To the best, they want it to become a capital to help them find a footing in the city, or they want it to become a base for them to enjoy the minimum living standards in the city. The bread and butter of the non-agricultural workers living in the villages mainly depends on non-agricultural jobs. For them it will be more convenient and appropriate if the land becomes a social security (security for minimum life standard or old age guarantee), thus saving them from the botheration of maintaining or transferring the little land they possess. Therefore, it can be seen that times have changed, and varied market subjects have even more varied requirements. This demands that the innovation in land system must satisfy the varied requirements of the varied market subjects.

Agricultural land reforms should also consider nations' requirements. What are nations' requirements? They are food security and life security of farmers. New farmland systems must safeguard nations' food policy. Food subsidies should directly go in the hands of the tiller, and then only food security can be ensured. The new land policy has to also ensure that all the farmers, irrespective of their choice of tilling or not tilling land, must have security of livelihood. Every year in China, a portion of farmers have to evacuate their land; this evacuation should be orderly and stable. Those people who evacuate their land must get unemployment benefits and assurance of minimum living standard. If the city cannot treat them equally without any discrimination, then they should be able to go back to their land.

Under such a requirement, I believe, "permanent land right" plan requires further discussion. The so called 'permanent land right' means ownership of the land belongs to the country, and the land use right permanently belongs to the farmers, and abolition of the system whereby land belongs to the village collectives. This right to use cannot be casually leased, transferred, or else it will produce non-tilling landlords and tenant farmers. Any citizen will be able to engage in farming on a land on parity, provided he conforms to the rental parameters. Those farmers who will conform to the conditions of surrendering the lease may surrender it, at the same time they will get security to maintain minimum living standard or old age guarantees, just like the people in the city (of course, the standard of security will be different owing to location). The extra land may be leased by willing individuals or industries at a negotiated price.

Advantages and terms of a state owned permanent rental system

The 'permanent land right' given to peasants under state ownership of land has avoided privatisation of land as well as the reforms in land, owned by collectives. Irrespective of what form is employed for managing agriculture production, for example, shareholding system, contracting, technological cooperation, leasing, etc, all of these can be summed into two categories. First, the agricultural enterprises hiring labour force; and second, self employment by the farmers' models. Therefore, the real user of the land, industry and farmers, getting land right directly from the state, is the most just as well as the most efficient mode. Other modes such as privatisation of land, permanent rent system, ownership of the collectives etc will most probably lead to a situation where those who engage in agriculture, will rent land from the "second landlords". The current land transfer system has created numerous "second landlords". In the case of state ownership of the land, any farmer will have the right to rent land on a minimal price or no price at all. At the same time, the absence of "second landlord" will guarantee the proprietorship and social security to the farmer. This will substantially reveal the superiority of a socialist country, and also prevent any conflict with the market mechanism.

Under such a land system, farmers will enjoy highest degree of freedom in production and proprietorship of the land. They can choose to cultivate, or not to cultivate; they can choose to live in the countryside or in the city; irrespective of what they choose, their subsistence would be guaranteed. The "state owned permanent land rights system" in other words is similar to the urban land system in China. The urban land is also owned by the state, different stakeholders enjoy different land rights (many enjoy permanent land rights, actually the present right to use residential land for 70 years is not appropriate, it should be changed to right to permanent use, the user should pay yearly utilisation tax, this way commercial housing price can be effectively brought down and the tax revenue of the local government can be increased). The user of urban land pays utilisation tax according to different criteria, for example, for commercial use one pays more, one pays less tax if the land is used for a school, etc. Similarly, a common farmer might not pay tax at all under a certain limit of land lease etc. The experience of urban land use can be a referral point for the rural land use. This type of rural land system also adheres to the principle of harmonious development of urban and rural areas, and will be beneficial to the process of urbanisation.

A uniform rural-urban land system demands for other corresponding measures in order to thoroughly eliminate the phenomenon of rural-urban segmentation, especially the dual residential system, dual employment system, dual education system, dual medical system, dual social security system and dual financial system. At the same time, the rural residential plot system must be reformed, the homestead and residential houses of the farmers should be treated at par with the urban commercial housing. The farmer will enjoy permanent land rights as regards his homestead and residential plot, but the possibility of paying utilisation tax cannot be ruled out. The homestead utilisation tax will increase progressively. In order to make the farmers wealthy, non-agricultural activities have to be encouraged and the basic requirement for this would be the uniformity in urban and rural employment system. The concept of 'rural migrant workers' has to be done away with quickly; a person who has handed over his rural land and has been working in the city must be provided unemployment benefits. A few people may argue that this will put enormous pressure on cities; however, if the proportion of the unemployment benefit and living expenses is not favourable, the city will not have the congregation of people seeking unemployment benefit.

Now, how can one solve the issue of land acquisition under the 'permanent land rights'? Regardless of any land system, all farmers are entitled to compensation if their land has been acquired by the state or other enterprises. However, what is crucial is the amount of compensation and the ratio in which the profits are split. Currently, the academic community seems to lean to one side that is to appeal for protecting the interests of farmers; they have accused the local governments and the developers for appropriating large profits. Although there are no precise country-wide statistics available, however, as per my individual observation and information, presently, the farmers whose land has been acquired are a more affluent group than their counterparts. This is because they are mostly located at the outskirts of the cities; the proportion of non-agricultural jobs is higher and the prices of homesteads and housing property are appreciating very fast. If the non-agricultural farmers own collective assets or businesses, they can earn a considerable amount of collective dividends and income. Many among them have already become part of the renter class, even to the extent that many are unwilling to give up their household registration even after being admitted into university. Once land acquisition has taken place, no matter which project is developed, they all grow several dozen times or even several hundred times more than agriculture. How to share such huge profits? Is it justifiable that the farmers who happen to live in that area should get the lion's share? Letting developers gobble up huge profits is certainly not fair, however, is it fair to give farmers the authority to hand over these profits to farmers? In fact, greater political transparency still remains the most effective tool to restrict illegal activity in land development. Instead of restricting high profits of the developers through privatisation of land and protect farmers interest, there is a need to utilise the profits obtained through market opportunity for providing public service goods and transfer of payment at regional level. In the view of this, the concept of "farmers who have lost their land" is also a contradictory one. If one doesn't have any land, can they still be called farmers? A person having neither the land nor the work, and all the while looking for a job, could fall under the category of unemployed population. Therefore, those people who do not own any land must register under non-agricultural households. In case they are unable to find employment, they should be treated at par with the unemployed population of cities and towns. If they wish to continue to work in the agricultural sector, the government must create conditions, provide them permanent land rights and land in other areas.

In brief, the Indian experience shows that the results of the privatisation of land in the developing nations with huge population has not been rewarding, on the contrary, it has created the naughty poverty issues. If China implements the system of privatisation of land, it will be difficult for it, to evade falling into similar plight. Since the present collective ownership of land has many shortcomings and problems, it is high time that reforms are initiated. Therefore, in order to ensure that the tiller has his land, permanent land rights must be given to the farmers by implementing a 'state owned permanent lease system'. Moreover, those who do not engage in agriculture must give up every kind of land right and extended social security. The dual segmentation of urban and rural areas should be abolished; there should be orderly diversion of the agricultural population, and the cities should shoulder even greater responsibilities.

References

"Land Reforms in Bihar and the Left", a seminar on 13 April 1997, Indian Institute of Marxist Studies (IIMS).

India 2006, a reference manual, Ministry of Information and Broadcasting (2007), Government of India.

Sheng Rong (2005), "Cong mubiao he xuqiu jiaodu shenshi zhongguo nongdi gaige" (Looking at China's land reforms from the angle of objectives and requirements). In Rural Economy, (Chengdu), 2005.11.

Sheng Rong (2005), "Nongcun zhaijidi gaige mubiao ji fangan fenxi" (An Analysis of Objectives and Plans of Rural Homestead Reforms). China Agriculture University Journal (Social Science Edition) 2005.

Timothy Besley and Robin Burgess (1998), "Land Reform, Poverty Reduction and Growth: Evidence from India" Report, 1998.

World Economy Yearbook Editorial Committee (2005/2006), Shijiejingji nianjian (World Economy Yearbook).

"China's Rural Land Reform, A Perspective from its Objective and its Requirement", Rural Economy, Chengdu, 2005/11.

"Mission and Solutions, Rural Housing Land Reform", Journal of China Agricultural University (social sciences edition) Beijing 2005/4.

"The Year book of World Economy 2005/2006", World Economy Yearbook Editorial Committee, Beijing, 2006.

Rajiv Nayan

China's Strategic Forces' Modernisation

The contemporary world is talking about the rise of Asia. China is one of the principal propellants in the rise of Asia. Like the rise of Asia, generally, the Chinese rise is seen in economic terms or in terms of the growth of Gross Domestic Product. Overwhelmingly, the literature on China is steadfast in studying its economic miracle - the sustained growth rate over the decades. However, a section of the international community has been looking into the aspects other than economic. The claim of peaceful rise by China is analyzed by scholars and policy makers all over the world, though a country like the United States (US) has committed its resources to study the multidimensional growth of China more than any other country. That the Chinese rise has a strategic and security angle has also been probed by the academic community and the security establishments of the countries which have security concerns with China.

China is growing militarily as well. The military modernisation of China is a reality which is being surveyed worldwide. Report after report have come, delineating different contours of the Chinese military modernisation. Some consider it a part of Asian military modernisation and some are focussed solely on China. Yet, there are some western writers who contextualise the Chinese military modernisation in the regional setting. However, majority of writers get a global mission for the Chinese military modernisation. Admittedly, the study on the Chinese military modernisation has been hampered by the lack of transparency in military affairs in general and the closed authoritarian political system of China in particular.

The Chinese military modernisation, too, is multidimensional in nature. One of the reports of the US Department of Defence finds: "The

People's Liberation Army (PLA) is pursuing comprehensive transformation from a mass army designed for protracted wars of attrition on its territory to one capable of fighting and winning short-duration, high-intensity conflicts along its periphery against high-tech adversaries - an approach that China refers to as preparing for 'local wars under conditions of informatisation." Though China maintains that its military modernisation is defensive in nature, a very few people are ready to accept the Chinese official claim.

For sure, the military modernisation of China is incomplete without the modernisation of its strategic forces. The Chinese Second Artillery is the strategic force of China, and the Second Artillery maintains that it is only managing strategic deterrence for China. The 2009 Chinese White Paper notes: "The Second Artillery Force is mainly composed of the nuclear missile force, the conventional missile force, the support force, educational institutions, research institutes and the headquarter organisations. The missile force is organised into missile bases, missile brigades and launch battalions." The Chinese policy, seemingly, is that without strategic forces' modernisation. China may not influence global developments in its favour. China is undertaking apparently fast paced modernisation of its strategic forces, too. This paper examines, first, what the contours of China's strategic forces' modernisation are and how is it modernising these arsenals and secondly, what would its implications be for Asia and the world, at large?

Contours

One of the American writings acknowledges, " The People's Liberation Army (PLA), once widely dismissed as a bloated, poorly trained military with an enormous, but largely antiquated collection of weapons and equipment, is becoming a leaner, more professional, and increasingly operationally capable fighting force." Some view that through modernisation of strategic forces which essentially may mean modernisation of nuclear forces as well, China is trying to give teeth to the paper tiger. Mao had called nuclear weapons as paper tigers. Several Western writers believe that China has taken a somewhat puzzling route towards its strategic forces' modernisation.

China is the only NPT-defined nuclear weapon country that is still expanding its nuclear arsenals. The other four countries have declared a moratorium on their fissile material production. Russia and the US also have drastic plans to cut their nuclear arsenals. There is general global consideration that China does not have a modernisation programme for its warheads or if at all it has a modernisation programme, it is rather slow. However, this line of argument is contested by others. It is argued that China may not be going for the actual nuclear testing, but like the US it also has a very advanced scientific programme for nuclear warhead modernisation without explosive testing. One of the studies notes that China is carrying out stockpile stewardship activities. Hydrodynamic testing is an integral part of the stockpile stewardship programme. Media reports suggest that China is probing safety enhancements like integration of insensitive high explosives.

China is a signatory of the Comprehensive Test Ban Treaty (CTBT), but it has not ratified it. China maintains that it would ratify the treaty only after the US does. On the other hand, the US Senate does not have the required 67 Senators' support to ratify the treaty. The treaty can enter into force only when all the 44 countries listed on the Annexure 2 of the treaty sign and ratify the treaty. There are at least three countries, including India, which have neither signed the treaty nor ratified it. A few more countries have signed but not ratified the treaty. However, for China, it is the US that matters and for the treaty, other than the US ratification, it is the decision of North Korea that is very crucial. North Korea has already withdrawn its membership from the Nuclear Non-Proliferation Treaty (NPT). It is highly unlikely that it would join the CTBT before rejoining the NPT. And there is no indication yet about its rejoining the NPT. On balance, China may be benefited from the international inaction on the CTBT. The general understanding is that China had already conducted its nuclear tests before joining the NPT. It may resume testing a new generation of nuclear warheads only after the US does it. In recent years, it has been trying to demonstrate that it is a stakeholder of the international system in general and the non-proliferation system in particular. Yet, considering the recent assertive posture of the country, it is also possible that China may not wait for even the US action if it feels that nuclear test is needed for its national interests.

Commonly perceived analysis regarding the strategic forces' modernisation is that China is actually focussing on the modernisation of its nuclear delivery vehicles. Its old aircraft, including its indigenously built aircraft are proving useless. China has acquired a new aircraft like Sukhoi MKC. However, instead of the delivery vehicles, it is the modernisation of its ballistic missiles that appears to be the principal concern for the strategic community in the West and elsewhere. Of the ballistic missiles, it was generally believed that China is concentrating on short-and medium- range of ballistic missiles. For a long period, China did not seem interested in modernising its long-range missiles. However, the recent writings and reports are accepting that China is modernising its long-range ballistic missiles as well. Apparently, it is being done after overcoming its technological limitations. As per the conventional wisdom, modernisation of ballistic missiles may have the purpose of bolstering nuclear deterrence, yet the overwhelming writings on the Chinese military maintain that majority of the ballistic missiles are tipped with conventional warheads.

China is developing a new generation of missiles. It is replacing many of its liquid-fuelled missiles with the solid-fuel missiles. Solid-fuel missiles are considered compact, easy to handle and modern. However, in liquid fuel propulsion, too, advanced research is on. For China, development of solid-fuelled missiles became a priority in the 1980s. Even though China deployed solid-fuelled ballistic missiles system in the early 1990s, it did not stop its refinement. China is also shifting from the silo-based ballistic missile systems to the mobile systems. The idea behind the conversion to the mobile system is to make its nuclear assets survivable after an attack on it, either through conventional means or by nuclear weapons, and thus, increase its striking power.

China does not provide the true figure of its ballistic missile production. The Chinese media reports also indicate that China is proceeding with its missile development programme at a high speed, not at the 'glacial speed'. The number is increasing in almost all the categories of ballistic missiles. The Western sources believe that each category has hundreds of missiles and some even in thousands. China abandoned DF-2. It is in the process of replacing DF-5. Currently, China has DF-3/3A, DF-4, DF-5/5A, DF-11/M-11, DF-15/M-9, DF-21/21A, DF-21C, DF-21D, DF-25, DF-31, and DF-31A in the ballistic missile category. China also has JL-1 Submarine-Launched Ballistic Missile (SLBM). Another SLBM JL-2 is under development, whereas another ballistic missile DF-41 is believed to have been abandoned. Before deployment of a ballistic missile, China conducts experimental flight tests, designs finalisation flight tests, and batch production inspection flight tests. It is also raising new missile units and imparting its personnel advanced training to handle sophisticated strategic forces efficiently and effectively.

China has also developed the capability for manoeuvring re-entry vehicles, and Multiple Independently Targeted Reentry Vehicles (MIRV). A MIRV is one of the many warheads which are carried on the front end or bus of a ballistic missile. It can be sent separately and independently to different targets in succession. It is freed from the front end at different speeds and on different trajectories. China, apparently, is capable of mounting MIRV on DF-5. China is also capable of warhead miniaturisation. A miniaturised warhead diminishes the infrared signal of a reentry vehicle and thus, reduces its chance of detection by the missile defence interceptor of an enemy. Besides, China is also refining its cruise missiles. It is developing air-and ground-launched cruise missiles - the YJ-63 and DH-10 systems for stand-off, precision strikes. It also has the modern Russian-made SS-N-22 and SS-N-27B Anti-Ship Cruise Missiles. It has also upgraded the ground-launched YJ-62 ASCM. China is the only country which is believed to have developed anti-ship ballistic missiles.

Designation [given by NATO]	#	Range & Payload	Warhead and Yield	Propulsion and Guidance	Est .CEP	Comment
DF-2 [CSS-1]	0				1.9-3-.7 km	No longer deployed
DF-3/3A [CSS-2]	15-20	3,000 km 2,150 kg	Single nuclear warhead, 1-5 MT (3.3 MT) -Single conventi-onal warhead	Single-stage; storable liquid propellant (AK-27/UD-MH); Fully inertial strap-down guidance system	2.5-4-.0 km	120-150 minute launch prep. time; road-mobile

DF-4 [CSS-3]	15-- 20	5,400+ km 2,200 kg	Single nuclear warhead, 1-5 MT (3.3 MT)	Two-stage, non-storable liquid propellant (LOX/keros-ene)	3.0- 3.5 km	60-120 minute launch prep. time; also used as booster for Long March-1 (CZ-1) space launch vehicle (SLV); cave-based and rolled out to launch
DF-5/5A [CSS-4]	20	13,000-+ km 4000-5-000 kg	Single nuclear warhead, 1-5 MT (4-5 MT)	Two-stage; storable liquid propellant (N2O4/UD-MH); gyro-platform with onboard computer	0.5-- 3.0 km	30-60 minute launch prep. time; also used as booster for CZ-2, CZ-3, CZ-4 SLVs; deployed at silos at 3 locations; DF-5A (CSS-4 Mod 2),longer range and more mobile, continues to replace the DF-5 (CSS-4 Mod 1), which is silo-based
DF-21/-21A [CSS-5] [Mod 1&2]	50-- 80	2,100 km200-- 300kg	Single nuclear warhead, 200-300 kT - Single conventi-onal warhead	Two-stage; solid propellant; gyro - platform inertial guidance with onboard computer; working on terminal guidance system	0.3-- 0.4 km	10-15 minute launch prep. time; land-mobile; reportedly replacing DF-3 in some areas; same missile as JL-1 SLBM; longer range Mod 2 continues to replace Mod 1

DF-21C [CSS-5] [Mod 3]		1,70-0km 2,00-0kg	Single or multiple conventi-onal warhea-ds	Two-stage; solid propellant; combined inertial/GPS, coupled with terminal guidance		Road-mobile MRBM. Increased accuracy due to the combined guidance system.
DF-21D [CSS-5] [Mod 4]*		1,50-0+ km	Single or multiple conventi-onal warhea-ds	Two-stages; Solid propellant and a re-entry vehicle with a seeker, control fins and a warhead		Road-mobile delivered from a transporter-erector-launcher (TEL). The re-entry vehicle would use its seeker (possibly radar-homing or infrared) to locate and attack target.
DF-15/M--9[CSS-6/-CSST-600]	350--400	600 km 950 kg	Single nuclear-warhea-d,50-35-0 kT - Single or cluster conventi-onal warhead	Single-stage; solid propellant; strap-down inertial computer-di-gitized guidance system with terminal control	600 m	30 minute launch prep. time; M-9 version designed explicitly for export; enhancing accuracy with GPS technology
DF-11/M--11 [CSS-X-7]	700--750	300 km 800 kg	Single nuclear warhead, 350 kT -Single or cluster conventi-onal warhead	Two-stage; solid propellant; strap -down inertial computer-di-gitized guidance system with terminal control	150 m	30-45 minute launch preptime; M-11 version designed explicitly for export

M-7/86-10 [CSS-8]	?	180 km5-00 kg	Conventional warhead	Two-stage; solid propellant booster and storable liquid propellant main engine		Modification of HQ-2 (SA-2) surface-to-air missile (SAM);mobile
DF-25	0	1,70-0km 2,00-0kg	Single conventional warhead	Two-stage; solid propellant		Development thought to be cancelled in mid-1990s but may have been restarted sincethen; based on first two stages of DF-31; land-mobile
DF-31 [CSS--X-10]*	<10	7,20-0+km Paylo-ad un-k-nown	Single nuclear warhead,20-0-300 kT(100-200 kT) (500 kT).Possible future use with MRV/MIRV capability	Three-stage; solid propellant	0.5 km	10-15 minute launch prep. time; land-mobile; most likely cave-based; same missile as JL-2 SLBM; to replace the DF-4; could incorporate penetration aids such as decoys or chaff.
DF-31A	<10	11,2-00+ km Paylo-ad unkn-own	Single nuclear warhead, yield unknown. Potential for MRV/MIRV capability unknown	Three-stage; solid propellant		Launched from a road-mobile transporter-erec-tor-launcher (TEL).Incorpor-ates decoys and penetration aids to confuse missile defence systems.

DF-41-**	0	12,00-0+ km unkno-wn	Single nuclear warhead, 200-300 kT.Possibly equipped with MRV/MIRV capability	Three-sta-ge; solid propellant	0.7--0.8 km	Suspended and most likely cancelled; original design had 3-5 minute launch prep.time; was land-mobile and would have replaced the DF-5
JL-1 [CSS--N-4] SLBM	12	1,770-+ km 200 300 kg	Nuclear warhead, 200-300 kT (500 kT)	Two-stage; solid propellant; gyro-platf-orm inertial guidance with onboard computer	1.0 km	Sea-based version of the DF-21/21A
JL-2 [CSS--N-5] SLBM-*	0	7,200 km 200--300k-g?	Nuclear warhead, 200-300 kT. Possibly will be equipped with MRV/MIRV capability	Three-sta-ge; solid propellant	1.0 km	Under development; first credible sea-based nuclear strike capability once operational (projected by 2009-2010); warhead awaits certification; to be deployed on new 094 SSBN which is also currently under development

Notes:
"DF" stands for "Dong Feng" ("East Wind")
"JL" stands for "Julang" ("Great Wave")
"CSS" stands for "Chinese Surface-to-Surface"
"CSS-N" stands for "Chinese Surface-to-Surface Naval"
"CSST" stands for "Chinese Surface-to-Surface Tactical"
*Under development
**Probably Cancelled Ballistic Missile
Source: http://www.nti.org/e_research/profiles/China/Missile/index.html

Various official and unofficial reports emanating from China and other parts of the world inform that the Chinese government has highly advanced plans in space and anti-missile weapons. The January 2007 demonstration of anti-satellite capability by China made it clear that the country had developed very advanced capability in space technology and is willing to take it to a further height. Through a mobile missile system it launched a Kinetic Kill Vehicle to wreck an old Chinese weather satellite called Feng Yun 1C into lower earth orbit at an altitude of about 865 km. It has a highly advanced programme on laser weapons. China has developed space-based Command, Control, Communications, Computers, Intelligence, Surveillance, and Reconnaissance (C4ISR) along with the capability in imagery, reconnaissance, earth resource systems with military applications, BeiDou-system. The Chinese get enormous benefits from the Yaogan-1, -2, -3, -4, and -5, the Haiyang-1B, the CBERS-2 and -2B satellites, the Huanjing satellite constellation. The satellites in the Huanjing programme have visible, infrared, multi-spectral, and synthetic aperture radar imaging. In the coming years, it is expected to make use of commercial satellite imagery. A Pentagon report notes that as a result, China is 'closing gaps in the creation of a precision-strike capability.' Chinese counter space and cyber warfare are regarded as 'Assassin's Mace' programme.

Apart from developing its own ballistic missile defence capability and space programme, China is also developing systems and sub-systems to counter the ballistic missile interceptors of other countries. To beat ballistic missile defence China is developing decoys, enveloping balls, electromagnetic pulse, infrared stealth, and trajectory manipulation capabilities and so on. Through the refinement of spinning and rolling capability of its ballistic missiles, China is planning to deceive the targeting of its missiles. Lasers need some time to target any object. The manipulation of missiles may make it difficult for laser of an interceptor to target. Besides, laser which is vulnerable to smoke can become redundant by the smoke generated by the missile itself. Armed with accurate real-time target data from land and space-based sensors, Chinese warheads may easily trick the ballistic missile defence. Besides, the Second Artillery of China that is its real missile operating unit has very advanced, automated command system.

Realising the importance of naval power in modern warfare and for grand strategy, China has been modernising its naval power. It is changing doctrines, modernising weapons, giving new orientation to its old organisational structure and culture and imparting training to its forces. Apparently, it wants to develop a really professional naval force. It is developing complex naval platforms. It is mending its aging ships and giving them an advanced shape, developing a high-speed anti-ship cruise missile carrying patrol craft, building a large amphibious ship (Yuzhae LPD), renovating an aircraft carrier purchased from Ukraine, wire-guided and wake-homing torpedoes, launching several Jin-Class (Type 094) submarines and carrying out sea trials and so on. Of all the Naval forces, the Chinese development of submarines is quite noteworthy.

China is modernising its strategic forces through three methods - outright purchase of some systems, acquisition of technology and indigenous development of some systems. Russia is the principal arms supplier of China. But Europeans are generally accused of unintentionally helping the Chinese strategic forces' modernisation programme. However, the US relaxed its export control regulations and enhanced science and technology cooperation with China to promote its grand strategy in which China was a 'potential strategic counterweight' to the Soviet Union and the Warsaw Pact. This engagement started during President Nixon's tenure and continued afterwards. As a result, China was involved in high-technology trade with the United States, leading to increased instances of exception requests. Earlier in 1979, China and the United States also entered into a historic science and technology agreement, the text of which was subsequently revised, with the objective of promoting mutual interests. This agreement facilitated the evolution of an institutional framework as well as some rules and procedures, which in turn assisted subject-specific agreements in the form of protocols and memoranda of understanding. Although some initial assessments ruled out the possibility of any military implication of this agreement, yet later studies indicted the agreement for acquiring substantial dual-use and advanced technology capability because the agreement enabled the access of Chinese scientists to American advanced science and technology organisations. American industry accuses relaxed approach of European industry and less stringent rules of European countries regarding the supply of sensitive items, to the military modernisation of China

Implications

The modernisation of the Chinese military has made the international community busy with several key questions. One of the questions is regarding its impact on the region around China and the world in general. This forces us to study the motive and rationale behind the modernisation. Generally, the thinking is that China is modernising its arsenals to maintain its regional hegemony, to keep Asia unipolar and make the world multipolar. At the regional level, the Chinese forces are overcoming all the previously existing military gaps. Japan has one of the most sophisticated naval forces, and Russia is the dominant power of the region. Chinese have either overcome the gap or are fast overcoming it. This applies to other spheres as well. The idea seems to construct a new world order in which China emerges as a strong pole through fast development of national power. China would like to call this order a just order characterised by multipolarity. Chinese would like to project that in the new order no dominant power or the hegemony should shape the order.

The Chinese development of anti-access and area-denial capabilities has regional and global implications. Some policy analysts hold the view that the strategic modernisation of China may lead to greater strategic stability at the regional and the global level. The 2009 White Paper of the Chinese government explains: "Following the principle of building a lean and effective force and going with the tide of the development of military science and technology, the Second Artillery Force strives to raise the informationisation level of its weaponry and equipment, ensure their safety and reliability, and enhance its capabilities in protection, rapid reaction, penetration, damage and precision strike. After several decades of development, it has created a weaponry and equipment system with both nuclear and conventional missiles, both solid-fuelled and liquid-fuelled missiles, different launching ranges and different types of warheads." Expectedly, the Chinese government also claims that the military modernisation of China is completely defensive in nature; China is modernising its arsenals to defend itself and exist peacefully in the world.

Peaceful long-term security environment may be projected as the ultimate goal of the modernisation.

Admittedly, some elements of military modernisation may have been used for international cooperation efforts such as peacekeeping, humanitarian assistance and disaster relief and counter-piracy. A section of the strategic community dismisses the entire modernisation programme not more than 'possession mentality'. It is argued that pre-modernisation level of Chinese weapons, including nuclear is enough to deter its adversaries. No great power ever invaded the country. The modernisation is considered influence-neutral. The high-paced development, according to this section of the strategic community, does not add any value to the Chinese status. Whatever status or attention it is getting, it is only because of its rapid economic growth over the decades. Nevertheless the military modernisation in general and strategic forces' modernisation in particular is instilling fear in a larger section of the international community. The world is quite apprehensive about the intent of the strategic forces' modernisation.

Some may argue that the intent and action of the US are also aggressive. True, the US is also modernising its arsenal. Even Obama, during his election campaigns, quite frequently stated that his administration would pay serious attention to modernising its arsenals. In fact, after assuming the Presidency, he started working towards it. Notwithstanding Obama's peace overtures and support for nuclear disarmament, the security establishment is emphasising for the modernisation of American strategic forces, including nuclear weapons. But unlike the US, the Chinese system is not just authoritarian but also extremely opaque. For sure, the modernising Chinese military capability combined with its unpredictable political behaviour is worrisome for the world.

Officially, for China, the strategic forces' modernisation aims at providing a credible, stable and robust deterrence. The official Chinese line and the official American line may not appear very different if we take the fundamental objective of the strategic forces' modernisation by both the countries. Both the countries maintain that they have nuclear weapons for deterrence, not war. It is generally believed that China has 'access to several rungs of escalatory ladders' which it earlier lacked. Robustness of nuclear deterrence and its reliability and credibility are expected to provide stable external environment for economic development.

One question which has been widely discussed is a greater possibility that the modernisation of Chinese strategic forces may lead to doctrinal changes. Currently, China has given a very benign projection of its doctrine. As discussed, like other nuclear weapon countries, it assigns a deterrent role for its nuclear arsenals. But China has scored over other countries by declaring the doctrine of no-first use and no use of nuclear weapons against non-nuclear weapon countries. In fact, it is China that initiated the idea of negative security assurance. India, too, in its nuclear doctrine incorporated both the provisions. The US, in its recent nuclear posture review, promised to give negative security assurance. However, later statements of its officials sought to dilute the promise, and in the process made it ambiguous.

Some also fear that the strategic forces' modernisation may lead to change on Minimum Means of Reprisal or Credible Minimum Deterrence. China may get greater flexibility and military options for strategic strike with the military modernisation of naval forces, particularly of submarines. Jin class submarine is being watched very carefully by the concerned countries. In principle, the strong Chinese navy may resist sea-borne aggression and protect its national sovereignty. Reportedly, China has identified some offensive and defensive campaigns for its navy. These are: blockade, anti-sea lines communication, maritime land attack, anti-ship maritime transportation protection and naval base Defence. By strengthening naval-based deterrence, China may project that it has not deviated from its fundamental policy of reliance on the second strike capability. Formally, China may not renounce its credible minimum doctrine.

Would Chinese match the US document by making it more assertive and aggressive? Considering the current global mood and the pressure in favour of negative security assurance, it does not seem that China would change its doctrine notwithstanding the Chinese strategic forces' modernisation and the US ambiguity on the issue. China is aware that its nuclear doctrine is merely international public relations exercise. At present, China is investing its resources to increase its influence and convince the world that it is a stakeholder of the international system and the global nuclear order. China would not like to send a negative signal to the world by adopting any aggressive posture or image by abandoning no-first use or negative security assurance.

Then what can China do? Is China modernising its forces for power projection? Some argue that China may go for power projection at the regional level as well as at the global level. The international security community seems to be divided. The famous Pentagon 2009 report observes: "Today, while China has a few aerial refueling aircraft, it does not have the number of tankers, properly equipped combat aircraft, or sufficient training to employ this capability for power projection."

Some view that China would not induce any event or action that may cause regional dispute because it will adversely affect China's economic development. The Chinese ruling class, according to this thinking, has put economic development as its priority. However, the general understanding is that China is striving to acquire the complete system for war preparedness. The Chinese military establishment, armed with sophisticated military systems is expected to ensure access to resources or enforce claims to disputed territories. The countries such as India and Vietnam have already fought wars with China. True, since 1998, it had settled seven land territory disputes with six of its neighbours. Yet, it had territorial disputes with many countries. India has lost its territory to China, which India is reclaiming in different bilateral meetings. China has territorial disputes with South East Asian and East Asian countries as well. Exclusive Economic Zones, Senkaku Islands, Spartly and Paracel Island Groups, etc are the areas of dispute between China and these countries.

There are views that China, with a robust second strike capability, may behave aggressively towards some of its neighbours and Taiwan. The sophisticated arsenal may give enough capabilities to the Chinese, for regional strike or maritime interdiction operations. The Chinese military has accumulated hundreds of ballistic missiles, targeting Taiwan. One of the official US reports informs that China has stationed seven brigades, armed with more than a thousand short-range and medium-range ballistic missiles near Taiwan. The increase in the number and sophistication of short-range and medium range missiles has made Taiwan quite vulnerable to the aggressive design of China. Through a MIRVed system, China may hit soft targets. These soft targets are understood to be big cities and military installations.

Through the new systems, it is assumed that China may destroy the Taiwanese airfields quite easily. The destruction of the Taiwanese airfield is quite significant for the Chinese military strategy as it would deny Taiwan and its allies, required command and control and infrastructure to counter the Chinese attack in a possible battlefield scenario. For a long period, Taiwan enjoyed the dominance of the airspace over the Taiwan Strait. Now, the balance is altered in favour of China. Similarly, submarines, the submerged launching platforms, could be useful for counterstrike against the enemy's air raids. The purpose is to deny the enemy access to the region in time of crisis. In the Chinese military policy, annexation of Taiwan is the first priority. The western literature at this moment sees the possible crisis in the context of China, preventing Taiwan's de jure independence. Besides, China may project the possibility of limited war to force Taiwan to remain under constant fear of China, even if it is not annexed.

China expects that the allies of Taiwan, most prominently, the US may join the battle, if Taiwan is attacked. Although the US recognises one China, its military and other support to Taiwan have occasionally been causing tension between the US and China. The development and induction of longer range missiles by China are for targets beyond Taiwan. Conventional missiles could be useful for regional bases and aircraft carriers of its adversaries, especially the US. Even the continental US is well under the reach of Inter-continental Ballistic Missiles of China. As the purpose seems to have to be the countering of the US primacy in the nuclear field, there is a possibility that the US would make an attempt to maintain its primacy. This may lead to further modernisation of the US forces. Alertness or readiness of the strategic forces of the two countries may in fact create international disorder. There is a likelihood that with its newly found confidence, China may be quite venturesome and keep disturbing strategic stability. It has already demonstrated this tendency with its neighbours. So, instead of self-restraint, the Chinese strategic forces' modernisation may indulge in the intensification of the conflict.

Moreover, the Chinese priority or focus on Taiwan should not mean that China has no ill intention or aggressive design towards other countries in its neighbourhood. We have just discussed China's territorial disputes with its neighbours. Other countries may also face the Chinese brunt. Although China may be developing survivable system and increased striking power to counter the US missile defence system or the Taiwanese forces, yet it cannot be denied that other countries in the region which may appear adversaries to the Chinese leadership and which may have the ballistics defence system may become targets of the modernised Chinese strategic forces. Attacking surface ships like aircraft carriers with ballistic missile is also a possibility. Other targets in the neighbourhood may also come under the Chinese long range missiles. All the countries in its neighbourhood have to either accept its hegemony or keep facing one or another of the problem. Undoubtedly, China has been quite innovative in creating problems for its neighbours. Besides, China may also crush the internal dissent and will be more ruthless and insensitive to the human rights issue.

Conclusion

China has demonstrated a highly perceptible modernisation of its military and strategic forces. No sphere has been left untouched. The area where the level of modernisation is not very high, it is working hard through various means. In the strategic field, there are restrictions in import, but China has been able to beat it through innovations. Where it has not succeeded, it has developed or is developing indigenous technology. Formally, it does not seem that China is going to effect any change in its doctrine. However, in practice, it may continue with some provocative changes and signalling. China may change its posturing. The change of posturing may force its neighbours to review their defence and strategic weapons policy. In East Asia, as long as the US continues to spread its nuclear protective umbrella, Japan may not develop its nuclear weapons. The moment the American nuclear umbrella is withdrawn, we may see a high-paced modernisation of strategic forces. This may adversely affect the strategic stability in the region.

The strategic force modernisation may have implications for great-power relations. An economically emerging China is adding military dimension to its profile. Some have already started talking about the emergence of G-2, consisting of the US and China. More sober assessment could be for a multipolar world in which China would be playing an important role militarily as well. However, it may lead to a tense regional and international environment if the existing sole superpower and other competitors of China indulge in military modernisation to check the disturbing Chinese military modernisation. The balance of power in Asia may be in a constant flux. The equilibrium is going to be very dynamic. The world may have to devise a framework to maintain an Asian and global equilibrium which is going to be disturbed continually. India appears slow to respond to the Chinese modernisation. In 1998, it took a decision to go nuclear. There is some controversy regarding its thermo-nuclear device. India may have to refine the device by conducting a few more tests. It should not hesitate in doing so for its security. Although it has been developing ballistic missiles, it may have to dedicate more resources for increasing the range and sophistication of its delivery vehicles. Ballistic and cruise missiles may constitute the core. India also needs to develop other force multipliers and use revolution in Military Affairs. Ultimately, India may have to change its 1962 mindset. Today, India is quite advanced and its people far more confident. It needs to believe that China is not invincible.

References

http://www.Defence.gov/pubs/pdfs/China_Military_ Power_Report_2009.pdf

http://www.Defence.gov/pubs/pdfs/China_ Military_Power_Report_2009.pdf

http://www.china.org.cn/government/central_government/200901/20/content_1715 5577_9.htm

Michael S Chase, et. al.,"Chinese Theatre and Strategic Missile Force Modernisation and its implications for the United States", The Journal of Strategic Studies, Vol. 32, No.1, February 2009, p.67

RN Das

Indian and Chinese Diaspora

The increasing attention and focus to study the problems and potential of the expatriate population by the home countries can be attributed to a number of factors, the most important being the irreversible and unstoppable process of globalisation breaking the physical and emotional barriers of the nation state. The integration of world economy has brought to the fore, the sociol, economic and political issues, having a bearing on migration and reverse migration. While it is essential to address these issues carefully, it is equally important to harness the prowess and potential of the expatriate population as a strategic asset in the economic, social and educational development of the home country. A graphic illustration of this is the impact and influence of the Indian community in the USA, in facilitating the passage of the Indo-US nuclear deal even though the impact was minuscule.

It is in this context that the present article attempts to make a comparative study of attitude and policies of India and China towards their ethnic population abroad. Since comparisons are not always apt as there are dissimilarities and incongruities, therefore for better treatment of the subject, the article attempts to put in perspective, the evolution of the policies of the respective governments towards their ethnic population abroad. Firstly, the term diaspora includes ethnic Indians described as Persons of Indian Origin or PIOs and similarly Overseas Chinese, both of whom have adopted the citizenship of the host countries while retaining some kind of a primordial affiliation in terms of culture, emotion and possibly identity with the countries of their origin. Secondly, it also includes Non-Resident Indians (NRI's) and Overseas Chinese who have retained their respective nationalities but have gone abroad temporarily for education, career and professional advancement.

There are interesting similarities between the Indian and Chinese diasporas. Like the Chinese, the Indian diaspora maintained a historical taboo against overseas travel. Patterns of emigration in both Indian and Chinese communities have been similar in the 19th and 20th centuries. Indentured labour formed the bulk of Indian emigrants in the 19th century; a sizable professional segment emerged in the second half of the 20th century. Both communities have aroused feelings of envy in the areas where they live, as they have achieved more success, relative to the local populations. Both communities are also characterised by attachment and feelings of nostalgia for the countries they have left behind.

Like the Indian diaspora, the overseas Chinese constitute one of the largest diasporas in the world. The US, Canada and Australia receive more emigrants of Chinese origin than from anywhere else in the world. Indian Americans and Chinese Americans are some of the most successful ethnic groups in the Silicon Valley. It is pertinent to mention that according to a study done by the Duke University's School of Engineering and University of California's School of Information, Indians founded more engineering and technology firms in the US over the past decade than any other immigrant group. Between 1995 and 2005, Indian immigrants founded more companies in these sectors than Chinese, Taiwanese and British Immigrants put together.

A fourth of all engineering companies, founded in the US over the past one decade, were started by immigrants. According to press reports, the study reveals that as many as 26 per cent of these firms had Indian founders. The findings underline again, how skilled foreign workers hold the key to the development of technology and engineering industries in the US. According to Vivek Wadhwa, Executive in Residence at Duke University's Pratt School of Engineering and the author of the report, many of the huge waves of Indian immigrants who arrived in the US after 1980, were knowledge workers. This is borne out by two things, the fact that Indians obtained the most number of patents after the Chinese between 1995 and 2005 and that nearly half of all Indian-founded companies in the US are in the software sector.

These are the people who give the US its competitive advantage. "This shows that when Indians are given the environment in which they can succeed, they can stand head to head with the best of the best, in Silicon Valley and elsewhere", opines Wadhwa. Definitely the Indian diaspora has stolen the march over their Chinese counterpart.[1]

China: An Inclusive Nationality Policy

As far as Chinese diaspora is concerned, it may be mentioned that their policy and attitude towards ethnic Chinese or the Overseas Chinese have been more inclusive, as their policies and postures have been part of their ultimate goal - unification with what the Chinese call the 'compatriots' in Hong Kong, Macau and Taiwan in mind. Unlike China, India does not have this kind of an agenda.

Overseas Chinese traditionally consider themselves to be temporary absentees. The term for the Chinese who are staying abroad is, *huaqiao* or sojourners, meaning travellers. The terms 'overseas Chinese' has been used to refer to both Chinese nationals overseas and ethnic Chinese, who are citizens of other countries. It has also the connotation that the Chinese are sojourners who will eventually return to China. The Chinese Communist Party (CCP) used the term "overseas Chinese" in various ways. According to Stephen Fitzgerald, it was first used to include all ethnic Chinese overseas but by the mid 1950s, it was narrowing to a category comprising mainly Chinese nationals but also including all those who still maintained some attachment to the Chinese homeland". In fact, he suggested that the term was used beyond the concept of "nationality". It included both Chinese nationals and many ethnic Chinese, who were non-Chinese citizens.[2]

Indeed, Chinese leaders, in the 1950s, referred to the Chinese abroad as either Chinese people or Chinese nationals. Chou En-lai, for instance, used the two terms inter-changeably. This is understandable because China regarded the ethnic Chinese as citizens of China by law, unless a dual nationality treaty was signed between China and the country concerned.

For this reason the Kuomintang's (KMTs) policy was aimed at securing the support and allegiance of the Chinese abroad. A number of seats in the

---

[1] The Hidustan Times, 5 Jan 2007.

[2] Leo Suryadinata, China and the ASEAN States: The Ethnic Chinese Dimension,Singapore, 2005, p.1

Chinese parliament were reserved for the representatives of the overseas Chinese. Moreover, the KMT declared in 1929 that all Chinese including overseas Chinese, were China's nationals. The PRC initially pursued a policy towards the overseas Chinese that was similar to that of the KMT. The PRC constitution of 1954 states that: "The National People's Congress is composed of deputies elected by provinces, autonomous regions, municipalities directly under the central authority, the armed forces and Chinese residents abroad. It also states that "the People's Republic of China protects the just rights and interests of Chinese residents abroad."

The Chinese make a distinction between Chinese citizens residing abroad and Chinese who have given up their citizenship, which roughly corresponds with the NRI and PIO terminology used in India. Overseas Chinese who have invested or contributed in some way to China are also called 'returned overseas Chinese'. Currently, the major arms of the State, Legislature and Party have high level offices dealing with the Overseas Chinese through which preferential treatment is accorded to the latter.

The Chinese Constitution (Articles 50, 70 and 89) protects the legitimate rights of Chinese nationals residing abroad and the rights and interests of 'returned overseas Chinese'. It also mandates the Cabinet of the Chinese Government to exercise the above powers and functions as well as the setting up of the Overseas Chinese Committee of the Chinese Parliament.

The Chinese Communist Party has an office called the United Front Work Department of the Central Committee dealing with Taiwanese compatriots. One of the main national Chinese NGOs, the 'All China Federation of Returned Overseas Chinese' is under the leadership of the Chinese Communist Party, while the other national NGO 'China Overseas Exchange Association' also maintains close links with the government. There is also a 'Hong Kong, Macau, Taiwan and Overseas Chinese Affairs Sub-Committee' of the Chinese People's Consultative Conference (which has many non-Party members).

The Overseas Chinese Affairs Committee of the Chinese Parliament, the National People's Congress (NPC) functions under the NPC's Standing Committee when the NPC is not in session. The NPC has passed the following Laws [3]:

- The 1990 “Law of Protecting Rights and Interests of Overseas Chinese and their Relatives”, which safeguards their legal rights with a focus on political and civil rights, right to participation in politics, property, person, education and the right of visiting, settling and studying in China. Article 3 of this Law specifically mandates the State to accord appropriate preferential treatment to 'returned overseas Chinese' and the family members of overseas Chinese. Article 5 entitles 'returned overseas Chinese' to appropriate representation on the National People's Congress and local People's Congresses in places where there are relatively large numbers of 'retuned overseas Chinese'. Article 6 gives them the right to establish public organisations to safeguard their lawful rights and interests. Article 8 enjoins on local people's governments at all levels to support ‘returned overseas Chinese' and the family members of overseas Chinese who invest, inter alia, in the establishment of industrial and commercial enterprises. Article 9 allows preferential treatment of duty reduction or exemption to 'returned overseas Chinese' and the family members of overseas Chinese who receive donations made by their relatives and friends outside the country, for use in public welfare undertakings.

- The 1993 “Measures for the Implementation of the Law of the People's Republic of China on the Protection of the Rights and Interests of Returned Overseas Chinese and Family Members of Overseas Chinese” (that lays out the preferential treatment to be given by Governments at all levels, to Overseas Chinese when they return/invest in China).

Comparison with China, should not be on its face value, because theirs is a different political system in which the party is supreme, whereas India has a democratic system with all exuberance of democracy and compulsions of electoral politics.

---

[3] Report of the High Level Committee on the Indian Diaspora, Indian Council of World Affairs, 2001, pp 304-315

Policy and Attitude of India

Contrary to the view of many critics that India initiated a proactive policy towards its diaspora only after the government initiated economic reform and liberalisation, is it pertinent to mention that India had never abandoned its moral and emotional obligation to its expatriate population abroad, who had left the country in pursuit of greener pastures, fame and fortune. Yes, of course, compared to China, India's policy towards expatriate population especially in the post-Independent era and prior to the initiation of economic liberalisation and modernisation, can be described as best as one of benign neglect.

It was Mahatma Gandhi, who espoused the cause of Indian diaspora in an organised manner for the first time. It is worth recalling that Gandhi started his experiment of Satyagraha in South Africa, to highlight the injustice and unfair treatment meted out to the migrant Indians there. He valiantly fought for their rights, dignity and self-esteem. Gandhi was concerned not only with the problems of the South African Indians but with the lot of the Indians all over world.[4]

During his prolonged sojourn in South Africa, he made two trips back to India during which he wrote the 'green pamphlet' and addressed the Indian National Congress, the Chamber of Commerce and other organisations to rally support for their Indian countrymen, especially in South Africa. Gandhi's persistent campaign had sensitised the travails of the Indian Community to the Colonial authorities in India and the United Kingdom.

The national leadership of India who were fighting for the freedom struggle also attempted to raise the problems of the overseas Indians in the multilateral fora available to them. One such forum was the Imperial Conference where India made sure that the Overseas Indian problem figured prominently on the agenda. India also raised the issue of discrimination against Overseas Indians at the Imperial Conference of 1917. At the Imperial Conference of 1921, the Indian Government lobbied for

---

[4] M.C. Lal, India's Missed Opportunity, India's Relationship with Non-resident Indians, Asghate, 2001, p.79

the Overseas Indian population living in the Dominions to be conferred equal rights with the British. Indians were continuously denied the right of settlement in the Kenyan highlands, which were reserved for the white population. At the 1923 Imperial Conference, the issue of discrimination in South Africa was again taken up by Sir Tej Bahadur Sapru. India's lobbying at the Imperial Conferences had some success as it overcame a reluctance to discuss the problem of expatriate Indians in general and made it one of the Conference's major issues. It seemed that the empire could no longer lightly dismiss the problem, even if that did not lead to any dramatic results.

Despite the creation of the separate Department of Overseas Indians and its placing under an Indian member of the Viceroy's Executive Council, there was no substantial enlargement of the role of the Government of India. The separate Department of Overseas Indians had at its head Dr. N.B. Khare, who worked tirelessly.

In India, the Congress Party at its Amritsar Congress, declared that "this Congress is of the opinion that the anti-Indian agitation now going on in East Africa is utterly unscrupulous and trusts that the government of India will safeguard the right of free and unrestricted emigration from India to East Africa and the full civic and political rights of Indian settlers in East Africa, including the East African territory conquered by Germany". The 38th Indian National Congress Annual Session in December 1923 declared that unless India became independent, the grievances of the Indian Diaspora could not be properly remedied.

Role of Indian Diaspora in the Freedom Struggle

While Gandhi can legitimately be described as the first Pravasi Bharatiya who espoused the cause of the rights of the Indians abroad and fought for independence tenaciously, it is equally true of many other eminent freedom fighters who studied abroad and many of them who were settled abroad also fought for India's Independence. The role played by Lala Hardyal of Gadar Movement in San Francisco and that of the Shyamji Krishna Verma in the United Kingdom is well known. The contribution of Dadabhai Naoroji, the first Indian to become the member of the House of Commons, who espoused the cause of independence of India, is well-known.

It may be recalled that in June, 1940 in his 'Foreword' to Our Countrymen Abroad by Dharam Yas Dev, Secretary, Department of Indians Overseas, IACCC, Jawaharlal Nehru wrote, "ever since the national movement took shape in India, the problem of our countrymen abroad has been with us, as indeed it must be. And so it will remain till that movement triumphs and brings freedom and independence to India" and at the same time, admitted that "it is true that India has never forgotten her children abroad, but it is also true that she might have taken greater interest in them than she has done".[5]

Indian Policy in the post-independence Era

With the attainment of Independence, India's policy towards its expatriate population, particularly the PIOs, underwent a paradigm shift. Although India was committed to protect the legitimate interest of its ethnic population abroad, understandably, it could not do so beyond a point. This was acknowledged by no less a person than Prime Minister Jawaharlal Nehru himself, in the then Legislature called the Constituent Assembly on 4th December, 1947. Yet on another occasion while responding to certain issues relating to Indians Overseas, raised by Seth Govind Das on the floor of the House, Prime Minister Nehru said:

> Now these Indians abroad, what are they? Indian citizens? Are they going to be citizens of India or not? If they are not, then our interest in them becomes cultural and humanitarian, not political. That interest of course remains. For instance, take the Indians of Fiji nationals or Mauritians. The same question arises in regard to Burma and Ceylon. It is a difficult question. This House gets mixed up. It wants to treat them as Indians, and with the same breath it wants a complete franchise for them in the countries where they are living. Of course the two things do not go together. Either they get the franchise as nationals of the other country, or treat them as Indians minus the franchise and ask for the most favourable treatment given to an alien.[6]

---

[5] Chandrasekhar Bhatt, India and the Indian Diaspora: Inter- linkages and Expectations, in Ajay Dubey (ed.) Indian Diaspora Global Identity, New Delhi, p.17.

[6] Constituent Assembly of India (Legs) Deb. Vol.3, March 5-18, 1948, pp.1771.

Be that as it may, the post-Independence era witnessed exodus of qualified professionals to foreign countries, particularly the USA, Canada and the United Kingdom, resulting in the phenomenon called the 'brain drain' and there was no major initiative towards the diaspora, whether PIOs or NRIs.

A significant sensitisation effort was taken up in November 1977 when a Seminar was held at the India International Centre, Delhi, to consider the current status and problems of the Indian communities, living overseas. In his inaugural address, Atal Behari Vajpayee, the then Foreign Minister and the one, who subsequently became the Prime Minister of the country, setting the tone of the deliberation, said, “the subject of overseas Indians is one which is very dear to our hearts…Everyone of Indian origin overseas is a representative of India and retains many aspects of our cultural traditions and civilization. Though our sons and daughters have gone abroad to work or to reside there, India will never disown them or fail to appreciate and respect their essential loyalty to the culture and heritage of the mother country”.

With the economic reforms and liberalisation which India initiated during 1990s, the Government also initiated a proactive policy towards the expatriate population abroad, particularly towards the Non-Resident Indians with the goal to involve and associate them in the process of development and economic modernistion. It was against this backdrop that, the Ministry of Home Affairs launched the People of Indian Origin (PIO) Card in March 1999. The PIO Card Scheme was basically aimed to reinforce the emotional bonds of Indians who have made other countries their home, but who had a yearning to renew their ties with the land of their origin.

Under the PIO card scheme there was no need for getting a visa to visit India and for registering with the Foreigner's Registration Office if continuous stay did not exceed 180 days. The card also enabled the PIO's travel to India simpler, easier, flexible and hassle free. The scheme, however, did not evoke the desired response, apparently due to prohibiting fees.

In addition to the PIO Scheme which has since been improvised and the Overseas Indian Citizens (OCI) Cards following the policy of liberalisation, the Government also launched in 1998 what is called the Resurgent India Bonds (RIB) in 2000. A sum of U.S. 4.2 billion and US 5.51 billion were mobilised under these two schemes respectively, particularly to tide over the oil crisis which had affected the Indian economy to a great extent.

High Level Committee on Indian Diaspora

The government took a major initiative to address pressing issues pertaining to the diaspora when it constituted a High level Committee on Indian Diaspora in August 2000 under the Chairmanship of late Dr. L.M. Singhvi, a distinguished member of Rajya Sabha and the former Indian High Commissioner to the United Kingdom. The terms of reference of the Committee were as under:

(a) Review the status of Persons of Indian Origin (PIOs) and Non-Resident Indians (NRIs) in the context of constitutional provisions, laws and rules applicable to them both in India and the countries of their residence;

(b) Study the characteristics, aspirations, attitudes, requirements, strengths and weaknesses of Indian diaspora and their expectations from India;

(c) Study the role that the PIOs and NRIs may play in the economic, social and technological development of India;

(d) Examine the current regime that governs the travel and stay of PIOs in India and investment by PIOs in India, and recommend measures to resolve the problems faced by NRIs in these areas;

(e) Recommend a broad but flexible policy framework and country specific plans for forging a mutually beneficial relationship with the region or PIOs and NRIs and for facilitating their interaction with India and their participation in India's economic development.

The Committee submitted its Report in December, 2001 with a slew of recommendations, many of which have since been implemented.

The Committee recommended the celebration of 'Pravasi Bharatiya Divas' in recognition and appreciation of the constructive economic and philanthropic role played by the Indian diaspora and it also recommended conferring of the Pravasi Bharatiya Samman Awards on prominent persons of the overseas Indian Community in recognition of their valuable contribution in promoting the honour and prestige of India and in fostering the interests of overseas Indians.

Creation of Separate Ministry of Overseas Indian Affairs

The creation of the Ministry of Overseas Indian Affairs (MOIA) in May 2004 acknowledged the fact that the welfare of the Overseas Indians need mainstream attention. The mission of the Ministry is to promote, nurture and sustain a mutually beneficial and symbiotic relationship between India and its diaspora, which is estimated at over twenty five million, spread over 110 countries. The Ministry was earlier called the Ministry of Non-Resident Indian Affairs and was renamed as the Ministry of Overseas Indians Affairs in September 2004. The emigration division of the Ministry of Labour and Employment was attached to the new Ministry in December 2004. The NRI Division of the Ministry of External Affairs provides support to the Ministry of Overseas Indian Affairs and functions as the Diaspora Division in the Ministry.

Dual Citizenship

The Committee further recommended that dual citizenship should be permitted within the rubric of Citizenship Act, 1955. It was against this background that the Citizenship (Amendment) Bill, 2003 was introduced in the Rajya Sabha in December 2003. The Bill was subsequently referred to the Departmentally-Related Parliamentary Standing Committee on Home Affairs for examination under the Chairmanship of Pranab Mukherjee after being laid in the Lok Sabha. In 2004, by an amendment to the Citizenship Act, the facility of Overseas Citizenship of India (OCI) was made available to PIOs in 16 specified countries. At the Pravasi Bharatiya Divas 2005, held in Mumbai, the Prime Minister had announced Government's intention to PIOs of any country (except Pakistan & Bangladesh) that allows dual citizenship. This has since been given legal backing by the Indian Parliament, which approved the Citizenship

(Amendment) Act, 2005 in August 2005.

The amended Act enables the Central Government to register, as an Overseas Citizen of India (OCI), any person of full age and capacity:

(1) who is a citizen of another country now, but was a citizen of India at the time of, or at any time after the commencement of the Constitution of India, on 26th January 1950;

(2) who is a citizen of another country, but was eligible to become a citizen of India at the time of commencement of the Constitution

(3) who is a citizen of another country, but belonged to a territory that became a part of India after the 15th of August 1947;

(4) who is child or a grand child of such a citizen; or a child of a person mentioned in (1) to (4) above. No person who is or has been a citizen of Pakistan or Bangladesh shall be eligible to be registered as an OCI.

In an increasingly multicultural world, the importance of India granting the Overseas Citizenship of India status to PIOs cannot be over-emphasised. Unlike the post-Independence nation building years, when migration to foreign lands was considered brain-drain, the confidence of modern India is such that it now considers its non-resident citizens and PIOs as an asset that can only add to its growing stature in world affairs.

An Overseas Citizen of India is not entitled to the rights conferred on a citizen of India and will not have the right to equality of opportunity in matters of public employment and will not be a member of Parliament or of a State legislature. An Overseas Citizen of India will also not be entitled to agricultural land or plantation. Nevertheless it grants a life-long citizenship status and is a kind of psychological incentive for people to relate themselves with India.

Persons of Indian Origin (PIO) Card

Besides the OCI Card, the Government also refurbished the earlier Scheme of Persons of Indian Origin or PIO Card in August 2002. As per the revised Scheme, a PIO means a foreign citizen (not being a citizen of Pakistan, Bangladesh and other countries as may be specified by the Central

Government from time to time) if,

(i) He/She at any time held an Indian Passport; or

(ii) He/She or either of his/her parents or grand parents or great grand parents was born in and permanently resident in India as defined in the Government of India Act, 1935 and other territories that became part of India thereafter, provided neither was at any time, a citizen of any of the aforesaid countries; or

(iii) He/She is a spouse of a citizen of India or a person of Indian origin covered under (i) or (ii) above.

A PIO Card shall be valid for a period of fifteen years from the date of issue subject to the validity of the passport of the applicant. The fee for a PIO Card is Rs.15000/- (or its equivalent in local foreign currency of the country concerned), payable along with application; PIO Card to children up to the age of 18 years is issued at a fee of Rs.7500/- (or its equivalent in local foreign currency of the country concerned) for a fifteen year card.

Gratis PIO Card is also issued to an exceptionally eminent person of Indian Origin who plays an important role in building bridges between India and the country of his/her adoption, if he/she expresses a desire to obtain the PIO Card.

Facilities to be extended to a PIO Card holder:

1. A PIO Card holder shall not require a separate visa to visit India.

2. A PIO Card holder will be exempt from the requirement of registration, if his stay on any single visit in India, does not exceed 180 days.

3. In event of continuity of stay in India of the PIO Card holder beyond 180 days, he/she shall have to get himself/herself registered within 30 days of the expiry of 180 days with the concerned Foreigners Regional Registration Officer/Foreigners Registration Officer.

4. All PIOs including PIO Card holders, shall enjoy parity with NRIs in respect of all facilities available to the latter in the

economic, financial and educational fields except in matters relating to the acquisition of agricultural/ plantation properties. No parity shall be allowed in the sphere of political rights.

Voting Rights

The issue of granting voting rights to the Non-Resident Indians, particularly from the Gulf region has engaged the attention of Parliament, the media and the judiciary for quite some time. The issue has been raised in the Parliament. As a matter of fact in 1998, Mr. E. Ahmed, the then Minister of State for External Affairs, who himself is from Kerala had introduced a Private members' Bill in the Lok Sabha, securing voting rights for NRIs in the Gulf. However, the Bill never came up for discussion since the Lok Sabha was dissolved. Earlier, in 1998, in a writ petition filed in the High Court of Kerala by Shri K. Balchandran Nair, Chairman, Non-Resident Indian Welfare Association, Kochi, the Hon'ble High Court, in its judgement, directed the Union Government to consider the request for the Non-Resident Indians for inclusion of their names in the voting list and to grant them right to vote.

It is pertinent to mention in this context, that under Article 326 of the Constitution of India, the right to vote has been accorded a constitutional status. Article 326 stipulates that "every person who is a citizen of India and who is not less than eighteen years of age and is not otherwise disqualified under the Constitution or any law made by the appropriate legislature, is entitled to be registered as a voter. As per the provisions of the Constitution, non-residence, unsoundness of mind, crime or corrupt or illegal practice have been listed as disqualifications for restriction as a voter.

While Article 326 of the Constitution entitles voting right to the citizens which is in fact one of the most basic democratic rights, Article 327 of the Constitution empowers the Parliament to make provisions by law, with respect to all matters relating to, or in connection with, elections to either House of Parliament or to the House or either House of the Legislature of a state, including the preparation or electoral rolls. In exercise to such power, the Parliament has enacted the Representation of the People Act, 1950. Section 28 of the Act has conferred the power to make rules on the Union Government after consulting the Election Commission for carrying the purpose of the Act. In exercise of such power, the Union Government has promulgated the Registration of Election Rules, 1960.

Section 19 of the Representation of the People Act, 1950 prescribes the conditions of registration viz. (a) not less than eighteen years of age on the qualifying date; and (b) ordinary resident in a constituency. Section 20 of the Act deals with the term 'ordinary resident'. Sub-section thereof provides that "a person shall not be deemed to be ordinarily resident in a constituency on the ground only that he owns; or is in possession of it". It further stipulates that : "a person absenting himself temporarily from his place of ordinary residence shall not by reason thereof, cease to be ordinarily resident therein". Thus the Act only refers to the term "ordinarily resident" and exceptions thereto but it does not exactly define the term. The definition of the term has been left to be decided by the Central Government in consultation with the Election Commission of India through notification to the official gazette. Presently, under the directions of the Election Commission of India, it has been left to the decision of the Electoral Registration officers to decide about the ordinary resident status of a person, desiring to get his name included in the electoral rolls.

The Election Commission has issued direction to the Electoral Registration officers regarding the definition of 'ordinarily resident' which among other things mentions that, 'Persons who have gone out of the country for business or employment should be treated as having moved out of that place. Mere ownership or possession of a building or other immovable property will not allow the owner, the residential qualification. On the other hand, even persons living in sheds, and person living on a pavements in a particular area, do not change the place of residence and are otherwise identifiable. The list includes even students in hostels and leprosy patients. But implicitly it debars NRIs, who are temporarily outside the country.

It was against this background that with the objective of giving voting rights to the Non-Resident Indians, the Representation of the People (Amendment) Bill, 2006 was introduced in the Rajya Sabha on 17 February, 2006. The Government felt that conferring such rights will enable them to participate in the democratic process of elections in their motherland and will also boost their involvement in the nation building. Accordingly, having considered all aspects of their demand, the government proposed to make provision through legislation to enable the Indian citizens, absenting from their place of ordinary residence in India, owing to their employment, education or other occupations outside India, to get their names registered in the electoral rolls of the concerned constituency of their place of ordinary residence in India, had they been in India, so that they would be in a position to cast their votes in elections to the Lok Sabha and to the State Legislatures, in case they happen to be in their constituency at the time of polls. Accordingly the Bill sought to amend section 20 of the Representation of the People Act, 1950. As per Parliamentary practice, the Bill was referred to the Parliamentary Standing Committee on Personnel, Public Grievance, land and Justice by the Chairman, Rajya Sabha on 17 March 2006. The Committee in its sittings, heard the views of the representatives of the Ministry of External Affairs, Home Affairs and Overseas Indian Affairs, Law and Justice and the Election Commission of India. The Committee also studied the memoranda it received from the general public and submitted its report on 2nd August 2006.

After taking into consideration, the views and suggestions received from various quarters and the proposed amendment to the principle Act, the Committee recognised the fact that the Indians living abroad take keen interest in the affairs of the country and are participating in the nation building process through various methods and are also helping in mobilisation of the resources of the country, quoting the Ministry of Law and Justice, while elaborating on the need for conferring voting rights to the NRIs, the report mentioned that the estimated number of persons outside India due to employment is 5 millions and the granting of voting rights will boost their involvement in nation building.

However, the Committee felt that the proposed amendment in its present form has gotten far reaching consequences and may create some problems for a conservative society like India. It further observed that although, a citizen has been defined constitutionally and other categories of citizens in the Citizenship Act, 1955, the term NRI is not statutorily legally defined anywhere and is understood in common prevalence. The

Committee noted that Section 20 of the Representation of the People Act, 1950, already contained a number of exemptions to the term 'ordinary resident' and felt that it would have been more appropriate if all the exemptions were provided in a single exemption clause.

Pravasi Bharatiya Bima Yojana

Government of India had introduced an insurance scheme called the Pravasi Bharatiya Bima Yojana in 2003. This scheme covers a minimum of insurance of Rs.200,000 in the event of death or permanent disability, cost of transportation of the dead body with an attendant, in case of death abroad, provision of air passage in case of non-acceptance by the employer or premature termination, medical cover of a minimum of Rs.50,000 in case of accident or sickness. The Government had also decided to reserve certain percentage of seats across different disciplines, in educational institutions for the children of NRIs, in the Gulf and South-east Asia.

An Investment Friendly Regime

While there is no dearth of area or avenue where PIOs and NRIs can invest their resources, expertise and experiences, the plethora of Special Economic Zones (SEZs) being set up by the Union Government and State Governments independently and/or in collaboration with corporate houses offer excellent opportunities for investments by the overseas Indians. The provisions of the SEZs are a significant improvement upon the earlier scheme of Export Processing Zones, which had a number of bottlenecks. The new Act provides for establishment, development and management of the SEZs for promotion of exports and for matters connected therewith or incidental thereto. Under the provisions of the Act, any person who intends to set up SEZs, may after identifying the area, make a proposal to the State Governments concerned for the purpose of setting up these SEZs. The Act, inter alia provides for foreign collaboration and foreign direct investment (FDI), including investments by persons outside India for setting up a unit. The most attractive feature of the Act, pertaining to SEZs is the provision for single window clearance for setting up such units without hassles.

The government of India is also whole-heartedly committed to create an investment friendly regime to benefit from the human and material resources of the PIOs and NRIs. It is in this connection that the government is taking initiatives to bring about parity so far as FDI is concerned, between the PIOs and NRIs. For instance, the government is all set to usher in a more flexible FDI regime in domestic airlines. The move aims to treat PIOs' investments in domestic airlines at par with NRIs. In all other industries, PIO investments are treated at par with NRI investments, but in domestic airlines ventures, PIO inflows were treated as FDIs, which capped their equity holding at 49%. To rekindle the philanthropic instincts in the PIOs and NRIs, it is essential that such investment friendly policies are sustained and streamlined further.

Overseas Chinese and their contribution to China's Economic Development

There is generally a tendency to compare the role of Chinese and Indian diaspora in the economic development of their respective countries. There are glaring differences between the two countries and their populace. Be that as it may, about 70% of FDI in China in early 1990s, was from Overseas Chinese, mostly in labour intensive export processing sectors such as shoes, toys, electronic sub-assembled, food processing, textiles, Christmas decorations and other items on demand, in export markets and in real estate. Entrepreneurs in Hong Kong, Macau, Taiwan, South Korea and Southeast Asia shifted significant but initially low-technology manufacturing/assembly/export processing operations to Mainland China. About 80% of Hong Kong's labour intensive industry migrated to Southern China. This was followed by larger investments in infrastructure and real estate by bigger conglomerates. The Special Administrative Region of Hong Kong continues to be the main financial conduit for the PRC. The Overseas Chinese Communities' preference for investment reflects each group's historical roots and physical proximity to neighbouring provinces on Mainland China. The coastal areas account for about 75% of total FDI, with Guangdong alone accounting for 30% of total FDI. Hong Kong FDI mostly goes to the adjacent province of Guangdong, which has the same language, Cantonese. Taiwanese investors preferred neighbouring Fujian. Investment flowed to the coastal areas because of the export oriented character of FDI and because it minimised the costs of transporters. Later investors also preferred coastal locations, which by then had developed infrastructural facilities.

NRI Investment

As contrasted with China, investment by the Indian diaspora comes from the foreign remittances, mostly from the Gulf region. Yet another important aspect of the inflow of money from the Non-Resident Indians is that the NRIs have emerged as the largest overseas lender to India, surpassing traditional sources such as multilateral and bilateral foreign agencies. Throughout the 1990s and early part of this millennium, funds from multilateral organisations such as the World Bank, formed a major chunk of India's outstanding external debt. Since then, however, NRI deposits in India have grown manifold and they now form the largest share of the country's external debt.

The Homeward Mobility: The Return of the Native

If the Chinese, all along, held the view that they are only 'sojourners' to eventually 'return' to the motherland, the clock has turned the full circle in India, ushering in the reverse migration and now there is the phenomenon called 'brain-gain' instead of 'brain-drain' of the earlier decades of the Independent India. The process of reverse migration eloquently speaks of the churning process of social transformation of Non-Resident Indians which is so poignantly captured in Ashutosh Gowarikar's captivating movie 'Swadesh' and the character portrayed so well by Sharukh Khan. The homeward mobility of NRIs has started with a social message loud and clear - India Calling!

There is no dearth of such stories of philanthropy and social commitment. Vikram Akula, MA from Yale, Ph. D from University of Chicago and a Fullbright Scholar, threw away a promising and lucrative career in the affluent society of the USA and returned to India to set up Swayam Krushi Sangham (SKS), now internationally recognised as one of the world's fastest-growing micro finance institution. Akula is the founder and CEO of SKS which has disbursed Rs.240 crores to cover 2.2 lakh women across India. Time magazine, too, has added him in its list of the world's 100 most influential people. It won't be a surprise if he gets a Magassasy Award for his contribution to social service.

Yet another example of such supreme sacrifice and commitment is the duo Ramesh and Swati Ramanathan who returned from abroad to Bangalore to set up Janagraha, an NGO for improving the quality of public governance. Ramesh, an MBA from Yale was MD, Citi Bank, London and Swati a successful design professional when they decided to come back. Today Janagraha is credited with a large number of civic society initiatives. Over 5,000 volunteers have given their time, and over one lakh citizens have participated in its activities. The stories of Akula and Ramesh and Swati Ramanathan are only illustrative and certainly not exhaustive. Now there are many NGOs, directly and indirectly funded by the NRIs which are doing exceedingly good work in social sector. The graduates of IITs, IIMs and other prestigious and premier universities and institutions of India, who are abroad, are also contributing significantly to the sectors like education and health. They have also contributed generously during crises such as the Latur earthquake, the super cyclone in Orissa, the earthquake in Gujarat and during the Tsunami. These developments speak volumes for their philanthropy and social concern and commitment.

References

Primary and Secondary Sources

1. Report of the High Level Committee on Indian Diaspora, Indian Council of World Affairs, 2001.
2. Constitution of the People's Republic of China.
3. Constitution of India.
4. Representation of People's Act, 1960.
5. Report of the Department Related Parliamentary Standing Committee on Home Affairs (107th Report), 2003, Rajya Sabha Secretariat.
6. Report of the Department Related Parliamentary Standing Committee on Personnel, Public Grievance, Law and Justice, 2006, Rajya Sabha Secretariat.
7. Annual Report of Ministry of Overseas Indian Affairs, 2005-06.
8. Lok Sabha Debates.
9. Rajya Sabha Debates.

10. Judith, Brown, *Global South Asians: Introducing the Modern Diaspora.*
11. Dubey, Ajay (Ed.), *Indian Diaspora, Global Identity*, Kalinga Publications, New Delhi, 2003.
12. Ghosh, Papiya, *Partition and the South Asian Diaspora*, Routledge, London, 2007.
13. Lal, Brij V., *Encyclopedia of Indian Diaspora*, Oxford University Press, New Delhi, 2007.
14. Lal, M.C., *India's Missed Opportunity: India's Relationship with Non-Resident Indians*, Ashgate, Hamsphire, 2001.
15. Rajan, M.S. (Ed.) *India's Foreign Relations during the Nehru Era*, Asia Publishing House, 1976.

Yang Xiaoping & Zhang Guihong

The Road to Global Zero Perspectives from China and India

Introduction

In 1964, when China exploded her first atomic bomb, Chairman Mao advocated the complete prohibition and thorough destruction of nuclear weapons and undertook unconditionally, the decision not to use or threaten to use nuclear weapons against non-nuclear-weapon states or nuclear-weapon-free zones[1]. In 1988, at the United Nations General Assembly, India's Prime Minister Rajiv Gandhi presented a time-bound action plan for achieving nuclear weapon free world and called for a world, free of nuclear weapons[2]. And on September 23, 2009, during his speech to the United Nations General Assembly, the U.S. President Obama proposed to "outline a comprehensive agenda to seek the goal of a world without nuclear weapons and to support efforts to strengthen the NPT." [3]

However, without abolishing the nuclear weapons and undertaking universal nuclear disarmament, a world free of nuclear weapons seems just like a utopia. Therefore, is there any road towards global zero? What might be the possible path ways?

This paper first defines global zero as a kind of compact and manageable state and then explains the reasons why we should move forward towards it in the context of changing geopolitical environment and the new forms of threats. Subsequently, it examines the on-path obstacles towards nuclear free world from the strategic perspectives of both China and India, and

---

[1] Renmin Ribao (People Daily), 1964-10-22.

[2] http://www.indianembassy.org/policy/Disarmament/disarm15.htm

[3] http://www.whitehouse.gov/the_press_office/Remarks-by-the-President-to-the-United-Nations General-Assembly

reassesses the role of nuclear deterrence in the post-Cold War era. Finally, the paper explores the possible pathways guided by the idea of comprehensive governance. It argues that governance-orientated nuclear disarmament, balance between respect and monitoring and regional security, community building on the basis of mutual trust and confidence are very important on the road towards global zero, although the goal might be decades ahead.

What is Global Zero?

Global zero refers to the worldwide elimination of a weapons system, especially nuclear weapons.[4] In practice, it is often associated with nuclear disarmament or the worldwide elimination of nuclear weapons in arms control discourse. As a long-term agenda, global zero is not quite as simple as it may appear. The total elimination of nuclear weapons means much more than just dismantling all those in existence at the time. Instead, it has to include a package of arrangements and monitoring methods on all fissile materials removed from nuclear weapons, delivery system being dismantled in parallel to the destruction of warheads, as well as the dismantlement of military fissile material production facilities.[5]

Characteristically, global zero is a kind of state in which each state's security concerns are assured and all threats become more manageable in a geopolitical environment that is genuinely cooperative. It's not zero-sum thinking, but rather something like the idea described as a harmonious world.[6] Any measure towards it would certainly help the world create an environment in which other steps such as conventional arms control, restriction on modernisation of weaponry, placement of weapons in space, enforcement of highest standards for security of nuclear materials, creation of a global security system, etc. will become possible.

Why Zero: Nuclear Armaments as an Unmanageable Global Threat

Whether in the past or present, nuclear weapons are the most brutal

---

[4] http://en.wikipedia.org/wiki/Global_Zero

[5] See reference of the report "Eliminating Nuclear Threats" by International Commission on Nuclear Non-Proliferation and Disarmament, available at http://www.icnnd.com

[6] http://www.un.org/chinese/focus/wen/ga.shtml

weapons we have ever conceived, inherently indiscriminate in killing and maiming and leaving a lethal and fatal impact for generations to come. The World War II has proved the brutality of these weapons, for it devoured nearly one hundred million people in just a few minutes. Their use by anyone at any time, whether by accident, miscalculation or design, would be catastrophic for the whole planet. Compared with global warming or climate change, nuclear weapons have the capacity to destroy the whole life on this planet, and the arsenals we now possess are capable of doing this, many times over.

The changing international political ecology requires us to rethink the role of nuclear deterrence. During the Cold War, driven by the most primitive impulse of each state for absolute security, the emergence of nuclear weapons was thought to bring world peace through its specific deterrence effect. However, just as described by the Game Theory, the emergence of nuclear weapons actually resulted in security dilemma in which all states pursued security by the possession of nuclear weapons, but proved to be insecure all the time. Distinctively, each state's search for absolute security has in practice made or would make this world more insecure, unstable and immoral, because so long as any state possesses nuclear weapons, others will want them, no matter whether in the name of security consideration or other reasons. Therefore, as long as any such weapons exist, it defies credibility that they will not be used one day, by accident, miscalculation or design. This is the precondition of the deterrence effect.

In the 21st century, historical border disputes, ethnic and religious conflicts, as well as socio-economic problems have become much more complicated and complex due to the emergence of non-state actors and the fear of their getting easier access to nuclear technology and fissile materials. Nuclear non-proliferation has faced unprecedented challenges due to the failure of existing nuclear powers to commit themselves to real disarmament, and the incapability of international regime to prevent new states from acquiring nuclear weapons, as well as the inefficiency of the international community to stop any terrorist or any other non-state actors from getting access to such weapons. During the Nuclear Security Summit in Washington D.C in April 2009, there was consensus among the participants that the threat of nuclear terrorism has become real and that all responsible members of the world community should have a stake in ensuring comprehensive nuclear security. In his speech at the summit, while highlighting non-traditional security issues, Chinese President Hu Jintao clearly stated that "the potential threats of nuclear terrorism could not be ignored. The risks of the loss and illicit trafficking of fissile materials were increasing. It has become an important task facing all countries to properly deal with the challenges of nuclear safety, to protect the sustained and healthy development of nuclear energy and to maintain world peace and stability."[7]

While deliberating on global security in the 21st century, Paul Rogers posits that in the 21st century, new forms of conflicts primarily stem from three sources. The first is "potential source of conflict stems from a greater likelihood of increased human migration arising from economic, social and especially environmental desperation." The second area of conflict concerns "environmental factors, especially the control of physical resources." The last relates to "anti-elite violence, because an economically polarised and increasingly constrained global system will result in competitive and violent responses by the disempowered, both within and between states."[8] All these threats and challenges must be tackled with much more conviction and effectiveness than the world has managed so far, as people across the globe are linked with a shared fate.

Assessing the on-path Obstacles: Chinese and Indian Perspectives

Global zero should be the ultimate goal of the international community. However, when one focusses on primary and intermediate steps towards the nuclear free world, the primary concern is to diagnose the risks and obstacles on its path. In China's and India's context, it could be the national interests and strategic utility of the nuclear weapons in national Defence strategy on either side of the Himalayas, especially China's Taiwan issue and its sincere adherence to the No-First-Use (NFU) doctrine and NPT commitments, as well as India's view of nuclear weapons as a symbol of big

---

[7] Hu Jintao, "Work together on nuclear security challenges to promote world peace and stability" (xieshou yingdui he anquan tiaozhan, gongtong cujin shijie heping yu fazhan), http://www.fmcoprc.gov.hk/chn/wj/wjxw/t679411.htm

[8] Paul Rogers, Losing Control: Global Security in the Twenty-First Century, London: Pluto Press, 2002(second edition), pp.96-97.

power, and its practical consideration to pin down Pakistan.

On the one hand, in the context of globalisation, China and India have some shared national interest in the following aspects. First, both nations are focussing on domestic economic growth and development that requires a stable regional and international environment. Second, both have adhered to an independent foreign policy. Third, both are countering terrorism and actively participating in regional and global security cooperation. Finally, both require international flexibility and tolerance for their future developments as emerging powers, whether in the fields of energy, marine, space, soft power or other domains.

On the other hand, when specifically focussing on India's and China's perspectives on national interests, geopolitical factors should never be ignored, for the real nuclear disarmament has to be conducted in a long-term and holistic manner. Because of the unsettled territory problem between China and India, the long-term rivalry between India and Pakistan and traditional strategic ties between China and Pakistan, India is apprehensive of China's interest and intention in South Asia, though China's goal is to develop all-round relations with both India and Pakistan.

India not only considers its nuclear programme as a symbol of a big power, but also a way to balance China. From this point of view, it could be understood that the nuclear doctrine of both India and China is to maintain a credible minimum deterrence. The motivation behind it is the belief that credible deterrence is important for strategic stability, and by extension, for national survival.

In light of the above, the main obstacles on the path would be the following:

First, the U.S. and Russia refuse to follow the unconditional commitment to no-first-use policy. In 1964, when China exploded her first atomic bomb, it advocated not to use or threaten to use nuclear weapons against non-nuclear-weapon states or nuclear-weapon-free zones. China has always exercised utmost restraint on the question of using nuclear weapons. As far as other big powers are concerned, Moscow, after recognising its relative weakness vis-à-vis U.S. after the end of the Cold War in 1993, formally rescinded the no-first-use policy inherited from the Soviet Union (initially adopted in 1983). Now both the U.S. and Russian nuclear doctrines run contrary to the agreement of a No-First-Use Treaty. The United States, because it employs its nuclear weapons as a deterrent to chemical attacks, believes that an NFU policy could undermine deterrence. The U.S. didn't change its stated stand during the recently concluded nuclear security summit. As far as Russia is concerned, its nuclear forces are called upon to deter conventional conflicts.[9]

Second, American ratification of the CTBT is critically needed, as it could be regarded as a circuit-breaker and would have an immediate impact on other hold-out states and add a major yet new momentum to both the disarmament and non-proliferation efforts. Obama has stated that "my administration will immediately and aggressively pursue U.S. ratification"[10] of the CTBT. Beijing has also not ratified the treaty. India's perspective on this treaty has also been changing. Initially, India perceived that instead of being a step towards the eventual elimination of nuclear weapons, the CTBT only appeared to drive nuclear testing into the laboratories. Modernisation of existing arsenals is likely to continue through computer simulations by nuclear weapon states having such technological capability. Other states not equipped with such capabilities will have to freeze their weaponisation at current levels. Overall, there appears to be little willingness on the part of the NWS to actually give up their nuclear arsenals. But now this posture is changing.

Third, the universal compliance and enforcement of NPT has a long way to go. These challenges mainly cover three aspects: 1) the proliferation of nuclear materials to non-state actors and the fear of nuclear terrorism. Currently, the threat of terror groups acquiring nuclear technology has grown immensely and the failure of NPT appears imminent. In present times, the sense of panic over nuclear dangers is exacerbated by the acquisition of nuclear weapons by "states of proliferation concern" that perceive an asymmetric advantage in this weapon against a more powerful

---

[9] Cristina Hansell; Nikita Perfilyev, "Together Towards Nuclear Zero", p. 15, http://pdfserve.informaworld.com/171464__915796781.pdf

[10] "Remarks by President Barack Obama," April 5, 2009.

adversary and the growing apprehension of possible use of nuclear terrorism by non-state actors. These cannot be adequately addressed through classical deterrence, no matter how credible it might be. 2) The universal acceptance and compliance to NPT, especially the non-peaceful-purpose use of fissile material, nuclear materials, equipment and technology. Ironically, only four states like India, Pakistan, Israel and North Korea are out of it, but are known to be nuclear weapons capable states.[11] 3) The measures to strengthen NPT safeguards and verification, compliance and enforcement have not been very effective.

Last but not least, the trust and confidence building measures between key states, between highly-equipped nuclear states and lowly-equipped ones as well as between NWS and NNWS is yet to be strengthened. Now what is required is that the leaders should transcend the zero-sum thinking and learn to base their security on mutual trust rather than mutual fear. As we know, the primary motivation for nuclear proliferation is always a need to respond to a security threat perception. Once a state feels threatened by the nuclear capability or an overwhelming conventional superiority of another state, there is seldom any other way in which it can better address the security deficit than by developing nuclear weapons of its own to have deterrence. Nuclear weapons are increasingly seen as providing insurance against regime change imposed from outside the state, especially against the forcible changes of regime/rulers. Thus in practice, one of the reasons why some states refused to join the NPT or ratify the CTBT is that they fear they may be cheated to make commitments to remain non-nuclear at the expense of their security concerns. Therefore, providing security assurances, and engaging more states in arms control talks at some point might be a promising pathway towards understanding and trust building.

The Possible Pathways: Comprehensive Governance

As expounded in the preceding sections, the global zero, by definition, demands that the nuclear free world should include a package of arrangements for disarmament, non-proliferation and so on. The possible pathways should have the capability to create an environment in which all

[11]Manpreet Sethi, "Building Credibility for a Nuclear Weapon Free World", Delhi Policy Group Working Paper for ICNND, 31 July 2009.

the desirable steps become possible. Going by the above obstacles, the responses of states seemed pretty weak. Therefore, the states, still as the major players in international community, are faced with a critical choice between losing control and opting to cooperative global governance.

Hence, it is extremely important or rather necessary to develop a new paradigm to enhance peace and limit conflict. And, in the centre, there must be a process of enhancing common global security based on action to be taken to reverse the socio-economic polarisation (some believe a world free of nuclear weapons is a world free of hegemony[12]), enhance sustainable economic development and control processes of proliferation and militarisation.[13] This is the general definition of good governance. And the basis for global good governance, I hold, is the encompassing interests between various states. Mancur Olsen once identified encompassing interests as the basis for different groups to work together.[14] In this chapter, encompassing interests mainly refer to the sufficiently broad interest to include those of the other party, as also to such situations in which good outcomes of the interaction between two parties will benefit both while bad results of interaction jeopardise each other.[15]

Therefore, in order to realise a global zero, there should be a governance-oriented nuclear disarmament, or disarmament through governance at the centre, in which top states such as the US and Russia should play the leading role. We all know nuclear disarmament is indispensable, but we are all too shy to vote the leaders out. Firstly, to achieve a global zero, the international community has to achieve significant and permanent cuts in US-Russian arms stocks, and more importantly, the real disarmament, which would not only include a serious reduction in their nuclear stockpiles,

---

[12] Zhongguo zhengzuo touhao qiangguo xu baochi chaoren lixing yu lengjing http://mil.news.sina.com.cn/2010-02-16/1231584340_1.html

[13] See reference, Paul Rogers, Losing Control: Global Security In the Twenty-First Century, Pluto Press, 2002, p.119.

[14] Mancur Olson, *Power and Prosperity: Outgrowing Communist and Capitalist Dictatorships*, New York: Basic Books, 2000.

[15] For more about the definition of encompassing interest and evidence of its importance, see *Olson, Power and Prosperity: Outgrowing Communist and Capitalist Dictatorships*, New York: Basic Books, 2000,

but also include an agreement on a test ban as well as talks on a Fissile Material Cut-off Treaty including other nuclear states. As the US and Russia together possess more than 90% of the world's nuclear weaponry, initial commitments must be made in both Washington and Moscow to lead the global nuclear disarmament effort by example. Secondly, all states should sign and ratify the Comprehensive Nuclear-Test-Ban Treaty (CTBT) unconditionally and without delay. The US ratification is critically needed for circuit-break, for it would have an immediate impact on other hold-out states, and add a major and new momentum to both disarmament and non-proliferation efforts.

Then, good governance also means the balance between respect and monitoring, between rights and obligations. The rise of emerging powers globally is an irreversible reality, paralleling with it are the huge demands for energy and the increasing climate changes. Therefore, the right to peacefully use nuclear technology should be respected, while the global cooperation on the nuclear technology safeguards could be enhanced. The role of NPT and FMCT should be emphasised and as an interim step, all nuclear-armed states should voluntarily declare their fissile material stocks and the amount regarded as excess to their weapons needs, they should place such excess material under IAEA safeguards as soon as practicable. At the same time, some basic principles should be reconfirmed, such as accepting universal no first use, and thus extending those assurances to NWS and concluding a Convention on Prohibition on Use or Threat of Use of Nuclear Weapons. Otherwise, some states would be skeptical of most recent initiatives that emphasise arms control and non-proliferation but do not appear willing to go the full distance to zero. They would conceive of such measures not as ends in themselves, but as milestones towards the final destination of a truly Nuclear Weapon Free World. It should be fair and non-discriminatory.

Lastly, for those who have strategic geopolitical worries and distrust, sense of common security should be reassured and creating and sustaining such a politically and militarily stable world must be the underlying goal. If we could make the geopolitical environment more manageable, then there is a scope for genuine cooperation. In this context, the development of regional security community is very important from both China's and

India's perspectives, though the formation of regional security community requires trust building to promote a transformation of identities. To achieve global zero, security communities hold the key because they promise to replace nuclear threats by a new international politics in which force would be delegitimised as an instrument of state policy, although it may take decades to materialise.

Conclusion

Global zero not only means dismantling of all existing nuclear weapons, but also refers to a package of arrangements and monitoring methods. It is a kind of state in which each state's security concerns are assured and all threats become more manageable in a geopolitical environment that is increasingly and genuinely cooperative.

A world free of nuclear weapons is the natural result of global good governance in which top states play a leading role in governance-orientated nuclear disarmament, flexibilities are accorded to balance between respect and monitoring, and regional security community is built on the basis of trust and confidence building. For comprehensive governance, the basis includes, but not restricts to, the peaceful co-existence of different countries, the respect for diversified cultures as well as different development models, the non-use of force, and more importantly, the new understanding and conception of security and the role of nuclear weapons in the 21st century.

In order to make global zero, the ultimate goal for a better tomorrow, the advocators of disarmament, whether governmental, scientific, military, academic or non-governmental, all must come together to demand immediate action for the total abolition of nuclear weapons.

C. Raja Mohan

Power and Paradox: The Future of Sino-Indian Relations

Introduction

The world is witnessing the simultaneous rise of its two largest nations, China and India. Although the emergence of India is not as spectacular as that of China, it is significant enough to affect the geopolitics of the various sub-regions of Asia, influence the great power relations and contribute to systemic change in international relations. It has been recognised for a while that the rise of China and India was inevitable and that together they might change the world in many ways. But the perception of the scale, pace and consequences of the emergence of China and India as great powers has become more acute since the financial crisis that rocked the world at the turn of this decade. The slowdown of the Western economies, especially those of Europe and Japan, and the continuing relative decline of Russia has meant that China and India will catch up and overtake most of the developed economies much earlier than anticipated. The improved economic standing of China and India, in turn, will allow the two countries to devote significant resources to military modernisation, and beef up their hard power capabilities. Both countries will also steadily improve their soft power resources and bring greater weight to their diplomacy and cultural influence. Meanwhile, the sheer size of their billion plus populations and expanding economic weight would produce massive systemic impact on a range of issues - from energy, environment, and resource security to regional institutions and global governance. The world must also accept that China and India - given the sense of their own exceptionalism and a strong belief in their 'manifest destiny'- have more than the necessary political will to become great powers and shape world politics in this century. How exactly China and India may change the world will depend on two important factors. One is the kind of purpose that China and India might attach to their increasing power capabilities. Will their policies be similar to those of

France and Britain in the 19th century? Or would they look like America and the Soviet Union in the 20th century? Or may China and India become very different type of great powers? The other factor is the nature of the relationship between the two Asian giants. This short essay is a reflection on whether China and India would be partners or rivals. This question animates not just the strategic communities in Beijing and Delhi but the whole world, for the dynamic between the two giants could become the defining dynamic of the international system in the 21st century.

The Paradox

Even before they constituted themselves as modern states - India (1947) and China (1949) - the national movements in the two countries and their intellectual leaders reached out to each other to find enduring bases for cooperation. As two great civilizational states emerging out of colonialism, the Chinese and Indian nationalists believed, they were destined to reshape Asia and the world. That was the essence of the understanding that Jawaharlal Nehru arrived at when he met the Chinese delegations at anti-colonial congress in Brussels in 1927. After that the Indian national movement signalled its solidarity with the Chinese people as they resisted the Japanese occupation. Yet as the Second World War engulfed them, the Chinese and Indian national liberation movements found it impossible to cooperate. The structure of great power conflict in Asia and the fact that India and China faced different imperial powers prevented political cooperation between the two national movements. As Japan advanced closer to the Subcontinent in the 1940s, Britain got Chiang Kai-shek to travel to India and urge the Indian nationalists to ease their confrontation against London and focus on the war effort against Tokyo. The Indian leaders, including Gandhi, refused. At the intellectual level too, the big ideas that moved China and India did not always match, and despite their common struggle to cope with the new domination of the West, they did not see eye to eye on critical political and philosophical assumptions.

In the early years after claiming their independent nationhood, India and China once again embarked on a new effort to build political cooperation. Their romanticism was marked by the slogan of 'Hindi-Chini Bhai-Bhai' in the 1950s. Yet by the late 1950s, the turbulence in Tibet and their unresolved boundary dispute began to sour the relationship which culminated in a brief military conflict at the end of 1962. This was followed by a prolonged chill until efforts were made to normalise the bilateral relations in the 1980s. Through the final years of the Cold War, India and China were ranged on the opposite sides of the divide. While Chinese communists drew closer to the United States after their split from the Soviet Comrades, the democratic India found itself embracing the Russian Communists. While the boundary dispute dominated the relationship, China and India found that their world views were radically different, and their interests clashed in Southeast Asia and South Asia, as also their differences on the future of the security order in Asia and the Indian Ocean were strong. No wonder that Sino-Indian relations in the 20th century were characterised as 'protracted contest' and an unending rivalry.

As the 21st century dawned, Sino-Indian relations seemed to enter one of their best ever phases. The normalisation efforts in the final years of the 20th century seemed to bear fruit as two-way trade between the two countries galloped from barely 2 bn dollars in 1998 to nearly 60 billion in 2010. Sustained high level exchanges and broadening people- to-people contacts were supplemented by important efforts at military confidence building and a political effort at resolving the all important boundary dispute. Yet, the notion of an all-encompassing rivalry began to take hold of their bilateral relationship. Some have seen this rivalry rooted in the relentless logic of geography. Since they shared the same space in Asia and both nations sought to expand their influence on the nations across their borders, a contestation for influence in Central Asia, South Asia, and Southeast Asia became inevitable. The competition was not limited to land spaces but also extended to the Indian Ocean and the Western Pacific Ocean, as China and India with their new focus on trade, sought to protect their now vital sea lanes of communication. Nor was the rivalry limited to their immediate environments. It expressed itself in far flung places from Siberia in the Russian Far East to Columbia in Latin America and from Africa to the South Pacific, as Beijing and Delhi chased each other's tail in search of vital natural resources - both energy and mineral - far from their shores.

Mitigating the Rivalry

In their enhanced bilateral engagement at the turn of the 21st century, both China and India have sought to downplay the prospects for mutual rivalry. They continually declared that they were not a threat to each other. They also insisted that there was enough space in the world for the peaceful rise of both China and India, and that cooperation between themselves would be critical for the emergence of the Asian century. For all these, formal statement of these propositions and deepening mutual economic links, China and India constantly sought to limit the influence of the other. Despite the tall talk of building "Chindia", what has emerged in the last few years is an unmitigated rivalry. Delhi's traditional fears of China encircling it in the Subcontinent through special relationships with India's neighbours has increased rather than decreased in the 21st century. In the past India's focus was China's strategic partnership with Pakistan; it now extends to Beijing's relationships with Nepal, Bhutan, Bangladesh, Burma and Sri Lanka. Similarly, Beijing is looking warily at India's expanding naval and military profile in the South China Sea.

In their attempt to hedge against each other's rise, Beijing and New Delhi found that their bilateral relationship was increasingly sensitive to their relationships with other major powers. Both have used their relationships with the United States, Japan, and Russia to gain advantage over the other. As a consequence, the fear of hostile strategic alignments by the other has gained ground in both capitals and laid the basis for what international relations theorists call the "security dilemma". What one nation sees as a necessary step in protecting its own interests is seen by the other as an aggressive move to undercut its positions. The security dilemma thus sets off the two mutually suspicious nations on an ever escalating competition, resulting in reduced security for both.

The notion of a Sino-Indian rivalry is not new. What makes it different and consequential today are a number of factors. Rising China and emerging India are more powerful nations today on the cusp of great power status, have interests that are wide-ranging, are driven by a strong nationalist impulse, have staked their domestic political legitimacy on their ability to sustain high rates of growth, which in turn, depends on their ability to achieve external objectives in an increasingly inter-connected world. They have repeatedly found themselves at odds in reshaping regional and international institutions. India has been wary of China's increasing influence in the South Asian Association of Regional Cooperation. Beijing in turn, has sought to limit India's role in East Asian institutions. Delhi and Beijing have also clashed over the reform of the global nuclear and the

United Nations Security Council. The world is watching very closely the unfolding rivalry between the rising Asian giants. If the rivalry ends up in war or conflict, it is bound to diminish both China and India. While the talk of a grand eastern alliance between Beijing and Delhi was always far-fetched, the big question is whether the two can manage their competition by keeping it limited and peaceful. Without the wisdom to do so, China and India will find it difficult to realise their larger global aspirations.

Re-making the World

Six decades ago when China and India reconnected with the world as modern and free republics, they had a huge problem coming to terms with the existing international order that was dominated by the Western powers. As two great civilizational states, China and India had a sense of their self-importance despite the extreme underdevelopment that marked their societies. It was not easy, therefore, for Beijing and Delhi to seek a special place in the world. China and India, after all, had endured an extended period of relative decline amidst the rise of Europe and the West in the previous centuries. In the middle of the twentieth century, the Chinese and Indian economies were burdened by widespread poverty and their large populations were under-equipped to participate in the world economy. As a result, China and India constantly found themselves either having to obey the diktat of other powers or defy them at considerable cost. After much trial and error, China and India found a way to grow their economies rapidly. Three decades of high growth rates since the late 1970s have made China the world's second largest economy. India which followed a similar path a decade later, is on track to become the second fastest growing economy after China.

As their relative economic gains make them great powers, Beijing and Delhi now have the power and responsibility to reshape the world. No future set of international rules will be sustainable without the explicit support of Beijing and Delhi. That is quite visible in the current international negotiations on global warming. It will be even more evident in the coming decades as China and India position themselves at the top of the global power hierarchy. Peaceful coexistence and deeper bilateral cooperation between China and India, then, are the principal preconditions for a stable and sustainable world order in the 21st century.

Binod Singh

India-China relations: Could trade and economics pave way for the strategic cooperation?

In this chapter, the author argues that if Sino-Indian relations are steaming ahead today, this is largely because trade has become a key engine of diplomacy between the two countries. Developing a long-term economic partnership between India and China requires conducive political atmosphere where the mutual investment could be guaranteed and current restrictions on mutual investments are removed. This chapter has attempted to provide rationales as to why China and India should engage each other and endeavour towards building a trustful relationship. India and China will benefit more from their engagement rather than showing indifference or the 'psychological warfare' or the so called policies of 'containment'. The chapter also emphasises the historical cultural links between the two countries and concludes that the rising economic engagement between the two countries will enhance the bilateral and regional peace and stability and will also lead to a possible but far-distant solution of the border demarcation.

Introduction

In the 21st century, India has emerged as one of the three major economic powers in Asia along with China and Japan. From being an insignificant member of the world economy in 1990, today, India has emerged to be the world's third largest economy in terms of purchasing power parity (PPP). For the last one decade, it has been the fastest growing economy next only to China. India is also an important economy of the BRICS[1]

---

[1] A much quoted study by Goldman Sachs identified Brazil, Russia, India and China (BRIC) as the set of large emerging market countries projected to grow rapidly over the next thirty years. South Africa was invited to join the group in 2010 at Sanya conference, since then it became BRICS.

countries and is already playing an important role in the global economy. India will host the next BRICS Summit in New Delhi in 2012, bringing together the leaders of Brazil, Russia, India, China and South Africa. This will be the fourth BRICS Summit. Earlier Summits were held in Russia (Yekaterinburg, 2009), Brazil (Brasilia, 2010) and China (Sanya, 2011).

India and China are the two largest developing countries in Asia with a long history of cultural exchange between them. China is India's largest neighbour, sharing over 4000 km long Himalayan border area, the dispute over which led to a short-term border conflict in 1962. Since then, there is mutual distrust prevailing among the two countries. But in the recent times, booming bilateral trade, increasing people-to-people contact, and a sustained exchange of high-level visits indicate maturing of the ties. Recent scholarship has focussed on China and India as the world's fastest growing economies, their expanding bilateral trade, and the vast potential for closer cooperation.[2] There is, however, little attention devoted to what prevented cooperation in the past, how economic engagement factors into their respective grand strategy and how it influences the scope, pace and context of bilateral economic interaction. In recent years, the scholars of international political economy[3] had been asking each other one common question: will India and China trust each other, and sit down on a negotiating table for serious business between them? The two Asian giants, however, have recently realised the importance of economic cooperation at bilateral as well as international level.

What we notice is that in the first half decade of the twenty first century, a silent revolution is taking place in the economic realm between China and India, which is set to transform the political engagement between the two countries. The profound impact of increased economic interaction could be seen in almost each and every aspect of India-China bilateral relations. Increased trade between them transformed not only the bilateral relations but regional cooperation as well. However, despite these achievements there is still a huge potential for further increase of the bilateral

---

[2] The debate over China and India was fuelled by an article written by Professor Tarun Khanna of Harvard Business School, and professor Huang Yasheng of MIT (now at Harvard), which appeared in the Foreign Policy, 2003.

[3] See various articles published by Jhon Garver, and also Jonathan Hoslag.

trade between the two giants. We have not been able to realise this potential due to political roadblocks and some attitudinal problems from both the sides in equal measure. This paper is an attempt to address some of these political economic issues and provides some remedies and suggestions. The paper is divided into the following parts. First review of current economic relations between the two giants. Secondly rationale for a deeper economic engagement between the two. Thirdly the specifics of current and proposed engagement, including respective strengths and weaknesses. Finally the elements of current cooperation and competition, vis-à-vis the security considerations of both the countries.

Background of the Economic engagements

Sino-Indian economic engagement has a short history but a sharply rising trajectory. Although the two had signed an accord in 1984, granting MFN status to each other, bilateral trade was only about $332 million until 1992. It has grown steadily since then, except during 1998-99 following the Indian nuclear tests, reaching $5 billion in 2002, and $ 69 billion in 2011.[4] The target set for 2015 is 100 billion, which seems quite achievable in due time. China now ranks as India's largest trading partner, although India remains a distant 15th in China's foreign trade statistics. Between 1991 and 2005, India's share of world trade just increased from 0.4 percent to 1 percent,[5] whereas in the same period, the Chinese export share increased from 2 percent to currently 6 percent of the global trade. In each of the last three years, the increase in China's foreign trade has exceeded India's total foreign trade. Growing at high rate for decades, by the year 2010, China has already emerged as the world's largest trading nation and its GDP has surpassed that of Japan to become the world's second largest economy. India is still catching up as a trading nation and it continues to face a major competition from Chinese products in the global export market.

[4] Data taken from the Website of the Embassy of India in Beijing. www.indianembassy.org.cn; Last accessed on Dec .22, 2011.

[5] It is interesting to note here that just after independence in 1950,India's share was 2 percent in the global trade. But then it declined continuously and started rising only after 1991 reforms. At the end of 2008, China leads India on share of world exports of goods (8% versus 3%) and services (3.1 % versus 2.7 %), share of global manufacturing (13% versus 2%), current account surplus ($380 versus negative $23billion), foreign exchange reserves ($2000 billion versus $400billion), GDP in terms of PPP ($ 8trillion versus $2.4 trillion) and per capita GDP ($1800 versus $900).

India and China had also denied their market to each other due to estranged relations since the late 1950s. Hence there was a need felt among the two countries to open to each other and start a relation based on mutual benefit which has been termed as Buy-Buy relations.

Since the 1980s, India realised that it needs to engage China and the rapprochement came from Indira Gandhi when she met the Chinese envoy in Geneva and gave some signals for resuming the dialogue between the two Asian giants. Later her son and India's Prime Minister, Rajiv Gandhi visited Beijing in 1988 and together with Deng Xiaoping, dreamed of 21st century being the "Chindia"[6] century. Since then, their bilateral relations have been furthered by incremental measures with several high-level exchange visits. But, India's Pokharan-II test and its possible explanation by the then Indian defence minister George Fernandes, once again derailed the trust building exercise initiated decades ago. It was Prime Minister Mr. Vajpayee who visited China in 2003 and laid a road map for increased economic engagement between China and India. The bilateral trade volume between the two nations rose from 3 billion USD per annum to more than 69 billion USD at the end of 2011. As a result of this, China has been the largest trading partner of India for several years.[7] In fact, after China's entry to WTO, the growth in Sino-Indian relations has been miraculous. The

[6] Chindia is a portmanteau word that refers to China and India together in general and their economies in particular. It was coined by Indian Congress Party Politician, Jairam Ramesh in 2005.

[7] In 2009, China has emerged as largest trading partner of India by replacing USA. According to the figures provided by China Customs, India-China bilateral trade in 2008 totalled US$ 51.8 billion, which was an increase of 34% year-on-year. In 2008, Indian exports to China touched US$ 20.3 billion, rising by 39% over the figure for 2007. Chinese exports in the same period have expanded by 31% to reach US$ 31.5 billion. In the last five years, the total value of trade has increased almost seven fold from US$7.59 billion in 2003 to US$51.85 billion in 2008. This represents an increase of around 583%. During the last five years, the Chinese exports to India increased from US$3.34 billion to US$ 31.51 billion which is nearly a ten fold increase. While the export from India to China has also increased, it has been a fivefold increase from US$4.25 billion in 2003 to US$20.34 billion in 2008. This would reinforce the fact that bilateral trade has been increasing and rate of growth of Chinese exports to India has been maintaining a steady pace.In 2008, the growth rate of Chinese exports to India stood at 31.21%, which was highest in the top ten destinations of Chinese exports. The global financial crisis of 2007-09, has impacted the bilateral trade between our two countries. In the first six months of 2009, bilateral trade stood at US$19.61 billion, which is a decline of 32% y-o-y. Indian exports to China in Jan-June 2009 stood at US$ 6.60 billion, declining by 50%. In comparison, the Chinese exports to India during the first six months of this year stood at US$13.01 billion, declining by only 16%. The value of Chinese exports during this period is double the Indian exports, which in turn is almost equal to the size of India's trade deficit with China during this period which stood at US$6.41 billion. (All data from ADB website)

trade between them has grown at the rate of 60% annually. Indian Tariff towards Chinese products and anti-dumping measures has reduced significantly in the recent years. Still, India has filed the maximum number of anti-dumping cases against China at the WTO.

In order to solve trade disputes between them, both India and China have regular dialogue to discuss trade related issues. India has several bilateral dialogue mechanisms with China, including the Joint Economic Group at Ministerial Level, Joint Working Group on Trade at DG/Joint Secretary Level and India-China Trade Remedy Cooperation mechanism at DG/ Joint Secretary Level. In order to enhance mutual cooperation, India and China held its first strategic economic summit in Beijing in Sept. 2011, which was attended by the head of Indian Planning Commission, Sh. Montek Singh Ahluwalia, and Mr. Zhang Ping, the head of National Development and Reform Commission (NDRC). Apart from this, there is regular financial dialogue held between the two countries starting in 2007. But nevertheless, the mutual understanding between China and India remains shallow and there is a strong undercurrent of suspicion in Sino-Indian economic relations. To this author, the following four attitudinal problems must be addressed in order to take the relations to new horizons. These are: (1) The Indian Policy maker's attitude towards Chinese imports; (2) The Indian intellectual's recognition of China's economic rise; (3) The reaction of Indian business community to China's export; and (4) The Chinese attitude towards Indian IT and pharmaceutical sector. All the above four issues are victims of prejudice and have a biased approach towards each other and also suffer with the neglect by the academic communities in the two countries.

One of the unique features of the India-China research literature is that it is dominated by third world country scholars, especially those based in think tanks of US and EU. They have realised in quite advance that an important factor propelling China's search for closer economic ties with India, stems from Beijing's concerns over the rapidly improving US-India relations and the growing rift in Sino-US ties. China views expanded economic ties with India as a "hedge" against a future US-India coalition to contain China's rise in Asian and international affairs. In the same vein, the scholars of Mainland China and India are preoccupied with the realist paradigm of international relations and they have limited their study to the China-India boundary dispute, struggle for power and influence and strategic alliance with the world's only superpower, the United States. In recent years, the Chinese media and their think tanks have shown much more concern about India, Japan and USA coming closer to each other and bandwagoning against the PRC. But some of the young generation scholars have been influenced by the current economic growth trend in the two countries and have attempted to focus on the economic interaction between China and India. Although the professional discussion of China India economic cooperation has just taken off, but it is set to engage the new generation of scholars from the two countries to focus more on non-conventional issues between China and India. Chinese Scholars such as Wen Fude, Zhang Minqiu, Hua Biyun, Ren Jia, Guo Suiyan etc., all have focussed on increased economic cooperation and border trade between India and China. Efforts at regional level such as the provincial government in Sichuan and Yunnan province have been playing an important role in increasing trade with India, which will boost the pace of development in the Western region of China and in the North-East region of India (Ren Jia, 2003).

Economic Rise of China and India

There is an honest recognition in India that compared to India, China has achieved many milestones in its development, in a very-short time (last 30 yrs.) and had set a precedent for many developing countries, including India, to follow. The rise of China is supposed to be a tectonic shift of our time. Despite reservations in the west,[8] China has emerged as a comparatively

---

[8] Thirty years ago, not a single western economist could predict what China has achieved now, and they still continue to doubt the Chinese growth statistics and question the sustainability of the high growth rate. The responses range from outright pessimism about China's future to fear of a strong China. Lester Brown (1995) wonders who will feed China. As recently as 1999, *Foreign Affairs* could publish an article called "Does China Matter,"that seriously suggested the nation was globally irrelevant. (See, Segal, Gerald 1999 "Does China Matter?"*Foreign Affairs* 78(5) September/October 1999, pp. 24–36. See also the excellent debunking of this article by Harris, Stuart (2003) "Does China Matter: The Global Economic Issues", *Australian National University Working Paper* 2003/1.)

Gordon Chang (2000) announces the coming collapse of China. Callum Henderson (1999) sees China as on the "brink,"while Ross Terrill (2003) writes of the "illusory nature of the

successful example of industrialisation in a developing country. What China has achieved in the last three decades was indeed that which no neoliberal economist in the West could predict in advance. Most of them always raised doubt over the sustainability of the Chinese growth rate with the question mark: "Can China sustain its high growth rate?" In the West, the China collapse theory has been popular since the 1989 and recently it has gained further momentum in the backdrop of "Arab Spring."[9] But, China provided a counter-example to most of the economic theories whether it is her repressed financial system or the undefined property rights. Due to its economic rise, China's military and overall comprehensive power has also increased manifolds and is poised to become another important power with significant influence on the current geopolitics. As the latest U.S. intelligence assessment predicted (2009), China is "poised to have more impact on the world over the next 20 years than any other country."

Not to speak of a comparison with India, but also in international comparisons, China's achievements have truly been extraordinary.[10] China's economy has expanded thirteen fold in the last 30 years. As a result of China's "reform and opening" policy—more than 500 million citizens have overcome the curse of poverty although there are still 200 million or fewer

---

market in most of the Chinese economy" and that "a crash looms because the Leninist core of the regime is unchanged from Mao's construction of it in Yan'an six decades ago"(pp. 329, 313). Nicholas Lardy (1998) stresses the large economic problems and the unprecedented potential for social unrest due to ever more indebted state-owned enterprises, the extent of nonperforming loans, and a decline in government revenue. At the other end of the range are those who project a strong China. Geoffrey Murray (1998) describes China as the next superpower. A number of authors view an all-powerful China as a threat (Bill Gertz, 2000, or Edward Timperlake and William Triplett II, 2002). Emma Broomfield (2003) provides an overview over the"China threat"literature. Stanley Lubman (2004) documents the negative views of China in U.S. congressional debates.

9 See Gordon Chang's *The coming collapse of China*,2003, and various other writings.

10 Professor Arvind Panagariya of Columbia University have done a recent study titled "India and China: Trade and foreign Investment" in which he has concluded that it is unjustifiable to compare the performance of the external sector of India and China on the same graph. He feels that both India and China should belong to two different leagues (Panagariya, 2005). He is also the most devout champion of forming an FTA between India and China.Economist Nicholas lardy, a leading scholar of the Chinese economy has also done a comparison of Indian and Chinese export growth and he has shown through the data analysis that during each year of 2002, 2003 and 2004, the increase in China's export over the previous year was more than the absolute level of India's exports (Lardy, 2005).

citizens living in poverty. Through its state-owned corporate behemoths frenetically buying foreign firms, technologies and resources, China now accounts for an 8% share of global GDP compared with 1.8% in 1978 and also nearly 70% increase in grain production—which made it a self-sufficient country to feed her 1.4 billion people.

Most of the Indians feel that the rise of China is not a challenge or threat to India; on the other hand they believe that it gave an impetus for the need of liberalisation and economic reforms in India. In a survey conducted by a newspaper, 99.9% of Indians appreciate China's economic growth, only 0.1% deny it.[11] The current Prime Minister of India, Dr. Manmohan Singh, who initiated the large scale economic reform and liberalisation as Finance Minister in the year 1991, always refers to success story of China in order to get his reform agenda legitimised. One of the famous quotes from the speeches of Dr. Singh is that "There is no competition between India and China and there is enough space for both China and India to grow," which is perfectly true if we do not see in the narrow sense of competition in certain sectors such as energy. In fact India and China attempted to jointly bid and develop oil fields in Africa and Latin America but only with little success.

Although India and China have increased bilateral trade over the last decade, the amount is far less than the potential of trade possibility between them.[12] Harvard Business School professor Tarun Khanna blames India for this. India's fears about Chinese competition and unease over past border war result in procedural and other roadblocks to increase trade, is proving more disadvantageous to India than to China. The data shows that China benefits from the trade more than India, both by selling better products to India and by welcoming Indian investment in China (Khanna, 2007). The current trade deficit of India with China is alarming hence it should take more positive initiatives to engage China on the economic front. At the same time, India can leverage her cultural influence and create an

[11] Quoted from Jairam Ramesh, *Making Sense of Chindia*, 2005.

[12] China and India recorded $ 19 billion in bilateral trade by the Nov. 2006, much less than would be expected of countries similar in size, within geographic proximity, and with shared cultural ties.

atmosphere of bonhomie among the Chinese citizens. This will lead to more amicable bilateral relations between the two countries. Although, it is widely viewed that increased cultural and economic links will enhance mutual understanding and trust between China and India (Deshingkar, 1995). Scholars such as Surjit Mansingh[13] has written that "between hostility at one extreme and collaboration at the other, there is space enough for India and China to cultivate 'normal' state-to-state relations in response to their respective perceptions of national interest (Mansingh,1994). But the fact is that the civilizational paradigm has not been successful in bringing back the relations between the two giants on track.

Complementarities between India and China

India and China have close geographical proximity; both are the fastest growing major economies in the world. Together, they contain about one-third of the world's population. When the world economy, especially the EU and US market is under recession, they have been named as countries with the highest potential for growth in the next 50 years in a BRICS report. The economic strengths of these two countries are widely considered complementary - China is perceived to be strong in manufacturing and infrastructure while India is perceived to be strong in services and information technology. China is stronger in hardware while India is stronger in software. China is stronger in physical markets while India is stronger in financial markets. Culturally also, the two countries have seen continuous exchange between each other since the millennium. The countries share such historical interactions – as the spread of Buddhism from India to China and trade on the Silk route. However, there are also geopolitical, cultural, and political differences between China and India; the effects of the Sino-Indian War of 1962 have meant that relations between the countries have been cautious and slow developing, what has been termed as incremental relations (Acharya and Deshpandey, 2008).

But, despite mutual distrust prevailing between them, Indian and Chinese companies are making significant cross-border investments. For example, India's IT giants such as Infosys, TCS, Wipro and many others

---

[13] Surjit Mansingh, *India-China relations in the post-Cold war era*, Asian Survey, March, 1994).

have already invested more than a billion dollars in business development centres in southern China. At the same time, China's Huawei has built a research and development centre in Bangalore. There are many other similar investments taking place.[14] The result of these investments is a rapid expansion in trade in services such as IT related services. China and India are both moving toward similar goals, increasingly competing in the same industries, but at the same time trading and investing with one another. The notable thing is that the combined market size of these two countries offers huge potential for companies in each country. India and China are not only the two largest markets for the Western companies, but also for each other. When US economy faces recession and the consumer spending goes down, Chinese exporters must look for new markets for their products. The current global economic recession suits this case as never before. During his visit to India in March 2005, Chinese Premier, Wen Jiabao proposed an FTA between the two countries and a working group was constituted, the report of which is already published. Since, India as a democratic system is constrained by the business lobby groups, which perceive Made-in-China as a threat to their products; hence there is not much development on formalising an FTA between the two countries. During the 2010 visit of Wen Jiabao, several deals were signed between the Indian and Chinese companies, the total value of which touched $ 15 billion approximately. During this visit, the China Development Bank signed a $2 billion package

[14] More than 100 Indian companies have a presence in China today. Indian IT firms that have a presence in China include Aptech, Cognizant Technologies, Hexaware Technologies,I-Flex, I-Gate, Infosys, L&T Infotech, NIIT, Sasken Communications, Satyam Computer Services, Semindia, Tata Consultancy Services, Tata Infotech Education, Wipro, Zensar Technologies and 3iInfotech. Indian banks also have a strong presence in the People's Republic. They include Allahabad Bank, Bank of Baroda, Bank of India, Canara Bank, ICICI Bank, Indian Overseas Bank, Punjab National Bank, State Bank of India, UCO Bank, Union Bank of India, UTI Bank and Vijaya Bank. Pharmaceutical companies, including Aur obindo Pharmaceuticals, Dr Reddys, Matrix Labs, Orchid Pharmaceuticals, Ranbaxy and United Phosphorous also have a significant presence in China. Other Indian groups and businesses with a foothold in China include the Aditya Birla group, Apollo Tyres, Asian Paints, Bajaj Auto, Bharat Forge, Essar, Essel Propack, Gas Authority of India Ltd, Godrej, Jindal Stainless, JK Tyres, Jubilant Organosys, L&T, Mahindra & Mahindra, MMTC, Mphasis, MRF, Raymond, Reliance Industries, Subex Systems, Sundram Fasteners, Suzlon, Tata International, Thermax, Tube Investments, TVS Motors, Videocon and Voltas. As ties between the two countries improve, the list will keep increasing over the years. (source: India Brand Equity Foundation 2009)

loan for India's Reliance group. Currently Chinese firms such as Shanghai Electronics and Shandong Electronics are engaged in several billion dollar projects in India, supplying various electronic equipments for India's new coming power generation plants. Some of these projects have been given to Chinese companies, since they are known for their speedy execution of the projects. These are all positive developments between India and China which will take the importance of bilateral relations to a new level. As some analysts have predicted, by 2020, India-China bilateral relations will emerge to be one of the most important in the world. But despite this optimism there are several obstructions in the way to build a more stable and peaceful friendly relation between the two giants.

There are strong and clear differences in development approaches and economic management systems between China and India and that can make all the differences in future. Foreign investment dependent and export-oriented growth approach of China (accounting for 60% of its GDP) is quite different from domestic demand driven approach followed by India (constituting 57% of Indian GDP). India's service-oriented growth model (58% of GDP) is different from China's, which relies more heavily on the manufacturing sector.[15] Beyond doubt, India is emerging as a global software and IT services power in the 21st century. China, in contrast, with the help of massive FDI inflows from many sources, including its own diaspora and an open trade regime, has emerged as world's factory.

The evolution of China's manufacturing sector and the strategy to attain scale, competitiveness and a wide range of products has been unique story in the history of industrialisation. China has followed the "classic" pattern, moving from primary to manufacturing sector, which has doubled its share of workforce and tripled its share of output. Whereas in India, the move has been mainly from agriculture to services in share of output, with no substantial increase in manufacturing and the structure of employment has not changed much. Share of the primary sector in GDP fell from 60 per cent to 18 per cent in four decades, but share in employment still

[15] India could push this sector with the help of its overseas diaspora broad and soft infrastructure, but the country's leadership is not very assertive in courting its own diaspora. They are much more interested in inviting foreign giants like Walmart and Ikea which will end up eating up the domestic retail industry.

more than 60 percent. While its performance is not comparable with the record set by China, there are features about India's growth performance such as export in auto parts and pharmaceutical products, which are worth highlighting.

If we argue that China is more dependent on export for its economic growth,[16] then it is always valid to argue that India's software industry is also heavily dependent on its export, because almost 60-70 percent of the total revenue of the software and BPO industry comes from the overseas market (NASSCOM, 2007, 2008). Therefore the future growth trend in both countries is heavily linked to their external sector developments.

Until now reforms in India have been still very limited and it is hard to quantify how much India needs to do in order to achieve a sustained growth rate similar to that in China. Indian FDI policy has been reformed and liberalised in various sectors but it is still not very friendly to foreign companies thinking of investing in India.[17] Since both the economies are still in their transition state from the planned to the market oriented system, therefore, there is no consensus on their success as a model of development

---

[16] Chinese economy is more vulnerable to fluctuation in the global demand. Since Indian economy is growing led by its domestic consumption (almost 60 percent of the economy is for domestic consumption) therefore she is less vulnerable to the fluctuation in the global demand. China's economy is heavily dependent on global trade and investment flows. A slowdown in the global demand, especially in the U.S. economy would have significant effect on Chinese growth rate as in the current global financial crisis (sparked by US sub-prime crisis). Chinese exports of goods and services amount to about 40 percent of GDP and exports to the U.S. account for about one-third of the total. The Chinese government estimates that the foreign trade sector employs more than 80 million people, of which 28 million work in foreign-invested enterprises[16] Time and again a sharp fall down in the export sector had created sleepless night for communist party rulers. Thus, this is an important risk for the Chinese economy, especially given that net exports have made a sizable contribution to growth in last few years. The 11th Five-year Plan adopted at the 5th Party Plenum of the CPC held on October 2005, the Chinese leadership clearly specified the goal of restructuring the Chinese economic growth from an export-led economy to one that is more broad-based and more "balanced," and hence more "sustainable" in the long run.

[17] The physical infrastructure which has been improved in recent years is still not very competitive in attracting FDI compared to China. World class Infrastructure is one of the major factors in attracting the huge volume of FDI and driving the fast GDP growth rate in China.China used its vast reservoirs of domestic savings to build an impressive infrastructure and sucked in huge amounts of foreign money to build factories and to acquire the expertise it needed. The combination of foreign technology and investment with domestic cheap labour greatly boosts the development of non-farm employment and productivity.

for other developing countries. However, their growth record and achievements have been widely recognized by the world community. At the very least, the Chinese experience provides two lessons for India. First, it shows how far India has fallen behind, given the slow pace of reform. Second, it shows how quickly infrastructure can be improved in a more suitable regulatory environment, because, the availability of both physical and social infrastructure is central to sustainable economic growth.[18] As some other commentators (e.g. Huang, 2003) have argued that compared with China, India is less dependent on resource mobilisation and more dependent on human capital, therefore we can agree that in the long term, Indian growth may be more sustainable than the Chinese one.[19] However, without complementary progress on reforms on improving basic education and nutrition, boosting productivity in the agriculture sector and easing stifling labour regulations, India may be hard pressed to take advantage of its population windfall and realize the projections of India's optimists. India and China both have plentiful supplies of underutilised labour, though India faces greater challenges of raising educational attainment. In China, everybody can do any work whether she is a woman or from some particular clan of family; there is no social dogma or taboo as such as the caste system in India. In India, the caste system has defined the division of labour in the society and which used to be very immobile until recently. Most of the industries women were not allowed to work in, especially in the manufacturing sector and therefore if no agriculture work then the half of the labour force was unproductive. In China, the women contributed

---

[18] In the case of China, it has been found that the development of urban transportation and the related infrastructure in a city is directly proportional to the level of economic development of that city. For providing the basic public goods for the economic development, we find that decentralization and inter-regional competition has so far worked well in China, whereas centralized decision-making and redistributive allocations have stymied competition in India. India has under-invested in infrastructure and is now facing obstacles to broadening and deepening its growth process as a result.Kochhar et al. (2008) estimate that, India needs to mobilise another $500 billion in the next five years in order to finance the infrastructure development to sustain the current growth rate of eight per cent. However, as Zhang & Kanbur (2005) finds, that in case of China, there needs to be a balance between decentralization and withdrawal of government's role especially in the social sectors.

[19] It has been argued that "if India can turn into a fast-growth economy, it will be the first developing nation that used its brainpower, not natural resources or the raw muscle of factory labor, as the catalyst" (See, Kripalani and Engardio, 2003, p. 70).

shoulder-to-shoulder with their men and thus they constitute a major section of the labour force. China also had created a huge pool of skilled labour force which was very attractive for FDI. In India, either the engineers trained form IITs were very high-end and could be only employed by the foreign MNCs. The Chinese education system has also created a large pool of low skilled workers such as mechanics and operators that can be hired at a fraction of the cost of similarly-trained workers in the West. India needs to replicate this in order to achieve similar growth rate with that of China.[20]

The way ahead

The relative strengths and weaknesses of the two countries indicate that in the coming decades there is likely to be a significant degree of convergence[21] between both the economies. As evident that in the last one decade, India is also catching up with China in growth rate and improving her position in the global economy, it seems that, India will catch-up in manufacturing industry[22] in the coming decade and China will also develop its services sector.[23] We can reach the initial conclusion that China and India, rather than having different development trajectories, might simply have different starting dates, with Chinese reforms preceding those in India by a number

[20] There is a consensus among development economists that the most important factor behind China's higher growth rate than India is inflow of huge FDI. But, China this much FDI would have not come to China if there were no skilled labour force. It can be argued that although wages are even lower in India and other parts of the developing world, but only China has been able to attract such a huge inflow of FDI. The reason could be that China provides not only low wages but high productivity and a relatively advanced supply-chain infrastructure.

[21] The convergence hypothesis maintains that (1) if countries are similar in terms of preferences and technology, the steady state income levels for them will be the same and with time they will tend to reach that same level of income and (2) that provided technology is a public good equally shared, all countries will eventually attain the same steady state growth, where the steady states of the economies refer to the economy where per capita output, capital stock and consumption grow at a common constant rate equal to the exogenously given rate of technological progress. However, judging whether countries are in their steady states can be problematic. One way to bypass this problem is to examine the relationship between initial income levels and subsequent growth rates (as quoted in Chen Baizhu and Feng Yi, 2000).

[22] Until now, India's manufacturing sector has been able to provide just little more than 5 million jobs out of its 500 million work force, where as in China there are more than 100 million workers employed in its export-led manufacturing industry.

[23] History tells us that it takes some 60 years for a society to move from economic takeoff to maturity (Rostow, 1960). Low-income countries tend to grow faster than mature economies for a long time. Then their growth rate levels off and declines drastically when they approach

of years and finally converging. If India succeeds in providing better infrastructure, including reliable power, more flexible labor laws and an efficient bureaucracy, it is entirely possible that it will become more competitive. These institutional changes would allow India to accelerate its economic growth in an equitable manner during the next round of economic reforms.[24] India and China both face the formidable challenges of eradicating poverty, reducing unemployment and improving the quality of life of its citizens. The other challenge is to reduce vast disparities in per capita income level between and within India's states. Poverty reduction continues to be the main focus of India's development plans.[25] Some of the other most challenging issues they face are the issues of minorities and regional imbalances, energy security, environmental degradation, epidemic diseases, domestic and international terrorism and also their ailing financial sector and rampant corruption. Issues of minorities may be directly linked with the issue of equitable growth, as the regional inequality in China and India is at its all-time high.[26] The policy makers in both the nations have recognized the problem and are struggling to create a harmonious society (in case of China) and inclusive growth (in case of India). In its race to control the global production network and invite the foreign capital, China has so far ignored the socio-political as well as environmental issues, which

---

the technological frontier (Barro, 2003, Cooper, 2005). As Li and Bin (2008) have rightly predicted that since China and India are not yet even halfway through the catching-up period and their productivity gaps with leading economies are large, they are expected to enjoy high growth for the next three decades or more provided that no major disruptions or external shocks occur.

[24] India is now in the second phase of economic reforms. It refers to the reform such as labour law reform, disinvestment, financial sector reform, removal of agricultural subsidies, etc., In the current period, the focus is on achieving fiscal consolidation, amending outdated legislations, revamping public sector enterprises, strengthening basic and social infrastructure, developing India's comparative advantage in information technology and knowledge-based industries and increasing the strength and vibrancy of capital markets and financial institutions.

[25] The latest World Bank (2008) report on India pointed out rightly in that despite India's better performance in the recent decade, it still needs to make it more equitable among people in order to sustain it. India can grow faster if it provides equal opportunities to its sons and daughters, which is improving but not as expected.

[26] Here inequality is measured in terms of Ginni coefficient which has almost crossed 0.5 for China and 0.4 for India. Apart from state and provincial level data, the inequalities have increased in terms of rural and urban income levels.

can have very serious consequences in the future. It seems that relatively slower economic growth in India is based on stronger socio-economic foundations, although, there is disenchantment among the common people with the quality of governance in the country.

Under the current global financial crisis, one way of sustaining the high growth rate and achieving better results by both economies is economic and social cooperation and not rivalry. The two giant economies have several areas to complement each other.[27] At the same time they provide an ideal tourist destination for each other. Chinese people are now known for their spending power, they desire to see the land of Buddha. But Visa formalities and other safety reasons still make them rethink. Instant visa facilities on arrival for tourist and businessmen in both the countries should be a welcome step to promote a faster growth of trading relations. There is a much more space for leaders and civil society of China and India to cooperate on various issues such as energy resources, scientific research, epidemic controls, global warming and including security issues related to regional and international terrorism. The mutual distrust and hate against each other could be just a thing of the past. Given the huge size, long history and the multi dimensions of India-China relations, there is an urgent need for increasing the bilateral exchange of students and taking up joint projects between scholars and scientists of the two countries. The deepening of border trade between them through the Nathu-la pass and opening few more mountain passes for trade would provide a new direction to India-China rapprochement and trust building.

In conclusion, the primary political significance of increased economic engagement and interdependence between India and China would stabilise the political and economic architecture not only in Asia but also the world at large, and would also augment the economic development of the entire region. It will also help China and India to mitigate distrust and foster an

---

[27] In the 21st century, apart from 9/11 and the war against terrorism, the most covered news around the globe was the economic rise of China and India. It is true in the academic community when their attention was converged on China and India. While United States was engaged in countering terrorist threats posed by radical Islamic elements led by Bin laden, China and India had come up to consolidate their economic position and maintain a sustained high growth.

increased level of cooperation at international level in terms of political and military confidence building. Indian and Chinese leadership should shed away the ego of personality crisis and should join hands to take the responsibility of ensuring a peaceful and harmonious environment for the economic and social benefit of their people. India and China have been neighbours since times immemorial and there is no reason why they cannot coexist and prosper together in the current geopolitical order. To quote from Nehru's comments in in 1950[28] *"During these thousand years... each country (China and India) learned something from each other, not only in region of thoughts and philosophy, but also in the arts and science of life. Probably China was more influenced by India, than India by China, which is pity, for India could well have received, with profit to herself......"*

References

BusinessWeek; *"Chindia": China and India special feature* August 12, 2005

Chidambaram, P. "A Passage to Prosperity", *The Wall Street Journal*, A14, 4 March. Chinese Silk Majors form Group amid Indian Anti-Dumping Threats", Economic Times, 25 January 2005

Deshpande, G Pand, Achary, Alka. Crossing a Bridge of Dreams : 50 Years of India-China, Tulika (New Delhi 2001)

Sheth. Jagdish N. *Chindia Rising*. New Delhi, McGraw Hill India, 2007.

Jairam Ramesh. *Making Sense of Chindia: Reflections on China and India.* New Delhi, India Research Press, 2005.

Khanna, Tarun. "China & India - The Ponder of Two", Harvard Business Review 85 (12), (Dec. 2007)

Srivastava, Anupam, *"The Strategic Context of India's Economic Engagement With China"*, in Kulkarni et al ed. *Economic Development in India and China*, serials, (Delhi 2008)

[28] As quoted in Tarun Khanna (2008), "Billions of Entrepreneurs: How China and India are Reshaping Their Futures and Yours", HBS Press, 368 pages. Publication date: Dec 20, 2007.

Yasheng, Huang and Khanna, Tarun, "Can India Overtake China?" *Foreign Policy*, No.137, July/August, 2003

Virmani, Arvind, "From 'bhai-bhai' to 'buy-buy': For India and China, Sustainable Economic ties, not FTA, are best", *Indian Express*, April 13, 2005

The Sixty Years of India-China Relationship:

1. Chronology of India-China Relations (1950-2010)
2. Economic Complimentarities between India and China
3. Panchsheel Agreement
4. Rajiv Gandhi's Goodwill Visit to China
5. Agreement between India & China on the Maintenance of Peace and Tranquility along the Line of Actual Control.
6. Agreement between India & China on Confidence Building Measures along the Line of Actual Control.
7. Documents signed between India and China during Prime Minister Vajpayee's visit to China
8. Political Parameters and Guiding Principles for the Settlement of the India-China Boundary Question
9. Highlights of the Joint Declaration issued after the talks between Prime Minister Manmohan Singh and Chinese President Hu Jintao
10. A Shared Vision for the 21st Century of the People's Republic of China and the Republic of India
11. 60th Anniversary of the Establishment of Diplomatic Relations between India and China

Chronology of India-China Relations (1950-2010)

India and China had relatively little modern political contact before the 1950s. However, both countries have had extensive and close historical cultural contact since the first century, especially with the transmission of Buddhism from India to China. Trade relations via the Silk Route acted as economic contact between the two regions.

On August 15, 1947, India assumed independence from the British rule and became a federal, democratic republic after its constitution came into effect on January 26, 1950. On October 1, 1949, the People's Liberation Army defeated the Kuomintang (Nationalist Party of China) in a civil war and established the People's Republic of China (PRC).

India was the second country after Myanmar (Burma) to recognise the People's Republic of China.

April 1950: K.M. Panikker is appointed as the first Indian Ambassador to China.

April 1954: Nehru and Chou En-lai sign Panchsheel Agreement - the Sino-Indian Agreement on Trade and Intercourse between India and Tibet Region of China in Beijing.

June 1954: Chinese Prime Minister Chou En-lai visits India for the first time.

October 1954: Jawaharlal Nehru visits China. A Sino-Indian trade agreement signed by Nehru and Chou En-lai in Beijing. Sino-Indian Friendship Associations are established in both countries.

April 1955: Nehru and Chou En-lai pledge to promote friendly ties at the Asian-African conference at Bandung, Indonesia.

November 1956: Chou En-lai visits India for the second time on a goodwill tour.

September 1957: Indian Vice-President S. Radhakrishnan visits China.

September 1958: India officially objects to the inclusion of areas of Northern Assam and NEFA in the *China Pictorial*, an official organ of the PRC.

January 1959: Chou En-lai expresses China's claim on about 90,000 square miles of Indian territory, both in Ladakh and NEFA.

April 1959: Dalai Lama flees from Lhasa to India. India grants him refuge, relations with Beijing begin to sour.

25 August 1959: First bloodshed at a border post in the eastern sector; a 200 to 300 strong Chinese detachment crossed the frontier in the Subansiri Frontier Division near Longju, they surrounded and fired at the forward picket of a dozen Assam Rifles men. One person was killed and another seriously wounded, the rest were arrested.

September 1959: In Parliament, Nehru tables the First White Paper on India-China relations. It contains notes, memoranda and letters exchanged between India and China between April 1954 and August 1959.

September 1959: China refuses to accept the McMohan Line. Chou En-lai justifies this by stating that China was not a signatory between British India and Tibet.

21 October 1959: Second skirmish resulting in bloodshed, this time in the western sector. A three-member Indian police patrol party detained by the Chinese near Kongka Pass in the Western Sector. The party having not returned, on 21 October 1959, Karam Singh, Deputy Superintendent of Police, along with 20 men went out in search of the missing party. After some distance he left behind 4 of his men and moved with others towards Chang Chenmo river. Here the Indian patrol party was subjected to a ruthless attack by the Chinese troops, using rifles, mortars and hand grenades. Nine members of the Indian patrol party were killed, and one policeman seriously injured, who too was probably killed by the Chinese. The rest, including Karam Singh, were arrested and treated badly while in custody. In the firing, one Chinese soldier was also killed.

October 1960: Indian opposition leaders report 52 violations of Indian air space by the Chinese in NEFA, Uttar Pradesh, now Uttarakhand, and Ladakh.

December 1961: India adopts the Forward Policy to stem the advance of a Chinese frontier line. The Forward Policy involved the establishment of a few symbolic posts in Ladakh so that India might be in a position to take action to recover any territory within Chinese possession. It also sought to block potential lines of further Chinese advance.

June 1962: Indian and Chinese soldiers face off within 100 yards of each other in the Galwan Valley in Ladakh. An armed clash is narrowly averted.

September 1962: Chinese forces cross McMohan Line, skirmishes ensue.

October 1962: China engages in prolonged attack along the border from NEFA to Ladakh.

October 24, 1962: China proposes a three-point cease-fire: 1. Both parties would respect Line of Actual Control; 2. Armed forces would withdraw 20 km from this line; 3. Talks between Prime Ministers would commence to seek settlement

October 26-27, 1962: India proclaims national emergency. Nehru rejects Chinese three-point proposal.

November 15-18, 1962: Fighting breaks out in Eastern and Western sectors.

November 21, 1962: China declares unilateral cease-fire along the India-China border, withdrawing its troops to 20 km behind LAC.

December 8, 1962: Chou En-lai reintroduces three-point cease-fire; India accepts.

1970: Informal contacts between Indian and Chinese diplomats established.

March 1973: China sends a new Charges d'Affaires to New Delhi, resuscitating stalled Sino-Indian relations.

April 1976: After a 15 year diplomatic hiatus, India and China restore diplomatic relations to the Ambassador level. K.R. Narayanan is appointed India's Ambassador to PRC, while Chen Chao Yuan becomes the Chinese

Ambassador to India.

February 1979: Indian Foreign Minister Atal Behari Vajpayee visits China, had to cut short his visit, as China invades Vietnam.

June 1981: Chinese Foreign Minister Huang Hua visits India to discuss establishment of an annual dialogue at the level of Vice-Ministers.

August 1984: Indian Commerce Secretary Abid Hussain signs the "Most Favoured Nation Agreement" with Chinese Vice-Minister Lu Xuejian in Beijing.

1986: Differences surface over the limits of the McMahon Line in Arunachal Pradesh's Sumdorung Chu area.

May 1987: Indian Prime Minister Rajiv Gandhi sends PN Haskar as Special Envoy to China for high level discussion with Chinese leaders.

December 1988: Prime Minister Rajiv Gandhi visits China. Agreement to set up a Joint Working Group on Boundary question and a Joint Group on Economic Relations, Trade, Science and Technology is signed.

December 1991: Chinese Premier Li Peng visits India, pledges to resolve the boundary question through friendly consultations.

September 1993: Prime Minister P.V. Narasimha Rao visits China, signs agreement on Border Peace and Tranquility and the setting up of the India-China Expert Group of Diplomatic and Military Officers, to assist the work in Joint Working Group.

August 1995: India and China agree to pull back their troops to the Sumdorong Chu Valley in the Eastern Sector.

November 1996: Chinese President Jiang Zemin visits India, signs Agreement on Confidence Building Measures in the military field along the LAC in the India-China Border Areas.

August 1997: The India-China Joint Working Group meets in New Delhi; instruments of ratification in respect to Confidence Building Measures Agreement are exchanged.

11 May 1998: India conducts three nuclear tests in Pokhran range in

Rajathan.

13 May 1998: India further conducts two more underground nuclear tests.

14 May 1998: China strongly condemns India's nuclear tests.

July 1998: China urges India and Pakistan to give up their nuclear ambitions and sign the NPT.

August 1998: India officially announces talks with China on the re-opening of the Ladakh-Kailash-Mansarovar route.

June 1999: China displays neutrality on the Kargil conflict and agrees to establish a security mechanism with India.

November 1999: India and China hold detailed discussions in New Delhi on ways to settle the border dispute.

February 2000: India and China sign a bilateral trade agreement in Beijing to facilitate China's early entry into the WTO. A Memorandum of Understanding for setting up a Joint Working Group in the steel industry, is written.

March 2000: India and China initiate the first ever bilateral security dialogue in Beijing on global and regional issues of mutual interest.

April 2000: India and China commemorate 50th anniversary of their diplomatic relations.

May 2000: Delegation from India's National Defence College arrives in China, signalling resumption of military ties, suspended after India's nuclear tests.

January 2001: Sino-Indian leaders jointly agree to form India-China Parliamentary Friendship Groups in their respective Parliaments following the visit of the Li Peng, Chairman of the Standing Committee of the National Peoples' Congress to India. India and China agree to counter terrorism together to maintain security and stability.

January 2002: China announces the first Shanghai-Beijing-New Delhi direct passenger flight for boosting bilateral business ties and tourism. Chinese Premier Zhu Rongji visits India. Memorandums of Understandings signed in New Delhi covering cooperation in: science and technology; outer space; tourism; sanitary measures; hydrological information (Brahmaputra River). Premier Zhu Rongji calls for cooperation in information technology, economic cooperation, and trade between India and China. India and China agree in Beijing, to quicken the pace of LAC delineation in order to resolve the border dispute within a reasonable time-frame.

June 2003: Indian Prime Minister Atal Behari Vajpayee's landmark June 2003 visit to China. China officially recognises Indian sovereignty over Sikkim as the two nations move toward resolving their border disputes.

November 2003: India and China hold the first joint naval exercise in November 2003 off Shanghai on China's Eastern seaboard.

2004: For the first time, Sino-Indian bilateral trade reaches the $10 billion mark.

April 2005: Chinese Premier Wen Jiabao visits Bangalore to push for increased Sino-Indian cooperation in high-tech industries.

July 6, 2006: China and India re-open Nathula Pass, an ancient trade route through the Himalayas and part of the Silk Route, a pass that had been closed since the Sino-Indian War in 1962.

December 2007: The First Joint Training Exercise between the PLA and the Indian Army, 'Hand in Hand 2007', was conducted in Kunming, China. One Company each from the PLA and the Indian Army participated in the counter terrorism exercises. Lt Gen Ma Xiaotian, Deputy CGS PLA and Lt Gen Susheel Gupta, DCOAS represented China and India respectively as observers.

January 2008: Indian Prime Minister Manmohan Singh visits China, meets Chinese Premier, Wen Jiabao, and President Hu Jintao, for bilateral discussions on trade, commerce, Defence, military, and various other issues.

December 2008: Second Joint Training Exercise between the Indian Army and the PLA - "Hand in Hand 2008" - was conducted at Belgaum, India between December 4 and 14, 2008. The theme of the exercise was Counter Terrorism again. Lt Gen Ma Xiaotian, Deputy CGS of the PLA and Lt Gen Nobel Thamburaj, GOC-in-C, Southern Command were the senior most observers from the Indian and Chinese sides respectively.

January 2010: Minister of Commerce, Anand Sharma visits China to push India-China trade ties.

April 2010: External Affairs Minister, SM Krishna visits China to participate in the celebration of the 60th year of opening up of diplomatic relationship between India and China.

May 2010: President of India, Pratibha Singh Patil visits China. Chinese president Hu Jintao assures her that China is ready to discuss the complex issues relating to India's quest for a permanent seat in the United Nations Security Council.

December 2010: Chinese Premier Wen Jiabao visits India.

Economic Complimentarities between India and China

Substantial complementarities characterise the economic structures of India and China:

- India and China are the two largest countries in the world in terms of population; they are also the fastest growing economies in the world.
- India and China together are home to the world's largest pools of skilled human resources, and there is a general consensus that these two countries will continue to be the engines of global economic growth in the 21st century.
- Bilateral trade and investment between the two countries have grown rapidly over the few years indicating the presence of a vast potential for further growth. China is emerging as a significant link in the manufacturing chain of the world while India's potential for the knowledge-based services and manufacturing is being noticed. These complementary strengths of the two ecomomies can be further exploited for mutual benefit.
- Their geographical proximity, similar cultural values, and large size of their economies can facilitate exploitation of these synergies. They can also pool their resources for improving their international competitiveness and can fruitfully share their development experiences and cooperate in the critical area of energy security.
- India-China economic cooperation has the potential to benefit nearly two fifths of humanity with spill over effects on the rest of the world.
- India and China resumed trade officially in 1978. Both the countries

signed a Trade Agreement (Most Favoured Nation Agreement) in 1984. Since 1988, when it was decided to extend the India-China relationship at various levels, an elaborate framework for promotiong trade and economic relations has evolved over time.

Bilateral Trade

- While international trade has been growing at around 15% on an average, India-China trade has increased by more than 50% annually in the last five years. In 2008, China became India's largest trading partner and the bilateral trade between the two countries touched US$ 51.8 billion. India has emerged as the 7th largest export market of China and 10th largest trade partner.

- If the current growth rate continues, the bilateral trade between the two most populous countries may cross US$ 100 billion by 2015. Even if the growth rate in India-China trade slows down to 25% annually (a conservative projection) from the current rate of over 50%, bilateral trade between them is expected to be almost US $70 billion in 2011.

- Since it is projected that by 2050 India and China will be the two leading economies in the world, it is inevitable that bilateral trade between the two countries will be among the most important economic relationships in the world.

- The targets of bilateral trade set by the Prime Ministers of the two countries during the visit of Premier Wen Jiabao's to India in 2005 as US$ 20 billion by 2008 and US$ 30 billion by 2010, were met much ahead of the deadline. The target fixed during President Hu Jintao's visit to India in 2006, to increase the bilateral trade to $40 billion by 2010, was achieved in early 2008. In 2008, the target was again revised to US$ 60 billion by 2010, which is likely to be met by this year-end.

Future Prospects

- The trade between India and China is still concentrated in a few products, especially the low value added raw materials and minerals dominating India's exports. The challenge is to make trade more broad-based and diversified, in favour of manufactured goods rather than raw materials, while sustaining a healthy expansion of trade. For this, a great deal of attention needs to be paid to trade facilitation, besides addrressing the issues of relevant tariff and non-tariff barriers.

It is believed that trade facilitation itself could lead to further strengthening of the India-China economic linkages by bringing down the present level of high transaction costs. The steps that could be considered, include streamlining customs procedures and moving towards a more comprehensive electronic data interface in customs administration and information exchange, having a bilateral preshipment inspection agreement, mutual recognition agreements on standards and harmonisation of conformity assesment procedures among others. Trade facilitation could also cover cooperation to facilitate financing and cooperation between export-import banks of the two countries.

- A large potential exists for trade, in services and investment. Barriers to trade in services, need to be addressed systematically to exploit the potential of trade in services for mutual benefit. Such potential appears to exist in areas such as IT and IT enables services, biotechnology, education, financial sector, education, health care, tourism, etc. among other sectors. The potential is yet to be fully exploited. Investments can be undertaken by Indian enterprises in China, not only for supplying the Chinese domestic market but also for exports in the third countries. Similarly, Chinese companies can explore investment opportunities in India for domestic market and for exports. Bilateral investment flows could be facilitated by bilateral investment protection and promotion agreement, among other policies. In addition, an organised institutional promotion by business chambers and governmental agencies may be fruitful. Economic relations could be further strengthened with improved transport linkages and connectivity. While some progress has been made on air connectivity between India and China, the frequency of direct air links is still low.

- Economic cooperation between India and China also has to look beyond just promotiong trade and investment. It could cover much broader areas to strengthen cooperation and information exchange between Government agencies and related institutions; exchange development experiences and promote technology and industrial cooperation in the fields, such as agriculture and rural development, electrical and electronics sector, project contracting. Given the fact that both China and India are highly dependent on imports of petroleum and gas, mutual cooperation in energy security is also of strategic importance; exchange experiences in the management of economy, such as city management, poverty relief and social security, development of SMEs disaster management, water resource management.
- The cooperation between China and India will lay foundations for the two countries to establish a Regional Trading Arrangement (RTA). It is expected that India-China RTA will be conducive to bringing the potential of economic cooperation into full play. Furthermore, with mutual cooperation and coordination of their positions in negotiations in WTO, they make contributions to building a more pro-development multilateral trade and financial architecture. China-India cooperation has the potential to benefit one third of humanity and also promote a broader regional economic integration in Asia.

[Source: Report of the India-China joint Study Group on Comprehensive Trade and Economic Cooperation 2005 & Data released by CII, pertaining to India-China Bilateral Trade]

Panchsheel Agreement

(The agreement between The Republic of India and The People's Republic of China on Trade and Intercourse between Tibet Region of China and India, April 1954)

The Government of the Republic of India and the Central People's Government of the People's Republic of China, being desirous of promoting trade and cultural intercourse between Tibet Region of China and India and of facilitating pilgrimage and travel by the peoples of China and India, have resolved to enter into the present Agreement based on the following principles:

(1) mutual respect for each other's territorial integrity and sovereignty,

(2) mutual non-aggression,

(3) mutual non-interference in each other's internal affairs,

(4) equality and mutual benefit, and

(5) peaceful co-existence.

And for this purpose have appointed as their respective Plenipotentiaries: The Government of the Republic of India, H. E. Nedyam Raghavan, Ambassador Extraordinary and Plenipotentiary of India, accredited to the People's Republic of China; the Central People's Government of the People's Republic of China, H. B. Chang Han-fu, Vice-Minister of Foreign Affairs of the Central People's Government, who, having examined each other's credentials and finding them in good and due form, have agreed upon the following:-

Article I

The High Contracting Parties mutually agree to establish Trade Agencies:

1. The Government of India agrees that the Government of China may establish Trade Agencies at New Delhi, Calcutta and Kalimpong.

2. The Government of China agrees that the Government of India may establish Trade Agencies at Yatung, Gyantse and Gartok.

The Trade Agencies of both Parties shall be accorded the same status and same treatment.

The Trade Agents of both Parties shall enjoy freedom from arrest while exercising these functions, and shall enjoy in respect of themselves, their wives and children who are dependent on them for livelihood, freedom from search.

The Trade Agencies of both Parties shall enjoy the privileges and immunities for couriers, mail-bags and communications in code.

Article II

The High Contracting Parties agree that traders of both countries known to be customarily and specifically engaged in trade between Tibet Region of China and India may trade at the following places:

1. The Government of China agrees to specify (1) Yatung, (2) Gyantse and (3) Phari as markets for trade. The Government of India agrees that trade may be carried on in India, including places like (1) Kalimpong, (2) Siliguri and (3) Calcutta, according to customary practice.

2. The Government of China agrees to specify (1) Gartok, (2) Pulanchung (Taklakot), (3) Gyanima-Khargo, (4) Gyaniina-Chaltra, (5) Ramura, (6) Dongbra, (7) Puling-Sumdo, (8) Nabra, (9) Shangtse and (10) Tashigong as markets for trade. The Government of India agrees that in future, when in accordance with the development and need of trade between the Ari District of Tibet Region of China and India, it has become necessary to specify markets for trade in the corresponding district in India adjacent to the Ari District of Tibet Region of China, it will be prepared to consider on the basis of equality and reciprocity to do so.

Article III

The High Contracting Parties agree that pilgrimage by religious believers of the two countries shall be carried on in accordance with the following provisions:-

1. Pilgrims from India of Lamaist, Hindu and Buddhist faiths may visit Kang Rimpoche (Kailas) and Mavam Tso (Mansarovar) in Tibet Region of China in accordance with custom.

2. Pilgrims from Tibet Region of China of Lamaist and Buddhist faiths may visit Banaras, Sarnath, Gaya and Sanchi in India in accordance with custom.

3. Pilgrims customarily visiting Lhasa may continue to do so in accordance with custom.

Article IV

Traders and pilgrims of both countries may travel by the following passes and routes:

1. Shipki La pass, (2) Mana pass, (3) Niti pass, (4) Kungri Bingri pass, (5) Darma pass, and (6) Lipu Lekh pass. Also, the customary route leading to Tashigong along the valley of the Shangatsangpu (Indus) River may continue to be traversed in accordance with custom.

Article V

For travelling across the border, the High Contracting Parties agree that diplomatic personnel, officials and nationals of the two countries shall hold passports issued by their own respective countries and visas by the other Party except as provided in Paragraphs 1, 2, 3 and 4 of this Article.

1. Traders of both countries known to be customarily and specifically engaged in trade between Tibet Region of China and India, their wives and children who are dependent on them for livelihood and their attendants, will be allowed entry for purposes of trade into India or Tibet Region of China, as the case may be, in accordance with custom on the production of certificates, duly issued by the local government of their own country or by its duly authorised agents and examined by the border check-posts of the other Party.

2. Inhabitants of the border districts of the two Countries who cross the border to carry on petty trade or to visit friends and relatives may proceed to the border districts of the other Party as they have

customarily done heretofore and need not be restricted to the passes and route specified in Article IV above and shall not be required to hold passports, visas or permits.

3. Porters and mule-team drivers of the two countries who cross the border to perform necessary transportation services need not hold passports issued by their own country, but shall only hold certificates good for a definite period of time (three months, half year or one year) duly issued by the local government of their own country or by its duly authorised agents and produce them for registration at the border check-posts of the other Party.

4. Pilgrims of both countries need not carry documents of certification but shall register at the border check-posts of the other Party and receive a permit for pilgrimage.

5. Notwithstanding the provisions of the foregoing paragraphs of this Article, either Government may refuse entry to any particular person.

6. Persons who enter the territory of the other Party in accordance with the foregoing paragraphs of this Article may stay within its territory only after complying with the procedures specified by the other Party.

Article VI

The present Agreement shall come into effect upon ratification by both Governments and shall remain in force for eight (8) years. Extension of the present Agreement may be negotiated by the two Parties if either Party requests for it, six (6) months prior to the expiry of the Agreement and the request is agreed to by the other Party.

Done in duplicate in Peking on April 29, 1954, in Hindi, Chinese and English languages, all text being equally valid.

Plenipotentiary of the Central Government of the People's Republic of China - CHANG HAN-FU

Plenipotentiary of the Government of the Republic of India - N RAGHAVAN

[Source: from the Archives of the Ministry of External Affairs (meaindia.nic.in), Government of India]

Rajiv Gandhi's Goodwill Visit to China (December 1988)

After 34 years since Jawaharlal Nehru's visit in 1954, Rajiv Gandhi was the first Prime Minister to visit China. During his visit, the two Governments signed the Agreement on Cooperation in the Field of Science and Technology, the Agreement relating to Civil Air Transport, and the Executive Programme for the Years 1988, 1989 and 1990 under the Agreement for Cultural Cooperation.

During their talks and meetings, the leaders of the two countries had a wide exchange of views and ideas on bilateral relations and international issues of mutual interest.

They emphasised that the Five Principles of mutual respect for sovereignty and territorial integrity, mutual non-aggression, non-interference in each other's internal affairs, equality and mutual benefit, and peaceful coexistence, which were jointly initiated by China and India and which have proved full of vitality through the test of history, constitute the basic guiding principles for good relations between states. These principles also constitute the basic guidelines for the establishment of a new international political order and the new international economic order. Both sides agreed that their common desire was to restore, improve and develop Sino-Indian good-neighbourly and friendly relations on the basis of these principles.

The leaders of the two countries held earnest, in-depth discussions on the Sino-Indian boundary question and agreed to settle this question through peaceful and friendly consultations. They also agreed to develop their relations actively in other fields and work hard to create a favourable climate and conditions for a fair and reasonable settlement of the boundary question while seeking a mutually acceptable solution to this question.

The Chinese side expressed concern over anti-China activities by some Tibetan elements in India. The Indian side reiterated the long-standing and consistent policy of the Government of India that Tibet is an autonomous region of China and that anti-China political activities by Tibetan elements would not be permitted on Indian soil.

[Source: Sino-Indian Joint Press Communique, Beijing, 23 December, 1988]

Agreement between the Government of the People's Republic of China and the Government of the Republic of India on the Maintenance of Peace and Tranquility along the Line of Actual Control in the China-India Border Areas

The Government of the People's Republic of China and the Government of the Republic of India, (hereinafter referred to as the two sides), have entered into the present Agreement in accordance with the Five Principles of mutual respect for sovereignty and territorial integrity, mutual non-aggression, non-interference in each other's internal affairs, equality and mutual benefit and peaceful coexistence and with a view to maintaining peace and tranquility in areas along the line of actual control in the China-India border areas.

Article I

The two sides are of the view that the China-India boundary question shall be resolved through peaceful and friendly consultations. Neither side shall use or threaten to use force against the other by any means. Pending an ultimate solution to the boundary question between the countries, the two sides shall strictly respect and observe the line of actual control between the two sides. No activities of either side shall overstep the line of actual control. In case personnel of one side cross the line of actual control, upon being cautioned by the other side, they shall immediately pull back to their own side of the line of actual control. When necessary, the two sides shall jointly check and determine the segments of the line of actual control where they have different views as to its alignment.

Article II

Each side will keep its military forces in the areas along the line of actual control to a minimum level compatible with the friendly and good neighbourly relations between the two countries. The two sides agree to reduce their military forces along the line of actual control in conformity with the requirements of the principle of mutual and equal security to ceilings to mutually agreed. The extent, depth, timing and nature of reduction of military forces along the line of actual control shall be determined through mutual consultations between the two countries. The reduction of military forces shall be carried out by stages in mutually agreed geographical locations, sectorwise within the areas along the line of actual control.

Article III

Both sides shall work out through consultations, effective confidence building measures in the areas along the line of actual control. Neither side will undertake specified levels of military exercises in mutually identified zones. Each side shall give the other prior notification of military exercises of specified levels near the line of actual control permitted under this Agreement.

Article IV

In case of contingencies or other problems arising in the areas along the line of actual control, the two sides shall deal with them through meetings and friendly consultations between border personnel of the two countries. The form of such meetings and channels of communications between the border personnel shall be mutually agreed upon by the two sides.

Article V

The two sides agree to take adequate measures to ensure that air intrusions across the line of actual control do not take place and shall undertake mutual consultations, should intrusions occur. Both sides shall also consult on possible restrictions on air exercises in areas to mutually agreed near the line of actual control.

Article VI

The two sides are agreed that references to the line of actual control in this Agreement do not prejudice their respective positions on the boundary question.

Article VII

The two sides shall agree through consultations on the form, method, scale and content of effective verification measures and supervision required for the reduction of military forces and the maintenance of peace and tranquillity in the areas along the line of actual control under this Agreement.

Article VIII

Each side of the China-India Joint Working Group on the boundary question shall appoint diplomatic and military experts to formulate, through mutual consultations, the implementation measures for the present Agreement. The experts shall advise the Joint Working Group on the resolution of differences between the two sides on the alignment of the line of actual control and address issues relating to redeployment with a view to reduction of military forces in the areas along the line of actual control. The experts shall also assist the Joint Working Group in supervision of the implementation of the Agreement and settlement of differences that may arise in that process, based on the principle of good faith and mutual confidence.

Article IX

The present Agreement shall come into effect as of the date of signature and is subject to amendment and addition by agreement of the two sides.

Signed in duplicated at Beijing on September 7, 1993 in the Chinese, Hindi and English languages, all three texts having equal validity.

Confidence-Building Measures Along The Line Of Actual Control In The India-China Border Areas Agreement between the Government of the Republic of India and the Government of the people's Republic of China

November 29, 1996 (New Delhi)

The Government of the Republic of India and the Government of the People's Republic of China (hereinafter referred to as the two sides),

Believing that it serves the fundamental interests of the peoples of India and China to foster a long-term good-neighbourly relationship in accordance with the 'five principles of mutual respect for sovereignty and territorial integrity, mutual non-aggression, non-interference in each other's internal affairs, equality and mutual benefit and peaceful co-existence,

Convinced that the maintenance of peace and tranquility along the line of actual control in the India-China border areas accords with the fundamental interests of the two peoples and will also contribute to the ultimate resolution of the boundary question,

Reaffirming that neither side shall use or threaten to use force against the other by any means or seek unilateral military superiority,

Pursuant to the Agreement between the Government of the Republic of India and the Government of the People's Republic of China on the Maintenance of Peace and Tranquility along the Line of Actual Control in the India-China Border Areas, signed on 7 September, 1993,

Recognizing the need for effective confidence building measures in the military field along the line of actual control in the border areas between the two sides,

Noting the utility of confidence building measures already in place along the line of actual control in the India-China border areas,

Committed to enhancing mutual confidence and transparency in the military field, Have agreed as follows:

Article I

Neither side shall use its military capability against the other side. No armed forces deployed by either side in the border areas along the line of actual control as part of their respective military strength shall be used to attack the other side, or engage in military activities that threaten the other side or undermine peace, tranquility and stability in the India-China border areas.

Article II

The two sides reiterate their determination to seek a fair, reasonable and mutually acceptable settlement of the boundary question. Pending an ultimate solution to the boundary question, the two sides reaffirm their commitment to strictly respect and observe the line-of actual control in the India-China border areas. No activities of either side shall overstep the line of actual control.

Article III

The two sides agree to take the following measures to reduce or limit their respective military forces within mutually agreed geographical zones along the line of actual control in the India-China border areas:

(1) The two sides reaffirm that they shall reduce or limit their respective military forces within mutually agreed geographical zones along the line of actual control in the India-China border areas to minimum levels compatible with the friendly and good neighbourly relations between the two countries and consistent with the principle of mutual and equal security.

(2) The two sides shall reduce or limit the number of field army, border defence forces, paramilitary forces and any other mutually agreed category of armed force deployed in mutually agreed

geographical zones along the line of actual control to ceilings to be mutually agreed upon. The major categories of armaments to be reduced or limited are as follows: combat tanks, infantry combat vehicles, guns (including howitzers) with 75 mm or bigger calibre, mortars with 120 mm or bigger calibre, surface-to-surface missiles, surface-to-air missiles and any other weapon system mutually agreed upon.

(3) The two sides shall exchange data on the military forces and armaments to be reduced or limited and decide on ceilings on military forces and armaments to be kept by each side within mutually agreed geographical zones along the line of actual control in the India-China border areas. The ceilings shall be determined in conformity with the requirement of the principle of mutual and equal security, with due consideration being given to parameters such as the nature of terrain, road communication and other infrastructure and time taken to induct/deinduct troops and armaments.

Article IV

In order to maintain peace and tranquility along the line of actual control in the India-China border areas and to prevent any tension in the border areas due to misreading by either side of the other side's intentions:

(1) Both sides shall avoid holding large scale military exercises involving more than one Division (approximately 1 5,000 troops) in close proximity of the line of actual control in the India-China border areas. However, if such exercises are to be conducted, the strategic direction of the main force involved shall not be towards the other side.

(2) If either side conducts a major military exercise involving more than one Brigade Group (approximately 5,000 troops) in close proximity of the line of actual control in the India-China border areas, it shall give the other side prior notification with regard to type, level, planned duration and area of exercise as well as the number and type of units or formations participating in the exercise.

(3) The date of completion of the exercise and deinduction of troops from the area of exercise shall be intimated to the other side within five days of completion or deinduction.

(4) Each side shall be entitled to obtain timely clarification from the side undertaking the exercise in respect of data specified in Paragraph 2 of the present Article.

Article V

With a view to preventing air intrusions across the line of actual control in the India-China border areas and facilitating overflights and landings by military aircraft:

(1) Both sides shall take adequate measures to ensure that air intrusions across the line of actual control do not take place. However, if an intrusion does take place, it should cease as soon as detected and the incident shall be promptly investigated by the side operating the aircraft. The results of the investigation shall be immediately communicated, through diplomatic channels or at border personnel meetings, to the other side.

(2) Subject to Paragraphs 3 and 5 of this Article, combat aircraft (to include fighter, bomber, reconnaissance, military trainer, armed helicopter and other armed aircraft) shall not fly within ten kilometres of the line of actual control.

(3) If either side is required to undertake flights of combat aircraft within ten kilometres from the line of actual control, it shall give the following information in advance to the other side, through diplomatic channels:

(a) Type and number of combat aircraft;

(b) Height of the proposed flight (in metres);

(c) Proposed duration of flights (normally not to exceed ten days);

(d) Proposed timing of flights; and

(e) Area of operations, defined in latitude and longitude.

(4) Unarmed transport aircraft, survey aircraft and helicopters shall be permitted to fly up to the line of actual control.

(5) No military aircraft of either side shall fly across the line of actual control, except by prior permission. Military aircraft of either side may fly across the line of actual control or overfly the other side's airspace or land on the other side only after obtaining the latter's prior permission after providing the latter with detailed information on the flight in accordance with the international practice in this regard.

Notwithstanding the above stipulation, each side has the sovereign right to specify additional conditions, including at short notice, for flights or landings of military aircraft of the other side on its side of the line of actual control or through its airspace.

(6) In order to ensure flight safety in emergency situations, the authorities designated by the two sides may contact each other by the quickest means of communications available.

Article VI

With a view to preventing dangerous military activities along the line of actual control in the India-China border areas, the two sides agree as follows:

(1) Neither side shall open fire, cause bio-degradation, use hazardous chemicals, conduct blast operations or hunt with guns or explosives within two kilometres from the line of actual control. This prohibition shall not apply to routine firing activities in small arms firing ranges.

(2) If there is a need to conduct blast operations within two kilometres of the line of actual control as part of developmental activities, the other side shall be informed through diplomatic channels or by convening a border personnel meeting, preferably five days in advance.

(3) While conducting exercises with live ammunition in areas close to the line of actual control, precaution shall be taken to ensure that a bullet or a missile does not accidentally fall on the other side

across the line of actual control and causes harm to the personnel or property of the other side.

(4) If the border personnel of the two sides come in a face-to-face situation due to differences on the alignment of the line of actual control or any other reason, they shall exercise self-restraint and take all necessary steps to avoid an escalation of the situation. Both sides shall also enter into immediate consultations through diplomatic and/or other available channels to review the situation and prevent any escalation of tension.

Article VII

In order to strengthen exchanges and cooperation between the military personnel and establishments in the border areas along the line of actual control, the two sides agree:

(a) To maintain and expand the regime of scheduled and flag meetings between their border representatives at designated places along the line of actual control;

(b) To maintain and expand telecommunication links between the border meeting points at designated places along the line of actual control;

(c) To establish step-by-step medium and high-level contacts between the border authorities of the two sides.

Article VIII

(1) Should the personnel of one side cross the line of actual control and enter the other side because of unavoidable circumstances like natural disasters, the other side shall extend all possible assistance to them and inform their side, as soon as possible, regarding the forced or inadvertent entry across the line of actual control. The modalities of return of the concerned personnel to their own side shall be settled through mutual consultations.

(2) The two sides shall provide each other, at the earliest possible, with information pertaining to natural disasters and epidemic

diseases in contiguous border areas which might affect the other side. The exchange of information shall take place either through diplomatic channels or at border personnel meetings.

Article IX

In case a doubtful situation develops in the border region, or in case one of the sides has some questions or doubts regarding the manner in which the other side is observing this Agreement, either side has the right to seek a clarification from the other side. The clarifications sought and replies to them shall be conveyed through diplomatic channels.

Article X

(1) Recognizing that the full implementation of some of the provisions of the present Agreement will depend on the two sides arriving at a common understanding of the alignment of the line of actual control in the India-China border areas, the two sides agree to speed up the process of clarification and confirmation of the line of actual control. As an initial step in this process, they are clarifying the alignment of the line of actual control in those segments where they have different perceptions. They also agree to exchange maps indicating their respective perceptions of the entire alignment of the line of actual control as soon as possible.

(2) Pending the completion of the process of clarification and confirmation of the line of actual control, the two sides shall work out modalities for implementing confidence building measures envisaged under this Agreement on an interim basis, without prejudice to their respective positions on the alignment of the line of actual control as well as on the boundary question.

Article XI

Detailed implementation measures required under Article I to Article X of this Agreement shall be decided through mutual consultations in the India-China Joint Working Group on the Boundary Question. The India-China Diplomatic and Military Expert Group shall assist the India-China Joint working Group in devising implementation measures under the Agreement.

Article XII

This Agreement is subject to ratification and shall enter into force on the date of exchange of instruments of ratification. It shall remain in effect until either side decides to terminate it after giving six months' notice in writing. It shall become invalid six months after the notification.

This Agreement is subject to amendment and addition by mutual agreement in writing between the two sides.

Signed in duplicate, in New Delhi on 29 November, 1996 in the Hindi, Chinese and English languages, all three texts being equally authentic. In case of divergence, the English text shall prevail.

Documents signed between India and China during Prime Minister Vajpayee's visit to China (June 2003)

Memorandum between the Government of the Republic of India and the Government of the People's Republic of China on Expanding Border Trade

The Government of the Republic of India and the Government of the People's Republic of China (hereinafter referred to as the two sides), with a view to promoting the development of friendly relations between the two countries and two peoples, pursuant to the Memorandum between the Government of the Republic of India and the Government of the People's Republic of China on the Resumption of Border Trade signed on 13 December 1991, and Protocol on Entry and Exit Procedures for Border Trade signed on 1 July 1992, desirous of opening another pass on the India-China border and setting up an additional point on each side for border trade, have agreed as follows:

Article I

The Indian side agrees to designate Changgu of Sikkim state as the venue for border trade market; the Chinese side agrees to designate Renqinggang of the Tibet Autonomous Region as the venue for border trade market.

Article II

The two sides agree to use Nathula as the pass for entry and exit of persons, means of transport and commodities engaged in border trade. Each side shall establish checkpoints at appropriate locations to monitor and manage their entry and exit through the Nathula Pass.

Article III

All the provisions of the Memorandum on the Resumption of Border Trade signed between the two Governments on 13 December 1991 and the Protocol on Entry and Exit Procedures for Border Trade signed between the two Governments on 1 July 1992 under the Memorandum, shall also be applicable to the border trade through the Nathula Pass.

Article IV

This Memorandum may be amended or supplemented by agreement, in writing, between the two sides.

Article V

This Memorandum shall come into force as from the date of its signature and shall be valid during the validity of the Memorandum on Resumption of Border Trade, signed between the two Governments in New Delhi on 13 December 1991.

Memorandums of Understanding signed:

1. Memorandum of Understanding on Cooperation between the Ministry of Law and Justice of the Government of the Republic of India and the Supreme People's Prosecution Service of the People's Republic of China.

2. Executive Programme on Educational Cooperation and Exchange between the Ministry of Human Resource Development, Government of the Republic of India and Ministry of Education, the People's Republic of China.

3. Protocol of Phytosanitary Requirements for Exporting Mangoes from India to China between the Ministry of Agriculture of the Republic of India and General Administration of Quality Supervision, Inspection and Quarantine of the People's Republic of China.

4. Memorandum of Understanding on Simplifying Visa Procedures between the Government of the Republic of India and the Government of the People's Republic of China.

5. Memorandum of Understanding for Enhanced Cooperation in the field of Renewable Energy between the Ministry of Non-

Conventional Energy Sources, Government of the Republic of India and the Ministry of Water Resources, Government of People's Republic of China.

6. Memorandum of Understanding for Cooperation in the field of Ocean Science and Technology between Department of Ocean Development, Government of the Republic of India and State Oceanic Administration, People's Republic of China.

7. Memorandum of Understanding between the Department of Science and Technology of the Republic of India and the National Science Foundation of China.

8. Memorandum of Understanding between the Government of the Republic of India and the Government of the People's Republic of China on the Reciprocal Establishment of Cultural Centres in their Capitals.

9. Executive Programme of Cultural Exchanges between the Government of the Republic of India and the Government of the People's Republic of China for the years 2003-2005.

[Source: from the Archives of the Ministry of External Affairs (meaindia.nic.in), Government of India]

Political Parameters and Guiding Principles for the Settlement of the India-China Boundary Question

(Agreement between the Government of the Republic of India and the Government of the People's Republic of China, 2005)

The Government of the Republic of India and the Government of the People's Republic of China (hereinafter referred to as the two sides), Believing that it serves the fundamental interests of the peoples of India and China to foster a long-term constructive and cooperative partnership on the basis of the Five Principles of Peaceful Co-existence, mutual respect and sensitivity for each other's concerns and aspirations and equality, desirous of qualitatively upgrading the bilateral relationship at all levels and in all areas while addressing differences through peaceful means in a fair, reasonable and mutually acceptable manner, reiterating their commitment to abide by and implement the Agreement on the Maintenance of Peace and Tranquility along the Line of Actual Control in the India-China Border Areas, signed on 7 September 1993, and the Agreement on Confidence Building Measures in the Military Field along the Line of Actual Control in the India-China Border Areas, signed on 29 November 1996, reaffirming the Declaration on Principles for Relations and Comprehensive Cooperation between India and China, signed on 23 June 2003, recalling that the two sides have appointed Special Representatives to explore the framework of settlement of the India-China boundary question and the two Special Representatives have been engaged in consultations in a friendly, cooperative and constructive atmosphere,noting that the two sides are seeking a political settlement of the boundary question, in the context of their overall and long-term interests.

Convinced that an early settlement of the boundary question will advance the basic interests of the two countries and should therefore be pursued as a strategic objective,

Have agreed on the following political parameters and guiding principles for a boundary settlement:

Article I

The differences on the boundary question should not be allowed to affect the overall development of bilateral relations. The two sides will resolve the boundary question through peaceful and friendly consultations. Neither side shall use or threaten to use force against the other by any means. The final solution of the boundary question will significantly promote good neighbourly and friendly relations between India and China.

Article II

The two sides should, in accordance with the Five Principles of Peaceful Coexistence, seek a fair, reasonable and mutually acceptable solution to the boundary question through consultations on an equal footing, proceeding from the political perspective of overall bilateral relations.

Article III

Both sides should, in the spirit of mutual respect and mutual understanding, make meaningful and mutually acceptable adjustments to their respective positions on the boundary question, so as to arrive at a package settlement to the boundary question. The boundary settlement must be final, covering all sectors of the India-China boundary.

Article IV

The two sides will give due consideration to each other's strategic and reasonable interests, and the principle of mutual and equal security.

Article V

The two sides will take into account, inter alia, historical evidence, national sentiments, practical difficulties and reasonable concerns and sensitivities of both sides, and the actual state of border areas.

Article VI

The boundary should be along well-defined and easily identifiable natural geographical features to be mutually agreed upon between the two sides.

Article VII

In reaching a boundary settlement, the two sides shall safeguard due interests of their settled populations in the border areas.

Article VIII

Within the agreed framework of the final boundary settlement, the delineation of the boundary will be carried out, utilising means such as modern cartographic and surveying practices and joint surveys.

Article IX

Pending an ultimate settlement of the boundary question, the two sides should strictly respect and observe the line of actual control and work together to maintain peace and tranquility in the border areas. The India-China Joint Working Group and the India-China Diplomatic and Military Expert Group shall continue their work under the Agreements of 7 September 1993 and 29 November 1996, including the clarification of the line of actual control and the implementation of confidence building measures.

Article X

The Special Representatives on the boundary question shall continue their consultations in an earnest manner with the objective of arriving at an agreed framework for a boundary settlement, which will provide the basis for the delineation and demarcation of the India-China boundary to be subsequently undertaken by civil and military officials and surveyors of the two sides.

Article XI

This Agreement shall come into force as of the date of signature and is subject to amendment and addition by mutual agreement in writing between the two sides.

Signed in duplicate in New Delhi on 11 April, 2005, in the Hindi, Chinese and English languages, all three texts being equally authentic. In case of divergence, the English text shall prevail.

[Source: from the Archives of the Ministry of External Affairs (meaindia.nic.in), Government of India]

Highlights of the joint declaration issued after the talks between Prime Minister Manmohan Singh and Chinese President Hu Jintao (November 2006)

In order to promote the sustainable socio-economic development of India and China, to fully realise the substantial potential for their cooperation in a wide range of areas, to upgrade India-China relations to a qualitatively new level, and to further substantiate and reinforce their Strategic and Cooperative Partnership, the leaders of the two countries have committed themselves to pursuing the following "ten-Pronged strategy":

1. Ensuring comprehensive development of bilateral relations:

- Hold regular summit-level meetings
- Open additional consulate general offices at Kolkata and Guangzhou.

2. Strengthening institutional linkages and dialogue mechanisms:

- Concerned ministries shall intensify exchanges under the existing dialogue mechanisms.

3. Consolidating commercial and economic exchanges:

- Endeavour to raise volume of bilateral trade to $40 billion (about Rs 90.000 crore) by 2010

4. Expanding all round mutually beneficial cooperation:

- Agree to fully implement the provisions of the Memorandum of Understanding on cooperation in the field of oil and natural gas.
- Strengthen cooperation in the information and communication technology sector.
- Set-up expert-level mechanism to exchange flood season hydrological data.

5. Instilling mutual trust and confidence through defence cooperation:

- Fully implement provisions of MoU for exchanges and cooperation in the field of Defence, signed on May 29, 2006

6. Seeking early settlement of outstanding issues:

- Committed to resolve outstanding differences, including boundary through peaceful means in a fair, reasonable, mutually acceptable and proactive manner.
- Joint Working Group on the boundary issue to expedite work

7. Promoting trans-border connectivity and cooperation:

- China to provide greater facilitation to indian pilgrims for Kailash-Mansarovar yatra.
- Explore possibility of opening additional route.

8. Boosting cooperation in science and technology:

- Expansion of civil nuclear cooperation.
- Strengthen cooperation in the use of space-based technologies.

9. Revitalising cultural ties and nurturing people-to-people exchanges:

- Organise 'Festival of India' in China and 'Festival of China' in India.
- Establish India-China Exchange Foundation.
- Launch new Educational Exchange Programme
- Organise the India-China year of Friendship through Tourism in 2007.

10. Expanding cooperation on regional and international stage:

- Shall positively assess the trilateral dialogue mechanism among India, China and Russia
- Revitalise and broaden India-China dialogue mechanism on counter-terrorism.
- Share developmental experiences with other developing countries and the international community through two-part seminar in New Delhi and Beijing.
- Strengthen cooperation in the World Trade Organisation.
- India to coutinue to abide by 'One China' policy. India reiterates its recognition of the Tibet Autonomous Region as part of China and not to allow Tibetans to engage in anti-China political activities in India.

[Source: From the Archives of the Ministry of External Affairs (meaindia.nic.in), Government of India]

A Shared Vision for the 21st Century for the People's Republic of China and the Republic of India (January 2008)

On his visit to China in January 2008, Prime Minister Manmohan Singh and Chinese Premier Wen Jiabao signed a joint document, vowing to promote the building of a harmonious world. The following is the full text of the document:

A Shared Vision for the 21st Century of the People's Republic of China and the Republic of India

H.E. Mr. Wen Jiabao, Premier of the State Council of the People's Republic of China and H.E. Dr. Manmohan Singh, Prime Minister of the Republic of India, meeting in Beijing on 14 January 2008, resolve to promote the building of a harmonious world of durable peace and common prosperity through developing the Strategic and Cooperative Partnership for Peace and Prosperity between the two countries.

China and India (hereinafter referred to as the "two sides") are the two largest developing nations on earth representing more than one-third of humanity. The two sides recognise that both China and India bear a significant historical responsibility to ensure comprehensive, balanced and sustainable economic and social development of the two countries and to promote peace and development in Asia and the world as a whole.

The two sides are convinced that it is time to look to the future in building a relationship of friendship and trust, based on equality, in which each is sensitive to the concerns and aspirations of the other. The two sides reiterate that China-India friendship and common development will have a positive influence on the future of the international system. China-India relations are not targeted at any country, nor will it affect their friendship with other countries.

The two sides believe that in the new century, Panchsheel, the Five Principles of Peaceful Co-existence, should continue to constitute the basic guiding principles for good relations between all countries and for creating the conditions for realising peace and progress of humankind. An international system founded on these principles will be fair, rational, equal and mutually beneficial, and will promote durable peace and common prosperity, create equal opportunities and eliminate poverty and discrimination.

The two sides hold that the right of each country to choose its own path of social, economic and political development in which fundamental human rights and the rule of law are given their due place, should be respected. An international system founded in tolerance and respect for diversity will promote the cause of peace and reduce the use, or threat of use, of force. The two sides favour an open and inclusive international system and believe that drawing lines on the ground of ideologies and values, or on geographical criteria, is not conducive to peaceful and harmonious coexistence.

The two sides believe that the continuous democratisation of international relations and multilateralism are an important objective in the new century. The central role of the United Nations in promoting international peace, security and development should be recognised and promoted. The two sides support comprehensive reform of the United Nations, including giving priority to increasing the representation of developing countries in the Security Council. The Indian side reiterates its aspirations for permanent membership of the UN Security Council. The Chinese side attaches great importance to India's position as a major developing country in international affairs. The Chinese side understands and supports India's aspirations to play a greater role in the United Nations, including in the Security Council.

The two sides support and encourage the processes of regional integration that provide mutually beneficial opportunities for growth, as an important feature of the emerging international economic system. The two sides positively view each others' participation in regional processes and agree to strengthen their coordination and consultation within regional cooperation, mechanisms including the East Asia Summit, to explore together and with other countries a new architecture for closer regional cooperation in Asia and to make joint efforts for further regional integration of Asia. The two sides will strengthen their coordination under the framework of Asia-Europe Meeting, and are committed to strengthening and deepening Asia-Europe comprehensive partnership.

The two sides take a positive view on each other's participation in sub-regional multilateral cooperation processes between like-minded countries, including South Asian Association for Regional Cooperation, Bay of Bengal Initiative for Multi-Sectoral Technical and Economic Cooperation and Shanghai Cooperation Organisation. The two sides hold that this does not affect either country's existing friendly relations or cooperation with other countries.

The two sides welcome the positive facets of economic globalisation, and are ready to face and meet its challenges, and will work with other countries towards balanced and mutually beneficial economic globalisation. The two sides believe that the establishment of an open, fair, equitable, transparent and rule-based multilateral trading system is the common aspiration of all countries. The two sides favour the early conclusion of the Doha Development Round, placing the issues that affect the poorest of the poor at its core. The two sides are determined to strengthen their coordination with other developing countries in order to secure their shared objectives.

The two sides are convinced that it is in the common interest of the international community to establish an international energy order that is fair, equitable, secure and stable and to the benefit of the entire international community. The two sides are committed to making joint efforts to diversify the global energy mix and enhance the share of clean and renewable energy, so as to meet the energy requirements of all countries.

The two sides welcome the opportunity for their outstanding scientists to work together in the International Thermonuclear Experimental Reactor (ITER) project, which is of great potential significance in meeting the global energy challenge in an environmentally sustainable manner. As two countries with advanced scientific capabilities, the two sides pledge to promote bilateral cooperation in civil nuclear energy, consistent with their respective international commitments, which will contribute to energy security and to dealing with risks associated with climate change.

The two sides recognise the challenge that humankind faces from climate change. The two sides take the issue of climate change seriously and reiterate their readiness to join the international community in the efforts to address climate change. The two sides also stand ready to enhance technological cooperation between the two countries. The two sides welcome the outcome of the United Nations Framework Convention on Climate Change (UNFCCC) meeting in Bali in December 2007 and agree to work closely during the negotiation process laid out in the Bali Road Map for long term cooperative action under the Convention. The two sides emphasise the importance of addressing climate change in accordance with principles and provisions of the UNFCCC and its Kyoto Protocol, in particular, the principle of common but differentiated responsibilities.

The two sides appeal to the international community to move forward the processes of multilateral arms control, disarmament and non-proliferation. Outer space is the common heritage of humankind. It is the responsibility of all space-faring nations to commit to the peaceful uses of outer space. The two sides express their categorical opposition to the weaponisation and arms race in outer space.

The two sides strongly condemn the scourge of terrorism in all its forms and manifestations, and in all regions of the world. The two sides pledge to work together and with the international community to strengthen the global framework against terrorism in a long-term, sustained and comprehensive manner.

The two sides believe that cultural and religious tolerance and dialogue between civilizations and people will contribute to overall peace and stability of our world. The two sides endorse all efforts to promote inter-civilizational and inter-faith dialogues.

The two sides believe that their bilateral relationship in this century will be of significant regional and global influence. The two sides will therefore continue to build their Strategic and Cooperative Partnership in a positive way. As major economies in their region, the two sides believe that the strong growth in their trade and economic relations is mutually beneficial and welcome the conclusion of a Feasibility Study on a Regional Trading Arrangement (RTA) between the two countries. According to the report of the Feasibility Study, a China-India RTA will be mutually advantageous. Against the backdrop of accelerating regional economic integration in Asia, the two sides agree to explore the possibility of commencing discussions on a mutually beneficial and high-quality RTA that meets the common aspirations of both countries, and will also benefit the region.

The two sides will continuously promote confidence building measures through steadily enhanced contacts in the field of defence. The two sides therefore welcome the commencement of the China-India Defence Dialogue and express their satisfaction at the successful conclusion of the first joint anti-terrorism training between their armed forces in December 2007. The two sides also welcome their efforts to set an example on trans-border rivers by commencing cooperation since 2002. The Indian side highly appreciates the assistance extended by China on the provision of flood season hydrological data which has assisted India in ensuring the safety and security of its population in the regions along these rivers. The two sides agree that this has contributed positively to building mutual understanding and trust.

The two sides remain firmly committed to resolving outstanding differences, including on the boundary question, through peaceful negotiations, while ensuring that such differences are not allowed to affect the positive development of bilateral relations. The two sides reiterate their determination to seek a fair, reasonable and mutually acceptable solution to the boundary question and to build a boundary of peace and friendship, on the basis of the Agreement on Political Parameters and Guiding Principles for the Settlement of the China-India Boundary Question, concluded in April 2005. The Special Representatives shall complete at an early date, the task of arriving at an agreed framework of settlement on the basis of this Agreement.

The Indian side recalls that India was among the first countries to recognise that there is one China and that its one China policy has remained unaltered. The Indian side states that it would continue to abide by its one China policy, and oppose any activity that is against the one China principle. The Chinese side expresses its appreciation for the Indian position.

The two sides recognise the responsibilities and obligations of the two countries to the international community. The two sides are determined to enhance mutual understanding and friendship between the people of China and India, for the betterment of both countries and to bring about a brighter future for humanity.

[Source: From the Archives of the Ministry of External Affairs (meaindia.nic.in), Government of India]

60th Anniversary of the Establishment of Diplomatic Relations between India and China

Press Release of The Ministry of External Affairs, Government of India, 1 April, 2010

April 1, 2010 marks the 60th Anniversary of the establishment of Diplomatic Relations between the Republic of India and the People's Republic of China. On this occasion, messages of felicitations have been exchanged between the Presidents, Prime Ministers and External Affairs Ministers of the two countries.

Conveying "warm greetings and good wishes" to the leadership and friendly people of China, President Smt. Pratibha Patil, in her letter to the Chinese President, observed that "our bilateral relations have gained in strength and momentum and have assumed global and strategic dimensions as a result of efforts by the two sides".

In his message to the Chinese Premier, Prime Minister Dr. Manmohan Singh stated that "India-China relations have diversified into almost all areas of human endeavour. They have achieved a high level of maturity that serves the interests of both our people and the cause of peace, stability and progress in the region and the world. We share a Strategic and Cooperative Partnership for Peace and Prosperity. We are important trade partners. We cooperate closely on many global issues. The Shared Vision for the 21st Century which we signed in 2008 provides the roadmap for our continued interaction and cooperation in the years ahead." PM added that "we regard the future of India-China relations with optimism" and that he looked forward to working with the Chinese Premier "to harness the vast potential for the further expansion of our ties to realise the mutual aspirations of our two peoples".

In his communication to the Foreign Minister of China, External Affairs Minister Shri SM Krishna remarked that India and China "are rapidly developing countries which share the objective of improving the living standards of our people. In recent times, we have emerged as two of the fastest growing economies in the world". He reiterated "our resolve to work closely with China for the peace and prosperity of our region and the globe".

APPENDIX I

Editors: Sardar Vallabhbhai Patel's letter to Jawaharlal Nehru on 7 November 1950 not only deplored Indian Ambassador KM Panikkar's action but also warned about dangers from China. Following is the full text of the letter:

My dear Jawaharlal,

Ever since my return from Ahmedabad and after the cabinet meeting the same day which I had to attend at practically fifteen minutes' notice and for which I regret I was not able to read all the papers, I have been anxiously thinking over the problem of Tibet and I thought I should share with you what is passing through my mind.

I have carefully gone through the correspondence between the External Affairs Ministry and our Ambassador in Peking and through him, the Chinese Government. I have tried to peruse this correspondence as favourably to our Ambassador and the Chinese Government as possible, but I regret to say that neither of them comes out well as a result of this study. The Chinese Government has tried to delude us by professions of peaceful intention. My own feeling is that at a crucial period they managed to instill into our Ambassador a false sense of confidence in their so-called desire to settle the Tibetan problem by peaceful means. There can be no doubt that during the period covered by this correspondence, the Chinese must have been concentrating for an onslaught on Tibet. The final action of the Chinese, in my judgement, is little short of perfidy. The tragedy of it is that the Tibetans put faith in us; they chose to be guided by us; and we have been unable to get them out of the meshes of Chinese diplomacy or Chinese malevolence. From the latest position, it appears that we shall not be able to rescue the Dalai Lama. Our Ambassador has been at great pains to find an explanation or justification for Chinese policy and actions. As the External Affairs Ministry remarked in one of their telegrams, there was a lack of firmness and unnecessary apology in one or two representations that he made to the Chinese Government on our behalf. It is impossible to imagine any sensible person believing in the so-called threat to China from Anglo-American machinations in Tibet. Therefore, if the Chinese put faith in this, they must have distrusted us so completely as to have taken us as tools or stooges of Anglo-American diplomacy or strategy. This feeling, if genuinely entertained by the Chinese in spite of your direct approaches to them, indicates that even though we regard ourselves as the friends of

China, the Chinese do not regard us as their friends. With the Communist mentality of "whoever is not with them being against them", this is a significant pointer, of which we have to take due note.

During the last several months, outside the Russian camp, we have practically been alone in championing the cause of Chinese entry into UN and in securing from the Americans, assurances on the question of Formosa. We have done everything we could to assuage Chinese feelings,

to allay its apprehensions and to defend its legitimate claims in our discussions and correspondence with America and Britain and in the UN. Inspite of this, China is not convinced about our disinterestedness; it continues to regard us with suspicion and the whole psychology is

one, at least outwardly, of skepticism, perhaps mixed with a little hostility. I doubt if we can go any further than we have done already to convince China of our good intentions, friendliness and goodwill. In Peking we have an Ambassador who is eminently suitable for putting across the friendly point of view. Even he seems to have failed to convert the Chinese. Their last telegram to us is an act of gross discourtesy not only in the summary way it disposes of our protest

against the entry of Chinese forces into Tibet but also in the wild insinuation that our attitude is determined by foreign influences. It looks as though it is not a friend speaking in that language but a potential enemy.

In the background of this, we have to consider what new situation now faces us as a result of the disappearance of Tibet, as we knew it and the expansion of China almost up to our gates. Throughout history we have seldom been worried about our north-east frontier. The Himalayas have been regarded as an impenetrable barrier against any threat from the north. We had a friendly Tibet which gave us no trouble. The Chinese were divided. They had their own domestic problems and never bothered us about frontiers. In 1914, we entered into a convention with Tibet which was not endorsed by the Chinese. We seem to have regarded Tibetan autonomy as extending to independent treaty relationship. Presumably, all that we required was Chinese

counter-signature. The Chinese interpretation of suzerainty seems to be different. We can, therefore, safely assume that very soon they will disown all the stipulations which Tibet has entered into with us in the past. That throws into the melting pot, all frontier and commercial settlements with Tibet on which we have been functioning and acting during the last half a century. China is no longer divided. It is united and strong. All along the Himalayas in the north and north-east, we have on our side of the frontier, a population ethnologically and culturally not different from Tibetans and Mongoloids. The undefined state of the frontier and the existence, on

our side, of a population with its affinities to the Tibetans or Chinese, have all the elements of the potential trouble between China and ourselves. Recent and bitter history also tells us that Communism is no shield against imperialism and that the communists are as good or as bad imperialists as any other. Chinese ambitions in this respect not only cover the Himalayan slopes on our side but also include the important part of Assam. They have their ambitions in Burma also. Burma has the added difficulty that it has no McMahon Line round with which to build up even the semblance of an agreement. Chinese irredentism and communist imperialism are different from the expansionism or imperialism of the western powers. The former has a cloak of ideology which makes it ten times more dangerous. In the guise of ideological expansion lie concealed racial, national or historical claims. The danger from the north and north-east, therefore, becomes both communist and imperialist. While our western and north-western threat to security is still as prominent as before, a new threat has developed from the north and north-east. Thus, for the first time, after centuries, India's defence has to concentrate itself on two fronts simultaneously. Our defence measures have so far been based on the calculations of superiority over Pakistan. In our calculations we shall now have to reckon with communist

China in the north and in the north-east, a communist China which has definite ambitions and aims and which does not, in any way, seem friendly disposed towards us.

Let us also consider the political conditions on this potentially troublesome frontier. Our northern and north-eastern approaches consist of Nepal, Bhutan, Sikkim, Darjeeling and the tribal areas in

Assam. From the point of view of communication, there are weak spots. Continuous defensive lines do not exist. There is almost an unlimited scope for infiltration. Police protection is limited to a very small number of passes. There, too, our outposts do not seem to be fully manned. The contact of these areas with us is by no means close and intimate. The people inhabiting these portions have no established loyalty or devotion to India. Even Darjeeling and Kalimpong areas are not free from pro-Mongoloid prejudices. During the last three years, we have not been able to make any appreciable approaches to the Nagas and other hill tribes in Assam. European missionaries and other visitors had been in touch with them, but their influence was in no way friendly to India or Indians. In Sikkim, there was political ferment some time ago. It is quite possible that discontent is smouldering there. Bhutan is comparatively quiet, but its affinity with Tibetans would be a handicap. Nepal has a weak oligarchic regime based almost entirely on force: it is in conflict with a turbulent element of the population as well as with enlightened ideas of the modern age. In these circumstances, to make people alive to the new danger or to make them defensively strong is a very difficult task indeed and that difficulty can be got over only by enlightened firmness, strength and a clear line of policy. I am sure the Chinese and their source of inspiration, Soviet Union, would not miss any opportunity of exploiting these weak spots, partly in support of their ideology and partly in support of their ambitions. In my judgement the situation is one which we cannot afford either to be complacent or to be vacillating. We must have a clear idea of what we wish to achieve and also of the methods by which we should achieve it. Any faltering or lack of decisiveness in formulating our objectives or in pursuing our policies to attain those objectives is bound to weaken us and increase the threats which are so evident. Side by side with these external dangers, we shall now have to face serious internal problems as well. I have already asked Iengar to send to the External Affairs Ministry a copy of the Intelligence Bureau's appreciation of these matters. Hitherto, the Communist Party of India has found some difficulty in contacting communists abroad, or in getting supplies of arms, literature, etc., from them. They had to contend with the difficult Burmese and Pakistan frontiers on the east or with the long seaboard. They shall now have a comparatively easy means of access to Chinese communists and through them to other foreign communists. Infiltration of spies, fifth columnists and communists would now be easier. Instead of having to deal with isolated communist pockets in Telengana and Warrangal we may have to deal with communist threats to our security along our northern and north-eastern frontiers, where, for supplies of arms and ammunition, they can safely depend on communist arsenals in China. The whole situation thus raises a number of problems on which we must come to an early decision so that we can, as I said earlier, formulate the objectives of our policy and decide the method by which those objectives are to be attained. It is also clear that the action will have to be fairly comprehensive, involving not only our defence strategy and state of preparations but also problem of internal security to deal with which we have not a moment to lose. We shall also have to deal with administrative and political problems in the weak spots along the frontier to which I have already referred. It is of course, impossible to be exhaustive in setting out all these problems. I am, however, giving below some of the problems which, in my opinion, require early solution and round which we have to build our administrative or military policies and measures to implement them.

(a) A military and intelligence appreciation of the Chinese threat to India both on the frontier and to internal security.

(b) An examination of military position and such redisposition of our forces as might be necessary, particularly with the idea of guarding important routes or areas which are likely to be the subject of dispute.

(c) An appraisement of the strength of our forces and, if necessary, reconsideration of our retrenchment plans for the Army in the light of the new threat.

(d) A long-term consideration of our defence needs. My own feeling is that, unless we assure our supplies of arms, ammunition and armour, we would be making our defence perpetually weak and we would not be able to stand up to the double threat of difficulties both from the west and north-west and north and north-east.

(e) The question of China's entry into the UN. In view of the rebuff which China has given us and the method which it has followed in dealing with Tibet, I am doubtful whether we can advocate its claim any longer. There would probably be a threat in the UN virtually to outlaw China, in view of its active participation in the Korean war. We must determine our attitude on this question also.

(f) The political and administrative steps which we should take to strengthen our northern and north-eastern frontier. This would include the whole of the border, ie. Nepal, Bhutan, Sikkim, Darjeeling and the tribal territory in Assam.

(g) Measures of internal security in the border areas as well as the states flanking those areas such as Uttar Pradesh, Bihar, Bengal and Assam.

(h) Improvement of our communication, road, rail, air and wireless, in these areas and with the frontier outposts.

(i) The future of our mission at Lhasa and the trade posts at Gyangtse and Yatung and the forces which we have in operation in Tibet to guard the trade routes.

(j) The policy in regard to the McMahon Line.

These are some of the questions which occur to my mind. It is possible that a consideration of these matters may lead us into wider question of our relationship with China, Russia, America, Britain and Burma. This, however, would be of a general nature, though some might be

basically very important, e.g., we might have to consider whether we should not enter into closer association with Burma in order to strengthen the latter in its dealings with China. I do not rule out the possibility that, before applying pressure on us, China might apply pressure on Burma.

With Burma, the frontier is entirely undefined and the Chinese territorial claims are more substantial. In its present position, Burma might offer an easier problem to China, and therefore, might claim its first attention.

I suggest that we meet early to have a general discussion on these problems and decide on such steps as we might think to be immediately necessary and direct, quick examination of other problems with a view to taking early measures to deal with them.

Vallabhbhai Patel,
7th November 1950

Talks between Mao and Nehru

We publish here an abridged version of the one-to-one conversation between Mao Tse-tung and Jawaharlal Nehru that took place in Beijing, in two rounds, when Nehru visited China in October, 1954. The first text 'Foreign Policy and Fear Complex' is a summary of the first round of conversation with excerpts of the direct conversation which took place on 19 October, 1954. The second text 'War and Peace' is a first-hand account of the direct conversation which took place on 23 October,1954.

Those who were present on both the occasions were the Indian Ambassador to China, N. Raghavan; Premier Chou En-lai, Vice-Chairman C'hu Teh; Chairman of the Congress of Standing Committee, Liu Shao-chi; Vice-Chairman of the Standing Committee, Sung Ching-ling; Vice-Premier Chen Yun; Chinese Ambassador to India, Yuan Chung-hsien; V.V. Paranjpe and Pu Shou-chang acted as interpreters.

Foreign Policy and Fear Complex

Chairman Mao Tse-Tung enquired after Nehru's health and after the usual courtesies he said that he was very glad to meet the Prime Minister and had been looking forward to his visit. He dwelt on the age-old associations and the new friendship between China and India. He said that today both India and China were struggling for peace. He had read with great interest the Prime Minister's speech of 29th September, 1954, and appreciated what he had said then.[1] China and India had more or less common history in recent times. India had suffered from the effects of colonialism for the last 200 or 300 years; so also had China, for more than a hundred years. There were many common features. Both suffered from colonial exploitation and after both the countries became free, it was important for both the countries to have peace in order to carry on peaceful reconstruction of their economies. Both countries were backward industrially. India, he understood, was more advanced, but all the same with their large populations, industrial reconstruction had to proceed with quickness in both countries. Given peace it might take about twenty years for China to be an industrial nation. China wanted peace. Some other nations, however, did not like to leave China alone. Obstructions were placed in the way of her trade and her reconstruction. Trade even through the Chinese waters, was being interfered with. Just a few yards away from the Chinese mainland, islands which belonged to China were under occupation. US was carrying on a policy of increasing tension right around China. Part of China, viz., Formosa, US had virtually occupied and was extending all assistance and encouragement to it. Taiwan had to be liberated. She was a standing threat to the Chinese mainland. From Taiwan and other territories, air raids were made on China[2]

---

[1] *Selected Works of Jawaharlal Nehru,* (second series), Vol. 26, pp. 318-332

[2] On 3 September, 1954, an artillery duel broke out between Communist China and Nationalist China over Quemoy island. Air raids by both parties were started on 5 September. On 6 September, the US Seventh Fleet patrol was strengthened over 30 islands in possession of the Nationalists. The US Government reiterated its stand on defending the Nationalist hold from communist attack "at all cost."

and US had been air-dropping its agents in groups of seven and ten with wireless transmitters and other equipments. Various such groups had been rounded up and caught.[3] China was not a threat to anyone and wished to live in peace with other countries. US, however, did not permit her to do so. In this matter even countries like England and France were being forced and intimidated by US to follow their line. Even with regard to Chinese admission to the United Nations and the recognition of her status, these nations under pressure from the United States had, unlike India and other Asian countries and also some north west European countries, been supporting US in her attitude.

The Chairman then referred to the Manila Conference and SEATO, in which countries, like UK, supported the American Government. Nehru began by expressing his appreciation of the very warm welcome that he had received that morning from the people of Peking.[4] He said he was overwhelmed by the demonstration that he had received and thanked the Chairman, the Premier and members of his Government. He said it was true that both India and China had a tradition of close and friendly association dating back from the early ages. This association continued more or less till India lost her freedom about 150 or 200 years ago and when China also became subjected to similar forces as those to which India had been subjected. Another link between India and China was common or similar, resulting from such colonialism. Both India and China were great countries with vast populations. Both had similar problems and need for reconstruction. There was, therefore, much common ground between the two countries and there was a closeness of association, though they might differ in ideology. There might be differences in outlook or ideology, but there was great goodwill and friendship between our two countries and people. This was an important feature in a world full of strife. The

---

[3] According to a communiqué of the Chinese Ministry of Public Security. 230 KMT and US agents had been captured since 1951, of whom 106 were killed while being rounded up. The most controversial of these were the cases pertaining to thirteen American secret agents involved in air-dropping agents, maintaining contacts with agents and conducting reconnaissance etc.

[4] Over a million people lined the twelve mile long route from the airport and for the first time the Chinese dispensed with the bullet proof cars and Nehru rode in an open car. Desmond Donnelly of the Daily Mail described the reception as 'a Roman triumph'.

great need of the world today was peace and the people of India as well as the people of China were devoted to the cause of peace. However, Nehru said he wanted to mention that there was a certain amount of fear in the minds of smaller nations in Asia, fear of these two big and great countries, China and India. This might be baseless fear. The fact remained that there was such fear. The very strength of these two countries might be the reason for such fear and there might be other reasons also. Nevertheless, the fact had to be faced that there was fear of China and...

Mao Tse-tung: Of communism?

Jawaharlal Nehru: We cannot analyse this fear and find out what exactly causes it, but it is important that we should remove this fear from the minds of smaller countries. It cannot be completely explained, but there is no doubt that the fear complex has affected many countries and has influenced their policies.

Mao: But US cannot be afraid? On the other hand, US is intimidating others.

Nehru: Even in US some observers have seen that there was fear and policies were influenced by fear.

Mao: What are they afraid of?

Nehru: It might be that they are afraid of losing their vested interests. US is a very powerful nation today and perhaps they are afraid of losing their power. After the last World War, European nations had become weak and European colonialism became a diminishing quantity, which would ultimately disappear. Some European countries have already realised this though not sufficiently enough. America, on the other hand, has emerged out of the War as a very strong power and she is anxious that this power may not be affected or diminished by other powerful nations. It is this fear complex that is affecting them.

Mao: How can America be afraid? On the other hand, she is frightening others through her activities. We cannot even have good sleep, you know. She is intimidating Britain, France and other nations to follow her policy. She does not care for the opinion of others, but she wants others to follow her opinion. Even for the SEATO, she did not care for the opinions of India, Burma or Indonesia and intimidated or brought pressure on countries like Philippines, Thailand, Pakistan and others to fall in with her policy.

Nehru said as far as he could see, SEATO was the American reaction against the Geneva Conference. The Americans did not like the settlement that arrived at Geneva and wanted to show that their views still counted and that their strength and influence in Asia had not become less.[5] Mao said that he agreed that it was a sort of demonstration against the decisions at the Geneva Conference and American inability therein to make their presence felt. Nehru explained that all the same there was the fear complex in America. Perhaps, she was afraid of the Soviet Union and countries like Britain and France, who left to themselves, might follow a different policy and were following American policy for fear that they might not be able to stand by themselves, in the case of another war. They think that if they do not follow the US, US might leave them to their own fate, in case of another conflict. That is one explanation of British support to the United States. Otherwise the interests of European colonial nations and those of America, conflict in the East and in many countries, European colonial nations are losing ground to Americans. Yet, we find them supporting American policy.

Mao enquired as to why countries like India did not then follow the American policy. Nehru answered that India was not afraid of any country in the world. The one thing that India's great leader Mahatma Gandhi had taught Indians was not to be afraid and it was this fearlessness that enabled Indians to win their freedom from British imperialism. Yes, said the Prime Minister, India was not afraid and followed her own policy, that which she considered right and just. Mao said that America had so much of strength and wealth etc. Nehru said that slowly Western nations had to realise that it was not so much the money that counted. Both India and China put together, had about 1000 million people of the world and human beings counted. Mao agreed that human beings counted the most. Nehru

[5] The decision for cessation of hostilities in Indo-China, arrived at Geneva, went directly against the foreign policy priorities of the US. The Spectator commented: "The star of Peking has caused the star of Washington to pale in an area where only a few years ago General McArthur was usurping the functions of God. With care and skilled determination the SEATO could serve in some measures to rebuild this vanishing authority."

continued that ultimately US and other nations would realise that it was not possible to set at nought, such a great country with such vast populations as China and in the end Chinese legitimate rights would have to be conceded.

Nehru then again referred to the fear of isolation in the minds of West European nations in the event of any armed conflict with Russia. All that they could do now was to try and influence American opinion without leaving the American camp. Mao said that Eden, while at Geneva, was in favour of Eastern Locarno. All the same the British supported US at the Manila Conference.[6] Nehru said that according to his information the British were not happy about it. Nehru referred to the joint declaration made by Prime Minister Chou En-lai and himself while the former was in India.[7] If the principles which were embodied in this declaration were given effect to and if other countries in Asia were made to feel that those principles would be effectively implemented, a good deal could be achieved in removing suspicion and fear. If those principles of non-interference, respect for sovereignty and territorial integrity etc. are acted upon, many of the troubles, that afflicted nations would be removed. The nations in Asia would have, however, to be convinced that the principles would be effectively implemented.

Mao agreed that the principles had been stated in the declaration and they could watch and see that they would be implemented. However, he thought that it would be wrong to make war, an instrument of policy. He had a good deal to say about it and he would like to continue the conversation with the Prime Minister later.

War and Peace

Mao Tse-Tung: How are the talks between the two Prime Ministers proceeding?

---

[6] During the Geneva Conference, Anthony Eden had proposed that an arrangement could be arrived at for the defence of South East Asia-in line of the Locarno Treaty-in which both the superpowers stood guarantee for its working. At the Manila conference, Lord Reading, the British delegate, argued that while the Geneva Conference had put an end to war, Manila was to ensure that "sacrifices were not exacted a second time."

[7] Issued on 28 June 1954 in New Delhi, the statement laid down the mutually agreed principles -Panchsheel - governing the relationship between the two countries.

Jawaharlal Nehru: We have discussed a great variety of questions and the talks were very satisfactory.

Mao: It is but natural. We have no quarrels between us. We had some quarrels with the Labour Party Delegation.[8] We spent three and a half hours in talks with the Labour Party Delegation, out of which two hours were spent in quarrels. But we quarrelled happily. They then talked about a great variety of topics and they spoke of doubts and disagreements and we did likewise. They asked us whether we wanted to destroy or undermine the Labour Party. I said we would not and we could not do so. If British Labour Party is to be destroyed, that is to say, if that is to happen then British working class should do it. According to their observation, their course was better. They think they are socialists and we are communists and their road is better and effective. I said the question of their effectiveness may better not be talked about. However, if they insisted, then we would express our views. Their policy, I said, would not reach the goal of socialism. They were still an imperialist country. They denied it. They asked whether we could cooperate with such sort of people. And I said entirely so. We said cooperation between two countries of different ideologies is entirely possible. Not only the British Labour Party but even if Churchill's Party wishes to cooperate we will also cooperate. We are also willing to cooperate with America if they want it. And there were some other matters of dispute. This was the Attlee Delegation. They were further worried (concerned) about our population being too large. They seem to have the idea that greater population would mean aggression. In our view our population problem would be solved under the new social system. It could be solved within the country. Do any of the South East Asian countries have the same doubts regarding our population?

Nehru: Yes. I mentioned last time that some of the South East Asian countries have apprehensions. Even in the past the Chinese and Indian populations spread out to these countries and so there is not only the fear of population, but in addition, of the strong nation behind it. But their apprehensions are not the same as of some European countries. This applies

---

[8] The delegation from UK visited China from 15 to 31 August and met Mao on 24 August, 1954.

to India also. In Africa, European settlers are carrying on an anti-India campaign where they are describing India as "Indian imperialism" while actually it is they who are imperialists. I might mention that I met one or two members of the British Delegation who gave me a brief account of their talks held here.

Mao: Yes. We must talk out differences if any. That is good. Whatever places Labour Delegates wanted to see, we allowed them to see. We do not favour Hitler's assertion, also made by the Japanese before, regarding 'have not' countries.

Nehru: Even before Hitler, Kaiser Wilhem talked the same way in Europe. About fifty years ago he had drawn a cartoon, entitled "Yellow peril" in which he showed herds from Asia, marching against Europe and he himself defending it. And by that probably he referred to the Japanese.

Mao: Yes; ten years ago Japan was just this "yellow peril". Now we need at least scores of years of peace to develop our country and to raise the livelihood of our people. We do not want war. If we can create these conditions it will be good. We will cooperate with anyone who is in favour of this objective. India is undoubtedly in favour of this. So also Burma and Indonesia. Even countries like Thailand, we do not think, are contemplating aggression. We want to improve our relationship with the Thai Government, but the Thai Government is peculiar. They do not want to pay any attention to us. Another case is that of Philippines. They say that we want aggression, but they do not say anything when we say we want to establish and improve relations. On the one hand, they say, they are afraid but when we want to issue something like a statement issued by India and China, about non-aggression, etc., they do not do it. We cannot find any reasons for it. They are depending on America and follow the same track. Speaking of the United States, in the last conversation there was one question we did not finish, viz. the question of war. Do you think that US wants war and would use war to achieve her interests?

Nehru: The Chairman has made many observations and I refer to some of them. Countries like Burma, Indonesia, and India not only support peace but they entirely favour peace. It is not only because peace is good, but out of selfish reasons. It is an absolute necessity. Otherwise all these countries face danger and destruction and it is an urgent necessity. There is no European country which is not desirous of peace and not actively afraid of war. So is Asia too. As regards US, the question is too difficult to have a simple answer. Because there are many elements in the US policy. I believe the majority of people in the United States want peace and there are many even in the Government who want peace. However, in the last few years there has been a growing tendency in US towards war, especially in the Defence Department and the military officials who have gained far greater strength in their foreign policy. Many of these high military officers think in terms of war but many in the civilian administration, do not. Thus there is a conflict between civil and military administration and many military generals openly talk of war. Eisenhower does not want war but he may be driven into it. He is weak and he does not understand politics. I happened to meet Dulles in Paris six years ago.[9] Then the elections were to take place and he hoped to become the Secretary of State. However, in the elections Truman won and Dulles did not then become the Secretary of State. He then said that of course they did not want war but he thought war would come because of the aggressive activities of the communist countries. He said war will not solve any question or questions. It is ultimately the system which pays greatest dividends that will win. Of course, he was speaking in business language. What he meant was that the system which will show greater results, will win.

Mao: Indeed, Dulles spoke quite well!

Nehru: A man like Dulles is a great menace. He is a Methodist or a Baptist preacher who religiously goes to Church and he is narrow-minded and bigoted. He thinks every one must agree with him and a man like him might take any move. I had a long talk with Eisenhower when he was the President of the Columbia University. He then said to me that he had seen much of war and he no more wanted war. And it did seem to me that he meant it. But unfortunately he is so completely in the hands of third rate advisers that he moves from one opinion to another. In about one month's time elections will be held in America and I think Democrats will get

---

[9] Nehru was in Paris in October-November 1948 to attend UN General Assembly session and met Dulles.

majority in the Congress. It will mean a lessening of tensions and from the point of view of war it will be better. The only persons who think that they will really profit by war are, perhaps, Chiang Kai-shek and Syngman Rhee.

Mao: We must study the questions of the advantages of war. We have seen two Wars and we must study who profited from them. The last two Wars benefited three kinds of countries while all other countries suffered. We might perhaps classify them into three categories:

1. US imperialism: They profited by both Wars and made profits;
2. Countries led by Communist parties or the working class; and
3. Oppressed people led by patriotic groups and parties who are still not communists like India, Indonesia, Syria and even Egypt.

If war comes, people have to be mobilised and kept under constant tension but then organisation of the people gives rise to revolution as in China and India. By the way, do you call your struggle a revolution?

Nehru: Most certainly we do.

Mao: Our countries, China and India, achieved independence as a result of the Second World War. As a consequence of War, another group of countries like Japan, Germany and Italy became weak. But some of the other countries who won the War also became weak. Thus, Chiang Kai-shek weakened and we stood up; Britain weakened and India, Burma, Egypt, etc., stood up; France weakened and Ho Chi Minh rose. I do not know what the American military groups have in mind. They are probably benefited and advanced by the two Wars and they think they will profit in a Third World War. But as a result of the Third World War it is not certain that America will be benefited and on the other hand she may find herself in trouble. Majority of Islamic countries like Syria in Western Asia and countries in Latin America and even perhaps America proper, may possibly shake off the yoke of American imperialists. Revolutionary force of the people always needs a chance to come up. For example, the Bolsheviks. If they had no chance of the First World War, revolution would have been difficult. So also in China. We got a chance because of the Japanese War and we came up. This is also true of patriotic parties in the South East and West Asia. The real result of the two World Wars is like this and in our view if a third World War is started, it will be to America's disadvantage. If a third World War starts, major portion of the world will be in a revolutionary stage. I am not saying it to make the people afraid but because it is really so, as shown by the Second War. Coming to the weapons, US depends on artillery, navy and bombing. They think they are strong, but there is no basic change except that more people would be killed. In olden days they used "cold weapons" (i.e., knives, swords etc). Now hot weapons (rifles, guns etc.) are used. Cold ones kill less people and hot ones kill more people; atomic weapons will kill still more people. But besides increasing the rate of mortality they make no difference. In a third World War many more people would be killed. We have no atom bomb. I do not know whether you have it. We have just started scientific research and we have no money. We cannot possibly undertake it now. But the atom bomb is possessed by both America and USSR. So, regarding arms, both sides are equal. The deciding factor is the people, the people who handle these weapons. Most important thing is that what the soldiers think is to their best advantage. Communist Party like your Congress Party had no weapons to start with, but now we have. Another experience in both the World Wars is that countries on the defensive won and those who started the War were defeated. In the First War, Germany marched as far as Paris to the west and Petrograd to the east. In the Second War also the defensive side won though Britain and France were a bit weakened; i.e., to say wars have not been advantageous to the aggressor. Therefore, our conclusion is that there should not be another war. We should have long-term peace.

Nehru: Chairman has been good enough to give an analysis of wars and their effects. Chairman is an expert and his views deserve to be respected. I should say that there is a large measure of agreement between us on many points but with reservations on some.

(1) Even without war, India would have attained freedom. Actually war provided a pick-axe in the hands of the British to hold on for a long time in India.

(2) The US gained by War yet the position after War was not to her liking. USSR also had gained and America was facing many problems and although she had won, she was unhappy. Chairman's

arguments would lead to the conclusion that war, inspite of the fact that it is bad and needs to be avoided, should still be welcomed, if it comes. I venture to disagree about weapons. It is not a matter of quantity but of quality. It is not merely greater killing but more than that. For, the killing is on such a vast scale that America will not profit and no other country will profit also. I am not an expert but I have studied science and I am in charge of the work on atomic research in my country. I have studied a little about some of the new developments in European countries. If a war starts it will result in the destruction of military and industrial centres of both sides. America thinks that they can destroy every administrative (governmental), industrial, productive and Army Centre of the USSR. Of course, Soviets also will not keep quiet. They too will destroy American centres. But the hydrogen bomb releases a chain reaction which is uncontrollable. The mere process of that energy creates another energy which will kill and none will be able to control them. The nature of war will be quite different and it will essentially destroy the industrialised countries. I agree with Chairman's viewpoint that in the final analysis, human beings count. But the Third World War may bring in accompanying changes and enormous destruction and there might well be chaos. Again, if all highly trained persons were destroyed, we cannot easily start again. I am saying from a purely practical viewpoint, Third World War will be quite different from the ones before. We cannot measure its results now. Maybe, there is no peace at all because there is no one (i.e., to say no organised machinery or government) to make peace. Of course, this is all guess work. China perhaps might suffer less because it is the industrialised nations which will suffer most, since there are nerve centres which can be destroyed easily. There is another aspect to be considered and that is the brutalising effect of war on humanity. War may result in degradation of a large number of human beings. Therefore, on every count, war has to be avoided. Chairman is right when he says that in the two Wars, the aggressor was defeated and yet a little twist, speaking from a purely practical viewpoint, may have given advantage to the aggressor. Hitler was a foolish person and he lost many opportunities. It would have been better for him if he had been more patient and wise. In the First World War, Germany was defeated but it was just touch and go. It was not so sure. There are many forces at work in the world and some are exaggerated by war, but some are exaggerated even without War. Even today British and French imperialism exist. Of course, European imperialism today is a dying thing. The French imperialism ceased after the First World War, while the British imperialism ceased after the Second War. It was hastened by war. There is no doubt about it. I do not think European countries are likely to continue as imperialist powers, because there is no strength left in them to do so. Their source of strength has dried up. American imperialism, however, is of a different type.

Mao: They (Britain and France) are not strong. But still they have colonies and semi-colonies.

Nehru: Yes, but they are weakened and there is no strength left in them. Only place they can hold on to is Africa.

Mao: Is Egypt still under British direction?

Nehru: No. The American influence is more than the British influence.

Mao: Our conclusions are equal (the same). Regarding analysis, we agree on some and do not agree on others. Prime Minister Nehru's analysis of facts regarding US, viz., that US profited on one side and is facing difficulties on the other, is very good. As also is his analysis of weapons being qualitatively different - if we see the development of weapons there is the arrow stage, the cannon stage and the atom stage - this is also correct. But when I talked of war - about the result of weapons of war, whatever weapons are used - cold, hot or atomic and how large the scale of war may be - the result is destruction of the other side. But truce was arranged on the 38th parallel. Here, truce was arranged without any power being totally destroyed. If you look back on past wars, in most cases, the defeated suffered most destruction; the losing side lost not only men but also in material. So victory or defeat hinges on the scope of destruction suffered.

Nehru: May I venture to ask you a question? I should have thought that the scope of destruction suffered by the USSR in the Second World War was far greater than any other country, but because of perseverance it still won.

Mao: I was talking about final result when I said so. The German Armies were totally destroyed, but the Soviet Armies were not. Again the Prime Minister's estimate that as a possible result of the third world war one may find oneself in a chaotic situation, may be correct. It is also true that the energy released by an atom will destroy not only men but material, agriculture, and human beings in tens of millions. But if one government goes away there will be another and as long as there are people, men will always find a way out. The surviving people will also find a way to keep themselves alive. However, people at present, are different from those in the past. There is a high degree of consciousness and aspirations for liberation and independence. This is so even in the US. So, in the final analysis it is better not to fight. If we act as Chief of Staff to Eisenhower, we would advise him not to go to war. (All smile) This work, however, can be more easily done by the Prime Minister (i.e., Nehru) rather than us. If we do it, he will think we are intimidating him with revolution and he will say: "I am not afraid of revolution."

Nehru: We cannot directly influence America. But we may be able to influence her indirectly through countries like Britain, France or Canada. I recently received a message from Churchill which in brief said that he was anxious over the tendencies towards war and he was trying to curb such tendencies in America. He said he was also thinking about the final admission of China to the United Nations.

Mao: Not only war but tensions also may seem to be to the advantage of those responsible for them, but they are disadvantageous to them. Is it after all better to let people have peace or to allow them to stay in tense situation every day? Tense situation everywhere will awaken people and will be helpful to revolution. Between India and China there is no tension, there is no psychological war. We do not spread psychological war among the people. We do not guard against each other as US and USSR do.

Nehru: In the United States, the argument is advanced that they do not want war but they must keep up the tension so that the Congress will sanction money for the armies.

Mao: That is only one advantage they are considering but they are also making countries follow them by intimidation, building military bases, etc. It is not merely a question of appropriations. What do you think about convening a World Peace Congress? Do you think it is possible? Over a hundred nations all over the world can participate and there should be a sort of treaty for peace and non-aggression.

Nehru: Well, I cannot say. But with every passing year the possibility of war is getting less and if fifteen years pass without a war, the possibility will be very remote indeed. Not that it is the people who will have changed but nobody would dare use such destructive weapons and a time may come when war would be avoided by a world agreement and mutual adjustment.

Mao: Is there any hope within ten years?

Nehru: Fears of consequences of war are growing and they will grow as the people know more about the weapons and after fifteen years, the weapons will be such that no one dare use them for war. It would mean destruction of both sides. Of course, I am giving my assurances.

Mao: Naturally we cannot stand guarantee for what they are doing.

Nehru: If, for example death rays are invented, not to speak of nations, any group of people can destroy the world.

Mao: One thing is there that is fear of weapons, but there is fear of revolutions also.

Nehru: Of course. But weapons may even be in the hands of certain groups. And as the science of communications advances there may be more types of guided missiles. There is, for example, a machine which plays chess. There might be created a machine which can fight and of course a machine would do it more efficiently. As science advances rapidly it may give enormous power to a group or a small number of anti-social persons.

Mao: Finally we must work together for preventing war and for a lasting peace.

Nehru: Undoubtedly so.

Mao: We have just started our Five Year Plan. If there be a war, all our plans will be destroyed. We have spent all money on construction. If war should come we have to gather everything to wage the war and all construction will be stopped and war plan will have to come and it would postpone industrialisation of China. Of course, it is difficult to sink the entire China into the sea and so too India, no matter how many people are killed.[10]

[Souce :*Selected Works of Jawaharlal Nehru,* Volume 27]

[10] At the end of the minutes Paranjpe recorded that the discussions went on to subjects like evolution of humanity, geological past of India and China till dinner.

CONTRIBUTORS

MANI SHANKAR AIYAR, renowned Congress leader and former Union Cabinet Minister, is Member of Parliament (Rajya Sabha). He is a special invitee to the Congress Working Committee and Chairman of both the party's political training department and the department of policy planning and coordination.

ZHANG YAN is Ambassador of The People's Republic of China to India, New Delhi.

BR DEEPAK is Associate Professor, Centre of Chinese and Southeast Asian Studies, Jawaharlal Nehru University, New Delhi. He is also Managing Editor, Think India Quarterly.

WANG BANGWEI is Professor and Dean of Oriental Studies of the Department of East Asian Languages, Peking University, Beijing, China.

SUDHEENDRA KULKARNI was Media Advisor to former Prime Minister Atal Behari Vajpayee; also former national secretary of the Bhartiya Janata Party (BJP), he is currently Chairman of the Observer Research Foundation, Mumbai.

CHENG RUISHENG is former Ambassador of The People's Republic of China to India and Myanmar. He is currently Advisor to China-India Eminent Persons' Forum.

DP TRIPATHI, Editor-in-Chief, Think India Quarterly, is General Secretary and Chief Spokesperson of Nationalist Congress Party (NCP).

MA JIALI is Professor, China Institute of Contemporary International Relations, Beijing, China.

AMITABH MATTOO, former Vice-Chancellor of University of Jammu, is currently Professor of International Politics, School of International Studies, Jawaharlal Nehru University, New Delhi.

AN SHUANGHONG is Professor of Education, Zhejiang University, Zhejiang, China.

P. STOBDAN is Senior Fellow at Institute for Defence Studies and Analyses, New Delhi.

SHENG RONG is Associate Professor, Department of Sociology, China Agriculture University, Beijing, China.

RAJIV NAYAN is Senior Research Associate at Institute for Defence Studies and Analyses, New Delhi.

RN DAS, Additional Director, Lok Sabha Secretariat, is currently working as Senior Fellow at Institute for Defence Studies and Analyses, New Delhi.

YANG XIAOPING is Doctoral Fellow at Institute of International Studies, Fudan University, Shanghai, China.

C. RAJA MOHAN is Strategic Affairs Editor of *The Indian Express*, New Delhi and Adjunct Professor of South Asian Studies at Nanyang Technological University, Singapore.

BINOD SINGH is foeign faculty of India Studies at the School of Asian and African Studies, Beijing Foreign Studies University, Beijing, China.